WHAT IS A CHILD?

WHAT IS A CHILD?
Childhood, Psychoanalysis, and Discourse

Michael Gerard Plastow

Routledge
Taylor & Francis Group

LONDON AND NEW YORK

First published 2015 by
Karnac Books Ltd.

Published 2018 by Routledge
2 Park Square, Milton Park, Abingdon, Oxon OX14 4RN
711 Third Avenue, New York, NY 10017, USA

Routledge is an imprint of the Taylor & Francis Group, an informa business

British Library Cataloguing in Publication Data

A C.I.P. for this book is available from the British Library

ISBN-13: 9781780490557 (pbk)

Typeset by V Publishing Solutions Pvt Ltd., Chennai, India

To my family

As a child, I was other ...
In the one I became
I grew up and forgot.
From mine now I've got,
   a silence, a law.
Did I lose or gain?

Criança, era outro ...
Naquele em que me tornei
Cresci e esqueci.
Tenho de meu, agora,
   um silêncio, uma lei.
Ganhei ou perdi?

—Fernando Pessoa, *1934*
(p. 411, translated for this edition)

CONTENTS

ACKNOWLEDGEMENT

I wish to acknowledge the enormous contribution of Tine Nørregaard towards this work.

Tine was an integral part of the planning and elaboration of the project of work that has led to the production of this book. The regular meetings that she and I have had over these past years have been the source of many of the ideas and arguments that are put forward, and which come to fruition here. Tine has been part of this work from its inception, and through its production and revision. Hence, even if this book assumes its final form under the pen of one author, it nonetheless draws its impetus from Tine's active collaboration.

Hence I wish to thank Tine Nørregaard for her work, her valuable time and energy, and her ideas that draw on a background and formation quite different to my own, all of which give a richness and depth that I could not have accomplished alone. I express here my gratitude for her support in realising this project.

APPRECIATION

I would like to give my thanks to David Pereira for his generous assistance with the theoretical approach to this work.

I would also like to thank Debbie Plastow for her help and encouragement throughout the writing of this work.

ABOUT THE AUTHOR

Michael Gerard Plastow is a psychoanalyst working in private practice in Melbourne. He is an Analyst of the School, The Freudian School of Melbourne, School of Lacanian Psychoanalysis. He also practises in the public sector as a child psychiatrist at the Alfred Child and Youth Mental Health Service where he leads a multidisciplinary team. Over a number of years he has convened a seminar on *Psychoanalysis and the Child* with Tine Nørregaard, also a psychoanalyst in the Freudian School of Melbourne.

Michael has published extensively in the psychoanalytic, psychiatric, and academic literature. He frequently presents his work at colloquia and conferences in Australia, Europe, and Latin America. He has a particular interest in the question of translation in psychoanalysis and has translated a number of papers into English, from French, Spanish, and Portuguese. His translation into English of Jacques Lacan's seminar *The Knowledge of the Psychoanalyst* was published in 2013 as a bilingual edition by the Association Lacanienne Internationale.

INTRODUCTION

One of Sigmund Freud's most controversial discoveries was that of sexuality in the child. In putting forward a notion of the child as a sexual or erotic being, he dispelled the idea of childhood as an idyllic period, free from the troubles and concerns of adulthood. Such a discovery was destined to disturb the peace of the day, all the more so when Freud proposed that the structure of a child's sexual longings was to be found in his relation to the mother and father. Freud designated this structure as the Oedipus complex.

In giving it this name, he acknowledged that from antiquity, poets have spoken about such longings, albeit in tragic form. Most notable among these was Sophocles, in his play Oedipus Rex, to which Freud referred as early as 1897 in a letter to Wilhelm Fliess (Freud, 1950a, p. 265). To enter Thebes, after unwittingly slaying his father, Oedipus confronts the mythical female figure of the Sphinx. To avoid a certain death, he has to attempt to answer her riddle: "What is the creature that walks on four legs in the morning, two legs at noon, and three in the evening?"

When Oedipus answers her riddle in order to save his life, he responds that the being who has at times two feet, at others three, and at yet others four, is Man as an adult, an old man, and an infant. But this attempt to respond to the enigma of sexuality with the proposition of three ages of life poses a difficulty for clinical practice. This difficulty has been played out in the history of child psychoanalysis with a division between the two sides of Oedipus' struggle: on the one hand, the confrontation with the enigma of sexuality for the child and the attempt to give it meaning; on the other, a turning away from this riddle through a recourse to a developmental insistence upon ages and stages.

This developmental solution to an age-old difficulty has plagued the field of psychoanalysis of the child—and clinical practice more generally—by defining the child and childhood in this way. Here we endeavour to return to the riddle, and put into question this simplistic solution that might save our skins in the short term, but at the cost of letting out the baby—Freud's notion of the *infantile*—with the bathwater. Oedipus avoids death, but he also avoids the enigma of sex. In this way both sexuality and death become repressed, but he pays a heavy price for this after the scales fall from his eyes. To speak about the clinical practice of the child is to put forward that the being we have before us might have to be structurally defined in relation to the enigmas of sex and death.

This book is based, in part, on topics that have been addressed in the seminar *Psychoanalysis and the Child*, conducted for some years now by Tine Nørregaard and myself. This title, intentionally, puts the child in the singular because as soon as the child is referred to as "children", there is an immediate generalisation and normalisation that takes place. Similarly, the myriad of developmental approaches to the child have in common a generalising tendency: they make of the child a category that is subject to all the normalising tendencies of objectivising science. The endeavour of this work is to restore the place of the child as a singular being who must be taken in his or her particularity.

Starting from such deliberations, the question that grounds this work imposes itself: *what is a child?* We will proceed by examining the threads identified in psychoanalytic texts regarding what is referred to as the *child*. Freud's writings will be taken up in order to elaborate upon the beginnings of the conceptualisation of childhood for psychoanalysis, in particular the *infantile factor of sexuality* that Freud delineated. The question of the *child* will require a close re-examination of our conceptions of history, as well as the notion of time itself.

These questions will be further pursued in reference to the pioneers in the field of psychoanalysis of the child, such as Anna Freud and Melanie Klein. We will examine the history of psychoanalysis of the child and assert the importance of Hermine Hug-Hellmuth with whom the logical beginning of this field will be located. She was the first to theorise the place of the mother and father in relation to the psychoanalysis of the child. Hug-Hellmuth had, in 1921, already remarked on the demands that are placed upon the analyst by the parents for "active therapy" (p. 298). These very same demands are present today in the requests of the clinician for more and more strategies. For Hug-Hellmuth, however, the work with the mother and father was conducted in order for the analysis of the child to be able to proceed unhindered.

If the notions that we currently hold of the *child* and *childhood* are determined by prevalent discourses in our societies—whether we are aware of them or not—we need to question the way in which our notion of the child has been construed throughout the ages. Thus a significant portion of this book will be devoted to an examination of the particular way in which the discourses that shape our thought have emerged historically. We will examine, amongst other texts, Philippe Ariès' important work *Centuries of Childhood*, Jean-Jacques Rousseau's *Émile*, Condillac's *Treatise on the Sensations*, and Michel Foucault's *The History of Sexuality*. In doing so we will endeavour to determine the manner in which the modern notion of the child has been moulded. In the emergence of our society from the Middle Ages, the theses and opinions of Enlightenment thinkers have produced lasting effects, and continue to influence the conception we have of the child. We will recognise that the idealised place that is reserved for the child is also an effect of the repression of sexuality and death perpetuated by these discourses.

The emergence of psychoanalysis occurred at a particular juncture in history in which the child was not only perceived as a subject on a similar footing to that of the adult, but correspondingly as a being who was in one way or another imbued with his or her own sexuality. It is not possible to conduct psychoanalysis with someone whom we consider to be a minor; rather, we work with a being who is an analysand in the full sense of this term. The fundamental question at play here is how the being of the child can emerge from minority into a subject who is able to speak in his or her own name.

Since I have translated many psychoanalytic texts—and recently a seminar of Jacques Lacan (1971–1972)—I attach importance to the question of the translation of many of the sources utilised in this work. While some of the failings and distortions of translation in psychoanalysis are well known—such as the rendering in the *Standard Edition* of Freud's *Trieb* (drive) into "instinct"—others, including the problematical translations of Lacan from French, are less well appreciated. And because my reading of many of the sources in their original languages are psychoanalytical readings that put the emphasis on the signifier, and on the letter of what has been written, or said, I will necessarily refer to many terms in their original languages, and translate some passages myself. Language, after all, is the very stuff of psychoanalysis, the primary medium of the psychoanalytic encounter.

Freud's radical unveiling of child sexuality and its enigmas, in addition to the discovery of the unconscious, is the legacy that we pursue in psychoanalysis. This is the work of the chapters that follow, via an examination of the discourses pertaining to the child and childhood, as well as through the history of psychoanalysis of the child itself. In taking up this task, I do not in any way intend to give an exhaustive account of the field, nor of the literature, but to continue to work some of the themes that have been worked in the seminar *Psychoanalysis and the Child* with Tine Nørregaard and the participants of the seminar, and to give a close examination of important threads that have emerged from it. Hence this book is an argument that is incessantly woven regarding the place of the child in contemporary clinical practice, in the wake of the work of Freud and Lacan.

PART I

THE CHILD AND THE INFANTILE:
HISTORY AND TIME

CHAPTER ONE

The child: between history and structure

What is a child?

This question, at first glance, might seem trivial and superfluous. Usually there is an assumption that remains unarticulated, that we know what a child is. The answer seems self-evident. Surely one can define a child by age? After all, this is how the question is most often approached. And the age of a child also suggests that the child is at a certain stage of development and maturity. From the perspective of the law, a child's age implies that he or she is permitted to do certain things and not others. For there to be a child also suggests the presence of parents or carers who take responsibility for the child.

In the clinical setting the limits of childhood are not clear and the usual definitions of the child do not hold up when tested. They are also elastic according to political and other influences. For instance a group defined as *infants* has been separated out from child psychiatry to form a relatively new field now known as *infant psychiatry*. These terms *infant* and *child* no longer coincide as they did at times in Freud. At the other end of the age spectrum of childhood, some of our child and adolescent mental health services are being extended out from an upper age of eighteen, previously considered to be the limit of childhood and adolescence, to now encompass *young people* or *youth* up to the age of twenty-five. Moreover, it is a social reality that the period during which children continue to live with their parents is becoming more and more prolonged. The Australian Bureau of Statistics (2009), for instance, discerned that in 1986, nineteen per cent of young people aged between twenty and thirty-four were living with their parents, whereas twenty years later, in 2006, the figure had risen to twenty-three per cent.

The dividing lines of such partitions are fought out in a type of culture war by invested parties who claim the superiority of their particular clinical approach. Thus some advocate that a different division be enacted whereby adolescents are removed from child and adolescent psychiatric services to be placed in adult-like services. Such decisions are made by politicians, albeit with input from some mental health professionals with political influence. What matters here is that the categories defined by age such as *infant, child, adolescent, youth,* and so on, are arbitrary divisions that are subject to the evolution in the discourses of clinicians, society, ideology, and politics. These apparently self-evident categories cannot be taken as givens.

Ages and stages for the child are also defined by law. The law, for instance, determines the age at which the individual is deemed to be legally responsible and therefore no longer considered a child. There are different ages at which the child or adolescent is able to vote, to have consensual sexual intercourse, or is deemed to be fully responsible for criminal acts, for instance. That such ages have also evolved over time demonstrates once again that the defining parameters of childhood and adolescence are fluid, and the categories that they define are subject to variation and manipulation. Before the law the child is a *minor*, in other words, something small and diminutive. The rights and responsibilities of the child are accordingly diminished in relation to the law. In particular, a child is not considered to be responsible for his or her acts in criminal law. This is a status that the child shares with the madman.

Even as far as the law is concerned, the notions of *childhood* and *adolescence* are quite fluid. The ages at which the minor gains rights and responsibilities have changed over time. This has generally been in the direction of a lowering of ages: the right to vote in many countries, for instance, was previously twenty-one and is now eighteen. The age at which the subject is legally allowed to consume alcohol has also decreased. Ages at which the adolescent is able to legally have sexual intercourse have changed, and can also be different from one sex to the other, and from one state or country to another. And ages regarding criminal responsibility vary according to particular crimes and different legislatures, as well as changing over time.

Moreover, there is a certain irony in the fact that if the overall trend is to lower the age at which the child or adolescent has rights and responsibilities, our society—and this is true here in Australia—has seen fit to extend certain child and adolescent mental health services to precisely the same group. After all, the age group that is now referred to as *youth* or *young people* is specifically one that, at the same time, is experiencing a more prolonged period of dependency. In putting these two facts together we could hazard a hypothesis that the increasing rights and responsibilities at younger ages come at a cost: that of a certain disarray and anguish.

Nonetheless, what is recognised as deserving of the attention of clinical services is not so much the anguish and distress, but rather their end result. It is only their final common denominators that are given credence in society by the psychiatric, psychological, and pharmaceutical industry: those of drug use, depression, accidents—including those of the road—and youth suicide.

To go along with a notion of the child based on the parameters of age and stage, then, is to be on very shaky ground. Philippe Ariès notes that in our era, "adolescence is the favourite age" (1960a, p. 30). And the emblems of adolescence which were first the mark of a revolt, such as the wearing of jeans and T-shirts, various aspects of one's image including the contemporary trend of piercings, tattoos, and various hairstyles and colours, a taste for rock music, etc., have not only become institutionalised as popular culture and therefore commercialised, they have also been integrated into high fashion. Thus there is no contradiction in having a sixty-year-old adolescent. Even the term *pre-adolescent* has been invented for those who are adolescent before their time so that they need not miss out on this favourite age.

Let us give a couple of clinical examples of the difficulties and dissonances in endeavouring to separate out a notion of childhood based on age and stage.

In a group in a clinical setting for children with social difficulties, two boys were having a fight over who was the "boss" of the group. Another boy said to these first two, "Stop being childish," to which one of the boys who was fighting said, "But we *are* children". Of course this comment is amusing because of the literal way in which the word "childish" is taken. It draws our attention to the fact that one does not need to be within the ages of childhood in order to be childish. It also raises the question of what it is to be a *child*. What is it then to be *childish*? The Swiss linguist Ferdinand de Saussure puts forward that, "There is no difference between the literal and figurative meaning of words" (2002, p. 47). This is because, as articulated by Saussure, any meaning is a fundamentally negative phenomenon. The meaning of the word *childish* lies simply in its difference to all other terms such as *naive, immature, irresponsible* and so on. So, in this way, what amuses us in what is articulated by this young boy lies in a certain truth: that of the tenuousness of the whole question of what it is to be a child or to be childish. This is precisely what is being called into question here.

To take another clinical example, a sixteen-year-old girl was presented by her parents and the school as being very childlike. During her lunch break at school, she would play with mud and engage in other activities that were described as being childish. The girl was the only child of a mother who, as a child herself, had discovered the dead body of her younger sibling. The fragility of childhood had been emphasised by the multiple miscarriages the mother had incurred prior to the conception of this girl. But in the interview with the girl her childish stance and manner of presenting herself was belied by the fact that she constantly twirled her axillary hair, a so-called secondary sexual characteristic, a sign that she was no longer a child, at least physically, despite the appearance and behaviour that she cultivated.

The difficulty in considering the question, *what is a child?*, is also complicated by the fact that the child is imbued with the ideals of the parents and of society. It is not for nothing that Freud referred to "His Majesty the Baby" (1914c, p. 91), which in turn echoes his earlier formula of "His Majesty the Ego" (1908e, p. 150), whom he says is the hero of every daydream and every story. In other words, this baby, this child, always partakes in the ideal of the parents. And the ego, at whatever age, is the successor to the baby, in his idealisation by the parents, an ideal ego in the reflection provided by the Other.

The French psychoanalysts Jean Bergès and Gabriel Balbo note that for the parents, the child is "themselves, as they suppose themselves to have been as children" (1994a, p. 114). It is for this reason that it is possible for parents to say to their child that *schooldays are the best days of your life*. This retrospective nostalgia of the adult, projected back onto childhood, reconstructs this childhood as an idealised, trouble-free, and blissful period. Here we begin to perceive one of the discourses on childhood, a discourse that constructs a particular view of childhood, a particular type of childhood.

We can no longer take *childhood* or the *child* as what they are considered to be from a common-sense understanding. Childhood is, in one sense, a state determined by the societal, political, ideological, and even clinical discourses that prevail. Such discourses, implicit or explicit, weave our commonly held conceptions of the child in ways that are quite predetermined.

These considerations bring forward the whole question of how, in regard to clinical practice, we construe the notions of time and history. Usually, time is considered to be a linear dimension, and history, and consequently development, is taken as a type of *process*. If we are not to allow such customary modes of thinking to prejudice the way in which we are able to grasp the child and the notion of childhood in clinical practice, then we must call them into question.

The question of development

The common-sense notion that defines the child in terms of age is taken up in clinical practice and refined by a division into developmental stages and tasks. In most clinical disciplines concerning the child, the so-called *developmental approach* has become a touchstone in which clinicians believe as a doctrine. Far from being a modern notion as it is portrayed, however, the *developmental* approach is an inevitable— and symptomatic—fallback position, whenever the notion of ages and stages is not questioned. In some texts it is even proposed that the developmental model emerged from Sigmund Freud himself! The theme of the Ages of Man, which was already prominent in Ancient Greek and Roman times, however, is the font from which developmental theory springs. The developmental model was already present in Oedipus' reply to the riddle of the Sphinx. While such an approach is promoted as being modern and scientific, it is in fact an elaboration of the ideology passed onto us from the Dark Ages.

Freud is most frequently read in a developmental manner but this is far from the only way in which his works may be taken up. In particular, it is his notion of sexual stages that lends itself to such a reading. Nonetheless, if we examine the text in which this notion is most explicitly elaborated, the *Three Essays on the Theory of Sexuality*, we find that although Freud speaks of "phases of development", he describes these in relation to what he calls the "Pregenital Organizations" (Freud, 1905d, p. 197). This notion of *organisation* conveys the concept of a structure that does not limit itself to a particular moment of time in the development of the psyche. Rather, it is an organisation that persists over time, even if it might be more prominent at particular moments in the life of each subject.

On the other hand, the promotion of time as a linear *process* inevitably leads to the idea of infantile sexuality being a set of stages that the child must pass through in his or her *development* and in which he or she may remain fixated at certain points. Thus in the hands of many of Freud's followers, the psychosexual organisations have become fixed as *stages*. With Anna Freud (1965), for instance, these have become reified into more and more stages and sub-stages that serve as objectifying criteria to determine normality or pathology. One of the effects of the developmental discourse is the insistence on a supposed *normality*. Or, with Erik Erikson (1950) and others, there are prescribed tasks to perform in order to pass into the next stage. These tasks, though, effectively become the commands of the superego.

The inevitable counterpart of the developmental logic is that the proposed fixations at certain points are seen as signs of an illness, or a delay in regard to the norm. Hence what creeps into this type of understanding is the deductive logic of objective science in which there is a linear notion of *cause* and *effect*. The symptoms and signs of the adult are projected back onto the putative *causes* of such fixations in early childhood. This is precisely the idea that predominates in clinical circles and determines the predominant place of the *aetiological formulation*, a concept that will be critically evaluated here.

The unquestioning endeavour to understand the child through a notion of ages and stages has led most streams of psychoanalysis after Freud to pursue a developmental line. This inexorable developmental bent, in not being questioned, has continued to plague psychoanalysis and other forms of clinical practice with children. It has afflicted both the history of psychoanalysis as well as the clinical apprehension of the child. Freud himself was not always clear and consistent about what was to be understood by the term *child*. Nonetheless, we can say that if on the one hand he did not explicitly subscribe to the notion of *development*, on the other hand he does not make of *childhood* a theoretical category.

The disciplines of psychology and psychiatry that emerged through the nineteenth century were imbued with a nineteenth-century notion of *process*. Freud's psychoanalysis was also influenced by this idea. These ideas continue to permeate clinical practice, for example in the psychiatric concepts of *organic process* or *psychotic process*. Some streams of psychoanalysis propose that a psychoanalytic treatment is also a process. Today, however, the origin of this conception of *process* has been lost. We need to return to earlier texts in order to see this notion articulated more explicitly. Jaspers, for instance, expresses it in the following way:

> *Process.* When some *entirely new* factor arises from a change in the psychic life that is in contrast to the development of the individual's life so far, it may be a phase. However where this is a *lasting* change in the psychic life we speak of a process. (1913, p. 692)

Jaspers goes on to further articulate this notion in relation to the psyche:

> Apart from theory and to create a term which will characterize the whole matter and do justice to the fact that we can only approach this from a psychological point of view, we have termed these processes 'psychic processes', as distinct from organic processes, using this concept as a marginal concept and not a classificatory one .... These phrases however express the riddle but do not explain it. (p. 693)

Here, in a footnote, Jaspers refers to another paper of his called "*Eifersuchtswahn*—a contribution to the problem of 'development of a personality' or 'process'" (p. 693). The notion of *development* here is synonymous with that of *process* in so far as it refers to the trajectory of the individual and his or her personality. As I have noted elsewhere (2000a), such a notion of development of the personality can refer only to the development of the ego, and not the unconscious. Freud noted that one of the qualities of the unconscious is that of "*timelessness*" (Freud, 1915e, p. 187). Thus it would be an absurdity to speak of development as a diachronic *process* in reference to the unconscious.

However, in contrast to the riddle of which Jaspers writes, the notions of process and development have become so ingrained in clinical practice as to no longer be in any need of questioning or explanation. But how have such notions permeated the clinical disciplines to such a degree?

Giorgio Agamben, in his paper "Time and History: Critique of the Instant and the Continuum", notes that the idea governing the nineteenth-century concept of history is that of *process*. He asserts that this is something that was only able to be grasped by Nietzsche. According to this notion it is only *process* as a whole that has meaning, never the particular moment of what Agamben refers to as *now*. In fact this concept of process is explicated by Agamben as pertaining to the Christian notion of salvation with which our Western concept of history is imbued. Thus our idea of history becomes a before and after of salvation, literally a BC and an AD, promoting as it does the idea of a linear history. Agamben proposes that: "... the history of salvation has meanwhile become pure chronology, a semblance of meaning can be saved only by introducing the idea—albeit one lacking any rational foundation—of a continuous, infinite progress" (1978a, p. 106).

As we have noted with Jaspers, the introduction of a conception of development or process does not explain anything in itself. The question posed here, rather, is quite the contrary: what is it that is obscured by the insistence upon a linear notion of time and the corresponding concepts of *process* and *development*? Agamben gives us some inkling into these things. He goes on to say the following in regard to the introduction of the notion of *process* in the nineteenth century:

> Under the influence of the natural sciences, 'development' and 'progress', which merely translate the idea of a chronologically oriented process, become the guiding categories of historical knowledge. Such a concept of time and history necessarily expropriates man from the human dimension and impedes access to authentic historicity. As Dilthey and Count Yorck had observed ... behind the apparent triumph of historicism in the nineteenth century is hidden a radical negation of history, in the name of an ideal of knowledge modelled on the natural sciences. (p. 106)

Although Agamben does not mention him, we can hear echoes of Darwin in this. Nor is Darwin far away in Freud's theorisations. But this developmental ideal of knowledge in the clinical field, due in part to the prominence and success of the natural sciences, is translated by a recourse to so-called objective observations. We can cite tendencies such as the emphasis on infant observations in the object relations field, as well as attachment theory, as prominent examples of the way that psychoanalytic theory has often tended to be deviated in a developmental direction. But what is radically negated, to use Agamben's expression, in the rush to objectivise, is the singularity of each subject as articulated by his or her particular trajectory. It is the encounter of each subject with sex, as broadly defined by Freud, that is erased by the reification of developmental ages and stages and the insistence on normality. Such an encounter was brought to prominence by Freud's method but always seems to be eliminated in later revisions.

Let us look to Giorgio Agamben once more in attempting to draw some further conclusions from the tendency to reduce *time* to a continuous progress:

> This leaves ample scope for the Lévi-Straussian critique, which points to the chronological and discontinuous nature of historiographical codification, and denounces fraudulent pretensions to any objective historical continuity independent of the code (with the result that history ultimately assumes the role of a 'thoroughgoing myth'). (p. 106)

Here the notion of history can be taken as referring to both *history* as a branch of learning—including the history of our clinical disciplines—and also as the *clinical history* of any particular patient. And if *code* is taken as the medium through which the patient articulates him- or herself, in other words, language, the notion of history as the linear progression of a life must be questioned. Thus *history*, including the clinical history as recounted by a patient, must be regarded as a mythical story. This is not at all to diminish the place of history but rather to restore it to its rightful place.

The psychoanalyst Jean Allouch has been a prominent critic of the notion of *process* which has crept into psychoanalysis. He counters this notion with Lacan's act of renaming the unconscious *unebévue*, which he says is a transliteration—not translation—of the Freudian *Unbewusste*, the unconscious. This *unebévue* is literally *a blunder* or more correctly *ablunder*, in reference to Freud's notion of parapraxes and bungled actions. Allouch proposes that this approach, "offers psychoanalysis the perspective of being able to situate each manifestation of *unebévue* as a singular, subjective *event*, not assimilable to any other, resistant to any incorporation into a so-called process" (2007, p. 18).

In other words, for Allouch, as for Lacan, it would be a fallacy to speak of a *process* in relation to the unconscious, since the unconscious is only made present at the very moment of a blunder, a parapraxis, a slip of the tongue for instance. We might also recall that Freud uses the word *unassimilable* in his "Project for a Scientific Psychology" at a point in which he speaks of the perceptions being "dissected into an unassimilable component (the thing)" (1950a, p. 366), "the thing" or *das Ding*. It is this unassimilable component, irreducible to what is already known, that is of interest to us in this encounter with the unconscious.

Allouch (1995), similarly, is critical of the notion of *Trauerarbeit*, the work of mourning, or at least the work of mourning conceived of as a *process*, dedicating a large study to a critique of this concept. He puts forward that even though Freud creates this term in his paper "Mourning and Melancholia", he does so in a way that is integrated into the writing of the text and which is permitted by the German language. He notes that the term *Trauerarbeit* was advanced by certain of Freud's followers, promoting it as a theoretical notion. For instance, in 1924 Karl Abraham wrote "*Trauerarbeit*", or "work of mourning", in inverted commas, as a way of attributing this to Freud but in doing so he elevates it to the status of a theoretical concept. Against this notion, Allouch privileges mourning as an *act*, an act which occurs at a particular moment or moments, in the moment of an utterance or *ablunder: unebévue*. That is, the act occurs in a *now* to return to Agamben's word, in order to constitute an *event*.

The notion of *development*, in so far as it has been adopted by certain schools of psychoanalysis, confuses and conflates the nineteenth-century notion of time as *process* with the history of the subject. That is, two aspects of temporality become sutured together, which has the effect of stifling thought on the matter. It is our task here to tease apart the various aspects of temporality that have a bearing on the child, and thus the notion of childhood itself.

What is the place of history?

In what manner can the notion of history, as it pertains to psychoanalysis, be taken up? To address the question of history we must examine both the status of history in its more general sense, including the history of psychoanalysis, as well as the particular history as recounted by the patient, including the account given by the child.

History refers in some way to the historical or the chronological sequencing of events. The history also participates in what can be called the *horological*, in other words the time of the clock. Thus there is the time of the session in which the history is given, but also the time and the timing of the events that are recounted which can take on their own importance in the history. Even if what are determinative in a history are the "accidental factors" (Freud, 1905d, p. 131) rather than the steady progression of development, the history is still recounted to us in the guise of a sequence of events, an historical or chronological account. These are two aspects of the history which must be disconnected from each other. Here the question of the history of psychoanalysis can be introduced.

In the beginnings of psychoanalysis, the child first entered the stage via the retrospective accounts of adults in analysis. From the outset, for psychoanalysis, *childhood* has always been something different to the period itself in which one is a child. Rather, it is a fabrication of the adult based upon selective memory, amnesia, and a post hoc account that is determined by the desire of the subject. Freud himself refers to "the distortion and refurbishing to which a person's own past is subjected when it is looked back upon from a later period" (1918b, p. 9).

Nonetheless a difficulty arises when this account is conflated with the period of childhood itself. Such a confusion occurs when what is recounted by adults is taken as the cause of their suffering through a type of aetiological formulation: whether it is the formulation of the patient or that of the clinician does not matter. This method of producing an aetiological formulation, to endeavour to locate a cause in the past, is a very commonplace one, and, contrary to the view often held, has nothing to do with psychoanalysis. This method is no different to the approach of the man in the street who says *I am like this because of what happened when I was a child*. Moreover, to take this method to the letter would be to say that *childhood is the cause of the adult*. It is this approach that is so prevalent in clinical practice since what is produced is always an *aetiological formulation*: all must be explained in terms of the history.

Freud himself participated in such a conception. For instance in his preface to the fourth edition of *The Three Essays on the Theory of Sexuality*, he proposes that, "If mankind had been able to learn from a direct observation of children, these three essays could have remained unwritten" (1905d, p. 133). Here he apparently confuses the child who is observed, with the notion of the *child* that is sketched out in the retrospective accounts of adults. Nonetheless, Freud seems to have in mind a different understanding of *observation*, noting in his preface to the third edition of the same text that the exposition of the case history of Little Hans "is based entirely upon everyday medical observation" (p. 130). But this same *observation* consists essentially of listening to what little Hans has to say to his father over an extended period of time. This is clearly no ordinary observation in the usual sense of a visual inspection. Furthermore, Freud notes that in this account, "preference is given to the accidental factors" (p. 131). In giving weight to the accidents or incidents that punctuate the supposedly steady progress of the history, we see that the history recounted is not at all a linear progression of development.

Maud Mannoni, in introducing her book *The Child, His "Illness", and the Others*, recounts the following regarding how childhood emerged in psychoanalysis:

> In the beginning of psychoanalysis, childhood was presented in the recollection of adults only in the sense of repressed memories. What was at issue was not so much the real past as the way it was situated in a certain perspective; in reconstructing his childhood the subject reorganized the past according to his desire, like a small child at play who reorganizes his present or past world to suit his fancy. Words surge forth to make contact with a real or imaginary adult—indeed, an imaginary companion. In psychoanalysis, the verbal accounts of children as well as of adults refer us not so much to realities as to worlds of desires and dreams. (1967a, p. 4)

What strikes us here is the fact that Mannoni does not differentiate between the accounts of the adult and the child in psychoanalysis. The adult as well as the child has what we can call a *childhood*. A four-year-old child whom I treated in psychoanalysis, for instance, did a drawing, saying that it was of "mummy's penis, daddy's penis, my penis, and my penis when I was a baby". He then drew and spoke of a similar series of "bottoms". We see in this example that in an analysis, even a young child such as this proposes an earlier time, a previous time that cannot be remembered: "when I was a baby". So then if the adult speaks of a previous time as *when I was a child*, this young child speaks of a previous time as *when I was a baby*, or *when I was little*, or *when I was in Mummy's tummy*, and so on. In this sense there is no structural difference between the analysis of an adult and that of the child: each has a *childhood* or a *previous time*.

Such a *previous time* has an enigmatic status, since this is a time outside the history in the terms in which the subject recounts it. Given that this time is always a time that is shrouded in amnesia, myth, and fantasy, we can refer to it as "Once upon a time" (Plastow, 2012a). Freud refers to this mythical time in a number of different ways. In his *Three Essays*, he refers to childhood as a "primaeval period, which falls within the lifetime of the individual himself" (1905d, p. 173). This primaeval period is constituted by the influence of heredity, in other words, that which lies outside the individual's history. He refers to this factor as "phylogenesis" as opposed to "ontogenesis" (p. 131). Once again, it is evident that Freud is a reader of Darwin. Moreover, in the *Three Essays*, Freud comments that infantile amnesia "turns everyone's childhood into something like a *prehistoric* epoch" (p. 176, my italics). In other words, in giving this primaeval period the status of a prehistory, he thus places it *outside history*.

Freud refers to this particular notion, that childhood is a *prehistoric* epoch, as the "infantile factor" (p. 176). It is this term *infantile* that is repeated from the notion of infantile amnesia. David Pereira reads in Freud's *infantile factor* an element of remoteness and alterity, or otherness. In this way, the infantile factor functions as an historically remote reference point for the adult neurosis. For this reason he proposes that "psychoanalysis proceeds by interpretation and construction of this remoteness, not by observation" (Pereira, 1999, p. 62). We can take from this that the *infantile factor* has to be distinguished from the *child* or *childhood* as recounted by the adult. The *infantile* in this formulation is precisely that which lies outside history. It is specifically this point that will guide our investigations in this book.

Nonetheless, in Freud, the logic of the *historical* and that of the *infantile* or *prehistoric* continues to be played out, as it does in any analysis whether it be of an adult or of a child. Pereira proposes that Freud does this by maintaining a tension, the tension "between the historical and the prehistoric, the ontogenetic and the phylogenetic" (1999, p. 63). Without recourse to the logical apparatus that Jacques Lacan uses much later on, we can put forward that Freud's method of approaching this temporal logic is precisely through the tension that he maintains between the historic and the prehistoric.

Sex and the history

If the prehistoric is what is outside the history, it nonetheless has a particular flavour. Freud notes in his review of the literature on children that had been written up to the beginning of the twentieth century, that not a single author had clearly recognised the existence of the sexual drive in childhood, and that in their works, "the chapter on 'Sexual Development' is as a rule omitted" (Freud, 1905d, p. 173). Similarly, what is omitted through the process of infantile amnesia is also something particular to the subject's sexuality.

Maud Mannoni reminds us of the case of a child suffering from night terrors reported by Debacker in 1881 (1967a, p. 44), and referred to by Freud in the *Interpretation of Dreams*. This case concerned a thirteen-year-old boy who had had a two-year history of disturbed nights and other symptoms. By way of treatment, he was sent to the country for a year and a half and when he returned he had recovered, but still remembered his past fears. Upon reaching puberty he gave the following explanation of his symptoms: "I didn't dare admit it; but I was continually having prickly feelings and overexcitement in my parts; in the end it got on my nerves so much that I often thought of jumping out of the dormitory window" (Freud, 1900a, p. 586). Despite this rich account given by the child and reported in his own medical thesis, Debacker's final conclusion was that of an entirely organic aetiology, explaining that all the symptoms were due to "cerebral ischaemia" (Freud, 1900a, p. 587).

What Freud refers to as the *infantile factor* or *infantile sexuality* is specifically what is absent in the case history. It disappears both from the clinical history that is usually taken by clinicians, as well as from the history of medical and psychological studies on the child, including within psychoanalysis itself. In the Wolf Man case history. Freud struggles to utilise this case to demonstrate the veracity of infantile sexuality and its resulting psychopathological effects, because of the dissension at that time of both Adler and Jung upon precisely this point. A number of more recent approaches concerning children—such as attachment theory and so-called mentalisation, for instance—supposedly draw upon psychoanalysis, but in doing so effectively expunge the sexual from the child's history.

There is something quite symptomatic in a clinical approach that involves this insistent and repetitive disappearance of sexuality from the history of the child. This is something that we can note currently in clinical circles in which, in effect, children are not inherently considered to have a sexuality. As soon as there is some manifestation of overt sexual behaviour in the child, or indeed some sexual elements in the child's play, the question of so-called "sexual abuse" is raised by concerned clinicians (Plastow, 2012b, p. 71). In other words, as soon there is a question of a child's sexuality, a cause from outside the child is immediately sought to explain it. This is not at all to say that sexual interference or molestation of children does not exist. But the question that does concern us here is how the irruption of sexuality, whether it arises from within or without, is experienced in the child.

In Part II of this book, the history of the beginnings of child psychoanalysis will be examined in a similar manner. That history was also punctuated by an irruption of sexuality in its principal protagonists, including in their relation to their own children. Sexuality and the *infantile factor* play as great a part in the history and structure of child psychoanalysis itself, as they do in the clinical history of each child.

Freud started from the very same point: that of having to posit sexual molestation in each of the cases of hysteria that he was treating, in order to explicate sexual elements in the dreams and fantasies of his patients. In the nineteenth century and up to the time in which Freud began to write, the psychiatric theory of hereditary degeneration held sway. According to this notion, sexuality in children was seen as a type of moral and constitutional degeneration. Such degeneration was considered to develop over the course of a number of generations, with each generation passing on a more degenerate form to the next. But whether it is degeneration, heredity, or any putative organic lesion, what all these have in common is to place sexuality *outside the history* of the child.

Since sexuality disappears or is excluded from the history, it has a tendency to reappear from elsewhere, particularly in the proposition of sexual traumas. Given that the *aetiological formulation* is necessarily incomplete—since something that we call *infantile sexuality* is necessarily excluded—there is a tendency in clinical practice to cast back the notion of cause to more and more distant times. Even in Freud's era, Otto Rank proposed that "the true source of neurosis was the act of birth" (Freud, 1937c, p. 216). Since, the notion of *cause* has been cast even further back to intrauterine life, but always in the same formulation that we have already articulated, that *the child is the cause of the adult*. We have to keep looking further and further back for this supposed place of trauma or cause, given that the history is always inadequate to explicate the suffering of the subject. Something always lacks in the history and, in clinical practice, it has to be made good by the proposition of a previous event to which a causative effect is attributed. Such an event is said to be traumatic in that it exerts its pathological effect on the child from without, from outside the child.

We could put forward that, for psychoanalysis, the purpose of the history is to elucidate an intersection of the history with the structure of the subject as defined by his or her encounter with sex and death, in other words, with the elements of the Oedipus complex. "Death and sexuality", as we recall, are the two unknowables circumscribed by Freud from the very first chapter of *The Psychopathology of Everyday Life* (1901b, p. 3). In particular, the enigma of sex and the mystery of death—both conveyed in the riddle of the Sphinx—are easily reduced to *trauma* if it is posited that sex was introduced by an external agent.

Childhood as remembered is a childhood of desire in which the child takes up a place as a sexual being. Such a childhood is not to be confused with an historical period that is posited as being able to be objectively observed. The temporal logic of this childhood does not correspond to a linear chronology, but is necessarily put forward in terms of a chronology. This is a structure that pertains to the adult and child alike.

What, then, is the nature of history? Lacan notes that, "History is not the past. History is the past in so far as it is historicized in the present" (1998a, p. 12). In the film series *The Story of Film: An Odyssey*, the film's director Mark Cousins interviews Scottish film director Bill Forsyth, who proposes something similar in relation to stories in cinema:

> We spend our lives inventing stories but the story doesn't really exist. We exist and our apprehension of a story is how we explain the kind of meanderings that we take. So there's no such thing as the empirical story. It's just what happens to people. (Cousins, 2011)

We can say the same thing about *history*, and about the clinical history: it is a retrospective attempt—an always failing one—to explain what has happened to us.

There is no such thing as a history *per se*—whether it be the history of the subject or the history of psychoanalysis—there is no such thing as a history in and of itself. There is only a history when it is recounted, when it is written in the present as a retrospective account. What is in question is the particular way in which each subject historicises the past. A psychoanalysis must constitute a rewriting of this historicisation. In the next chapter we will further examine the retrospective nature of history—and thus of the account of a patient in psychoanalysis—in reference to Freud's notion of the *Nachträglichkeit*.

The hole in the history

When the history of any particular subject is examined, there is always a lack in the history that is encountered: there is a hole in the history.

This hole in the history is nominated in various ways. It can be called the *prehistory*, which is otherwise designated by Freud as the *primal* (*primal* scene, father of the *primal* horde), or the *ancient* or *archaic*. It can also be called the *constitutional factors*, or *phylogeny* as opposed to ontogeny. Finally, this hole in the history, as it will be developed here, can be designated as the *infantile*—derived from the manner in which Freud refers to *infantile amnesia* or the *infantile factor* as it pertains to that which is outside (the) history.

For Freud the *infantile factor* is the central factor of repression, whether in infantile amnesia or hysterical amnesia. This infantile factor of repression functions for the child as well as the adult. But it functions in such a way that this factor must continue to remain outside the history as something that is not able to be retrieved. For the subject, given that sex is ultimately one of the great unknowables, sexuality—including infantile sexuality—is always presented through a screen. This is the basis of the Freudian notion of *screen memory* (1899a). In addition, Freud notes that a fetish is also like a screen memory: "The true explanation is that behind the first recollection of the fetish's appearance there lies a submerged and forgotten phase of sexual development" (1905d, p. 154). Here we give this submerged and forgotten phase the status of being fundamentally absent through the notion of the *infantile*.

The tendency in clinical circles is to fill in this lack in the history with a presumed or imagined knowledge. This presumed knowledge that is posited as being a candidate to fill the lack is referred to in various ways. Freud himself endeavoured to retrieve the knowledge that he presumed repressed by *infantile amnesia*. Anna Freud (1927a), and subsequently others, proposed a *preverbal stage*, which continues to be put forward to this day. It has always been exceedingly common—as we discerned with Debacker—to attribute an organic cause to fill the lack of knowledge, a tendency once referred to by Karl Jaspers as "Brain Mythologies" (1913, p. 18). And it has been increasingly common and even fashionable to attribute what we do not know to *genetics, epigenetics,* or even *brain chemistry*. In clinical practice, these stand in for the unknowable, just as *constitutional factors* did for Freud.

The *infantile*, then, is precisely what lacks in the history. Infantile sexuality and infantile amnesia refer to that which is unable to be found and presumed to be missing in action. Freud, again in the *Three Essays*, notes that the object is always a missing object and thus, "[T]he finding of an object is in fact a refinding of it" (1905d, p. 222).

We have endeavoured to put into question the usual conceptions of the child and childhood based on the common-sense notions of ages and stages that our culture has inherited at least from Ancient Greek times and which became firmly established in the Middle Ages. By continuing to subscribe to developmental and aetiological notions of history and of cause, we remain in the clinical Dark Ages. The developmental notion proposes a progressive unfolding of abilities and functions. The temporality that is determining in the structure of childhood, however, is of a different order. The notion of a smooth progress of development, given an orderly rhythm by the tasks and achievements of the various stages, is an aspect of the history that gives it an imaginary consistency and is one of the prevailing mythologies of childhood. The fact that such a history is always retrospective also contributes to this mythology.

It is the *accidents* of history that are determining, through the weight of a particular *now* or *event*. Such intrusions into the orderly progress of history are encounters with the elements of structure that pertain primarily to sex and death. The history, as Freud has elaborated it, is fundamentally flawed, or lacking. This flaw punches a hole in the imagined or imaginary consistency of the history, and it is this hole that is designated by the term *infantile*.

In a social context, the child is always a *minor*: he or she has limited rights and responsibilities and is nominally under the tutelage of an adult or adults. However, in relation to psychoanalysis, the child participates in the same retrospective temporal logic as the adult. Hence the *child*, as such, cannot be an analysand, since he or she is a minor. The *child* must therefore be attributed a place as subject.

CHAPTER TWO

A change of discourse: Freud's abandonment of the seduction hypothesis

On 21 September 1897, Freud wrote to his friend and colleague, Berlin ear, nose, and throat specialist Wilhelm Fliess, "I want to confide in you immediately the great secret that has been slowly dawning on me in the last few months. I no longer believe in my *neurotica*" (Masson, 1985, p. 264). In this way, Freud articulated the fact that he was abandoning his previous theory of the neuroses. This theory had proposed that hysterical symptoms, and hysteria itself, were caused by sexual seduction in infancy. According to that earlier theory, Freud had sought to locate the cause of hysterical symptoms in such traumatic infantile sexual experiences, of which the father was usually identified as the perpetrator (1896c). This early history was considered to be obscured by amnesia, something he later came to refer to as infantile amnesia. Such a traumatic aetiology of symptoms, of course, continues to have a prominent place in clinical circles. It is nothing different to what is referred to, in contemporary parlance, as childhood sexual abuse. This theoretical turning point does not imply that Freud no longer believed that the sexual seduction of children actually took place. Rather, it marked the beginning of a more sophisticated appreciation of his hysterical patients and the nature of their suffering.

In Freud's assertion in this letter, we can mark the very beginnings of psychoanalysis itself in so far as psychoanalysis became a science of the unconscious, as opposed to a psychology of supposed historical events. It also implied a new questioning of the status of *cause* in psychical suffering. The *seduction hypothesis* could now be understood as an endeavour to define one's suffering through a reference to history, to actual concrete external events. In other words, even if Freud abandoned the seduction hypothesis as the cause of hysteria, the seduction hypothesis nonetheless remains a foundational axis around which the whole question of psychoanalytic treatment turns. And this question is of crucial import to us here since its principal focus is upon the experience of the child, including the place of the history for the child. Thus it also articulates a changing understanding and conceptualisation of the child for psychoanalysis.

Freud's neurotica *and the seduction hypothesis*

Let us continue with Freud's letter to Fliess. Freud explains the reasons for his new disbelief in his previous theory of the neuroses. His first reasons are the following:

> The continual disappointment in my efforts to bring a single analysis to a real conclusion; the running away of people who for a period of time had been most gripped [by analysis]; the absence of the complete successes on which I had counted; the possibility of explaining to myself the partial successes in other ways ... (Masson, 1985, p. 264)

Here Freud expresses his disappointment with a number of incomplete or partial aspects of his treatments to date: *not all* can be explained by the seduction hypothesis. As we have noted, his disbelief primarily concerns the veracity and explanatory power of historical events. This evokes what we have referred to as the *hole in the history*. Freud comes to what is the most striking of the reasons for his new disbelief, that is, that in positing the cause as an actual seduction, what is evoked is:

> ... the surprise that in all cases, the *father*, not excluding my own, had to be accused of being perverse—the realization of the unexpected frequency of hysteria, with precisely the same conditions prevailing in each, whereas surely such widespread perversions against children are not very probable. (p. 264)

What is striking is that Freud is informed by more than just the revelations from his patients. The psychoanalytic revelations from his self-analysis, and in particular his own seduction hypothesis concerning his father, are also in play. In this statement we also perceive an important epistemological change that takes place in Freud's thinking. His previous theory which concerns *all fathers* was a generalising theory of the type which remains at the heart of conceptualisations in psychology and psychiatry. In abandoning such a notion of "all cases", Freud moves towards psychoanalysis as a science of the singular subject, rather than the subject as an instance of a generalised category.

This letter forms part of the correspondence between Freud and Fliess; however, we have access only to Freud's part. And even this part is also very incomplete (Kahn & Robert, 2006, pp. 7–12) despite the title of Jeffrey Masson's version (1985). It has been asserted, initially by Didier Anzieu (1959), and subsequently reinforced by Octave Mannoni (1969), that Freud's self-analysis took place through his correspondence with Fliess. Even though the main source of knowledge regarding Freud's self-analysis comes from his letters to Fliess, it may well be a very misleading conclusion that it was there that his self-analysis took place. Erik Porge (1996a) calls such a notion a "myth and chimera" of psychoanalysis and goes so far as to say that this account, which has become a psychoanalytic myth, has led to specific difficulties within psychoanalysis. There remains a question of where Freud's self-analysis took place, if we can say that there was indeed self-analysis. I have, by way of contrast, proposed that Freud's self-analysis took place through his writing but in quite a different context: specifically in his working of Goethe's *Faust* throughout his opus and over the lifespan of his work (Plastow, 2012c).

Freud had an intense and particular transference to Fliess, but transference does not guarantee that analysis takes place with the person who is the supposed subject of knowledge. Freud, for some time, subscribed to Fliess' theory regarding the aetiology of neurosis that consisted of a binary logic of a feminine cycle, or period, of twenty-eight days and a masculine period of twenty-three days. Fliess claimed that this corresponded to similar periods in animals and plants (Porge, 1996a, p. 19). This theory constituted an "all" as it was applicable to all individuals. Porge puts forward that it was the all-encompassing certainty of Fliess' delusional *binary logic* that ultimately pushed Freud to question the cause of neurosis and its relation to sexuality. Freud's "Project for a Scientific Psychology" contrasts starkly with what is described by Porge as Fliess' *organology*, with its absolutely determined concept of neurotic suffering.

It is in part, then, the unshakeability of Fliess' certainty—which Porge proposes was a delusional certainty—that induced Freud's disbelief in his own *neurotica*. Such disbelief in an historical, and thus also predetermined notion of causality, took the form of the disbelief in the perversity of his own father, as well as that of "all" fathers of his hysterical patients. This disbelief introduced another element, specifically that of the unconscious as the purveyor of an enigmatic or unknown truth. If the history inadequately explains the suffering of the subject, then what remains is an enigmatic surplus. This is where we can locate the unconscious as elaborated by Freud: the *Unbewusste*, which we can also coin, in good English, as the *unbeknownst*. We might even compare the step that Freud makes here, in refusing to follow Fliess' madness, to that of René Descartes in his methodology of hyperbolical doubt. After considering the delusional beliefs of the insane, Descartes concludes, "but then they are madmen, and I should appear no less mad if I took them as a precedent for my own case" (1641, p. 62). Here we might pinpoint the function of belief in clinical practice, and the methodological step introduced by Freud's hyperbolical doubt, "my doubt about my own matters" (Masson, 1985, p. 266), as he refers to it. Thus Freud's singular truth was allowed to contravene a generalised truth, the truth of the universal aetiology of the seduction hypothesis, as well as that of Fliess' delusional logic.

The effects of an epistemological rupture

This step by Freud led to a different epistemology in that it gave birth to psychoanalysis as a new discourse. Such a radical change of direction has the status of what Michel Foucault described as an *epistemological rupture* in knowledge, giving rise to what he referred to in *The Order of Things* as a new *episteme* (1966). It is an epistemological rupture in that the seduction hypothesis is no longer posited as the overall aetiology of neurosis, but is taken as a specific construction in each analysis. The seduction hypothesis is henceforth, within the analysis, located in the unconscious phantasy—to use Freud's term—of each analysand.

Freud's abandonment of the seduction hypothesis has of course been the subject of many critiques, including most famously that of

Jeffrey Masson in his book, *The Assault on Truth* (1984). The basis of such critiques is usually that Freud ceased believing that sexual seductions actually occurred. These critiques, moreover, continue to place their emphasis on the history as an adequate explanation for the subject's suffering. They are also misguided in that they misrepresent Freud's opinion. As clarified by Laplanche and Pontalis, "Right up to the end of his life, Freud continued to assert the existence, prevalence and pathogenic force of scenes of seduction actually experienced by children" (1967, p. 406).

Such critiques, most importantly, miss the point of Freud's radical discovery. As we have noted, they continue to be raised in clinical practice when sexual abuse is posited as the cause of a child's suffering, even in the absence of any material evidence of such. Rather, Freud's discovery implies that it is the encounter with sexuality itself that is traumatic, regardless of how it is experienced. And, in psychoanalysis, it is through the manifestations of the unconscious that we are able to read something of the specific way in which this trauma of sex has been structured for each subject and construed as historical occurrences.

For Freud himself, the abandonment of the seduction hypothesis gave rise to a completely new consideration, leading to, as he writes, "the certain insight that there are no indications of reality in the unconscious, so that one cannot distinguish between truth and fiction" (Masson, 1985, p. 264).

This is not to say that seduction or sexual abuse does not happen, or that it may be a traumatic occurrence. Rather, whether sexual abuse has occurred or not, a seduction hypothesis is posited by the subject in every case as an historical occurrence. And such a seduction hypothesis is a manifestation of the unconscious phantasy. However, what we have referred to as the *hole in the history* is a type of remainder, or leftover from the aetiological hypothesis. It is Freud who tells us what the function of such a remainder is: "[T]here would remain the solution that the sexual fantasy invariably seizes upon the theme of the parents" (pp. 264–265). This is, of course, the basis of what Freud would later refer to as the Oedipus complex.

Many years later, in the paper "On the History of the Psycho-Analytic Movement", Freud laid claim to the discovery of psycho-analysis precisely through his apprehension of the unconscious truth of sexuality—as a cause of hysterical suffering—that was transmitted to him by others. He grasped this in the anecdotes of the gynaecologist

Chrobach, the physician Charcot, and his own colleague Breuer. These clinicians, unbeknownst to themselves, conveyed to Freud a knowledge of the sexual nature of hysterical suffering. Freud states that, "These three identical opinions, which I heard without understanding, had lain dormant in my mind for years, until one day they awoke in the form of an apparently original discovery" (1914d, p. 13).

What is striking in this account is the temporal aspect of Freud's discovery. Even though this knowledge had been transmitted to Freud, it was only many years later that he retrospectively discovered it. Thus his discovery of the sexual aetiology of the neuroses was apprehended in a retroactive movement that Freud called the *Nachträglichkeit* and which Lacan would later name an *après-coup*. Already, in this very same letter of 21 September 1897, Freud was able to articulate this, although not yet in a theoretical manner:

> It seems once again arguable that only later experiences give the impetus to fantasies, which [then] hark back to childhood, and with this the factor of a hereditary disposition regains a sphere of influence from which I had made it my task to dislodge it—in the interest of illuminating neurosis. (Masson, 1985, p. 265)

In other words, Freud's abandonment of the seduction hypothesis as an actual historical traumatic occurrence is also an abandonment of the notion of a strict chronological ordering in the unconscious. Instead, the seduction is redefined as a scene of unconscious phantasy that is retroactively constructed. This notion was articulated by Freud with the term *Nachträglichkeit*, a term that we will here retain in preference to the translation given in the *Standard Edition*, as well as Jeffrey Masson's version of the correspondence, as "deferred action" (pp. 280, 316). The latter is a poor translation as it misconstrues the *Nachträglichkeit* as a forward temporal movement, or a "delayed discharge" (Laplanche & Pontalis, 1967, p. 114). It was in order to combat such a misconception that Lacan introduced the term *après-coup* into psychoanalytic theory in the French language. As there has been no adequate term to translate *Nachträglichkeit* in English, we will continue to emphasise Freud's term in the original German.

The epistemological rupture that was articulated by Freud is that it is the encounter with sexuality per se, an encounter to which each of us is subjected, that is the basis of the seduction hypothesis. And it is through this epistemological shift that Freud abandons the seduction hypothesis as an overall aetiological theory. In its place he nonetheless maintains the seduction hypothesis as a singular hypothesis for each subject in analysis. In this quest for origins, the truth for each subject can then be located through the accidents of history, not via a linear chronology, but rather by way of the retroactive logic of one's own *Nachträglichkeit*.

Let us then turn our attention to the manner in which Freud elaborated his notion of the *Nachträglichkeit*, a notion that became a key to the understanding of the temporal logic of the unconscious. It is the concept of the *Nachträglichkeit* that makes sexuality into a traumatic event, in the retelling of the accidents of history.

The temporal logic of the Nachträglichkeit

Freud first elaborated the notion of the *Nachträglichkeit* in his "Project for a Scientific Psychology", in the case of the girl referred to as Emma (1950a). The editors of the French edition of the correspondence suggest that this Emma was in all likelihood Emma Eckstein, who figures prominently in the Freud–Fliess correspondence. This "Project" was, in fact, part of Freud's correspondence with Fliess and was not published until the correspondence was posthumously retrieved from the Fliess family. It follows the correspondence in the Standard Edition (Freud, 1950a), but is absent from Jeffrey Masson's version of the correspondence (1985), as well as that published in German (Schröter, 1986). The more recent French version (Kahn & Robert, 2006) does include the "Project for a Scientific Psychology". Thus in taking up this question of Emma and the *Nachträglichkeit*, we must read the "Project" in reference to the rest of Freud's correspondence with Wilhelm Fliess.

In the "Project", Freud develops the idea of the *Nachträglichkeit* according to what he refers to as the *proton pseudos* πρῶτον ψεῦδος). Freud borrowed this term from Aristotle's *Prior Analytics* in which Aristotle proposed that, "A false argument comes about by reason of the first falsity [*proton pseudos*] in it" (Book II, 66a, Ch. 18, line 17, in Barnes, 1984a, p. 105). According to Freud it is with such a "first falsity", or false premise, that repression functions as the barrier to the unconscious and sexuality, in the retroactive logic of the *Nachträglichkeit* (1950a, pp. 352–356). In this case, a false premise leads to a false conclusion, but a false premise, for Aristotle, is also capable of generating a true conclusion.

Freud's patient Emma was an adolescent girl who suffered from a phobia of going alone into shops. She remembered an incident from when she was twelve years old, shortly after the onset of puberty, of seeing the two shop assistants laughing together. She recalled that they were laughing at her clothes and that, "one of them had pleased her sexually" (p. 353). In relation to her current symptom, Freud considered that the unpleasure she had experienced from being laughed at for her childish clothes had long been corrected. As an adult she no longer felt ridiculed for her manner of dress, and, moreover, the question of how she dressed was seemingly immaterial to whether she went into a shop alone or accompanied. Thus Freud considered that the memory alone—and thus the history as given—was inadequate to explain her symptoms.

During the analysis Emma revealed a second memory of which she was not conscious at the time of recounting the previously described scene. On two occasions, when she was eight years old, she had gone into a shop to buy sweets and a shopkeeper had grabbed at her genitals through her clothes. She herself noted that the laughing of the shop assistants had reminded her of the grin with which the shopkeeper had later accompanied his assault. Despite this experience, Emma had returned to the shop. "She now reproached herself for having gone there the second time, as though she had wanted in that way to provoke the assault" (p. 354). Freud posited that her "oppressive bad conscience" (p. 354) was to be traced back to this retroactive experience: "The memory aroused what it was certainly not able to at the time, a *sexual release*, which was transformed into anxiety" (p. 354).

This term "anxiety" translates the word "*Angst*" from the original German (Freud, 1895, p. 446). Here, however, we render this word in English as *anguish*, a term devoid of both the psychiatric and commonplace connotations of *anxiety*, as well as the references to *Angst* in the translations of existential and other philosophical traditions. *Anguish* does not implicate the existence of an object of anxiety or fear. It is a subjective state, that is, an experience to which one is subject. *Anguish* does not have an object, therefore is not necessarily *about* anything in particular, and therefore most apt here. It is also the most pertinent word in English to translate the term that Lacan used in French to elaborate upon Freud's notion of *Angst*, that is, *angoisse*. Emma experiences *anguish*: she is subject to an anguish that remains enigmatic.

As we have noted, Emma's onset of puberty had occurred between the two scenes. It is useful to note that the term *Nachträglichkeit* is derived from the verb *tragen* (literally *to carry*) and *nachtragen* (*to carry behind*) in German, which are etymologically related to the English verb *to drag*. It is this release of sexuality in puberty which is *nachträglich*, that is, it literally carries or drags the previous memory along behind it, transforming the prior experience with a new signification. Thus the *Nachträglichkeit* is the retroactive—and unconscious—effect of a current experience upon the earlier experiences forgotten behind the story, or history, that is told.

Freud proposed that it was the element remembered consciously, in this case, *clothes*, that had made two false connections in the material at its disposal. Firstly, Emma was being laughed at because of her clothes, and secondly, one of the shop assistants excited sexual pleasure in her. These false connections, a consequence of the *Nachträglichkeit*, led to the apparently rational outcome of the phobic symptom, that is, of running away.

In the recounting of this first scene of Emma's experience of sexuality—in other words through language—it acquired a false connection with the later scene. Freud thus outlines what he designates as the *proton pseudos* as this first falsity for psychoanalysis. According to Aristotle, the *proton pseudos* is the prior false statement, that, in his logic, can lead to a true conclusion (Barnes, 1984a). Thus to cite Aristotle: "From true premises it is not possible to draw a false conclusion; but a true conclusion may be drawn from false premises" (Barnes, 1984a, p. 85, 53b, lines 7–8).

To follow this propositional logic, it is because Freud proposed that a first false statement can effect a true conclusion that he was able to deduce that second, and earlier, scene from Emma's associations. The truth that resided in the symptom lay in the effect of the earlier memory that was hidden behind the later one. Freud's conclusion regarding the sexual nature of the symptom was precisely that of the *Nachträglichkeit* of the latter scene upon the prior. It is not a question here of the historical truth of an event, which is the aetiological manner in which the history is usually taken. If Freud had proposed that the truth of the symptom lay solely in the historical veracity of the earlier scene, then he would have remained at the level of the seduction hypothesis. Thus it is Freud's implication of the *proton pseudos* that enables the real of sex for the subject to be introduced. This is something that confronts each and every subject, but tends to be reduced to a sexual traumatic event posited as being external to the subject.

It is the very concept of the *Nachträglichkeit* that changed the place of Freud's seduction hypothesis in regard to history and cause. Rather than remaining with the seduction as the true premise in a particular history—a true premise that according to propositional logic cannot produce a true conclusion—the seduction hypothesis is the necessary first false statement that constitutes any history. This *proton pseudos*, then, gives a mythical form to the difficult encounter with the real of sexuality, however it may be experienced. This is where Freud's notion of the family romance and infantile sexual theories take their form and provide a retrospective and fictionalised version of the child's encounter with the riddle of sex. This is an enigma that pertains to the manner in which the child experiences sexuality. In this way, sexuality is linked to the child's own body, as well as to his experience of the body of each of his parents. Nonetheless, the *Nachträglichkeit* also implies that screen memories and infantile sexual theories contain a kernel of truth, even though the explanation, as well as the notion of cause attributed to them, is false.

The child and the seduction hypothesis

But how does Freud's initial proposition of a seduction hypothesis, and its abandonment, as well as a temporal logic of the *Nachträglichkeit*, pertain to the child, in particular the child in analysis? Let us examine some of the effects of Freud's discovery on our contemporary practice with children.

As we have noted, the childhood that we remember is a childhood of desire, not to be confused with a supposedly objective historical period. Thus the temporal logic of this childhood does not correspond to a chronology, but is necessarily posited as a chronology. Each neurotic, in some way, posits that, *I am like this because when I was little ...* . In other words, this chronology, put forward as causative, is considered to determine the way we are. It is a structure that pertains to both the adult and child alike. The more apparently circumscribed the past event to which we ascribe causality, the more striking and apparently determinative it is. This is literally to propose a seduction hypothesis. What is being put forward here is that each and every subject proposes a seduction hypothesis in this manner. This is most evident when it is able to be heard from an analysand within psychoanalysis.

Freud was also such an analysand, through his self-analysis. Even if we can say that Freud abandoned the seduction hypothesis as the aetiology of hysteria, we can also say that each analysand must propose a seduction hypothesis in each and every analysis. This hypothesis is both the screen across infantile sexuality as we have referred to it, and simultaneously the very—and only—means of discovery of the *infantile*, that is, the very structure of desire itself, for each one of us. In reference to the terms already introduced, the seduction hypothesis can be equated to *history* in the sense that this is an account of an historical event, posited in terms of *when I was little*. The structure of fantasy and desire can likewise be equated with *time*: time as the synchronous structure of the signifier. Hence, clinically, it is not a question of abandoning the seduction hypothesis but rather of maintaining the tension between the diachrony of *seduction* (as a nominally external historical event), and the synchrony of *fantasy* (through which desire is in part apprehended).

Giorgio Agamben separates out the two terms *time* and *history* in the following way: "Every conception of history is invariably accompanied by a certain experience of time which is implicit in it, conditions it, and thereby has to be elucidated" (1978a, p. 99). It is infantile sexuality, or what Freud calls the *infantile factor*, that is at stake in the notion of time. But the passing of time is marked by a periodicity that Man imposes on it. This periodicity for each being, nonetheless, is faulty: it has a hole in it. This hole is the void from which the child is created; it is the infantile sexuality that is always out of reach of lived experience, and it is also the ineluctable march towards death.

In another paper, entitled "In Playland", Agamben refers to a section of Collodi's novel *Pinocchio* in which Pinocchio arrives at a place that is aptly called Playland. We can immediately hear in the name of this place a reference to something that is already outside the realm of history as lived. We could also call this place fantasy-land—in reference to the notion of phantasy in Freud, and that of the fantasm in Lacan. What interests us most in Agamben's account is that he puts forward, in reference to time and history, a correspondence and opposition between *play* and *ritual*. Rituals, such as those of the New Year and other feast days that are repeated each year, mark the calendar in a predictable and periodic way. Agamben cites the ethnologist Claude Lévi-Strauss who proposes that, "[R]ites fix the stages of the calendar, as localities do those of an itinerary [and that] the real function of ritual is ... to preserve the continuity of lived experience" (Agamben, 1978b, p. 77).

This "continuity of lived experience" is thus a type of *synchrony*, a continuity that exists outside the subject's experience of history, or *diachrony*. The events of the calendar preserve an experience of time that is outside any one individual's account of history. By being marked on the calendar, rites or rituals are able to transform events, historical or mythical, into a structure, namely the synchronic structure of time. Even if these events have an historical veracity, they become mythologised by the yearly ritual, as occurs for any national holiday. This ritual is also what Freud refers to as *repetition*. And repetition has, by its very nature, the retrospective structure of *Nachträglichkeit*. In repetition, including that of *repetition compulsion*, a nominally historical event is ritualised. That is, the repetition is inscribed as a type of memorial or monument to a putative historical event, just as an important event is marked on the calendar by a public holiday or some other ritual. This production of a ritual, nonetheless, ensures that such an event remains structurally intact and therefore synchronous.

Agamben opposes ritual to play, noting that each is engaged in a relationship with time, but that this relationship is in each case an inverse one: "Ritual fixes and *structures* the calendar; play, on the other hand, though we do not yet know how and why, changes and *destroys* it" (Agamben, 1978b, p. 77; italics in original). He notes that play "is a machine for transforming synchrony into diachrony" (Agamben, p. 83). Thus in our terminology, we can say that play transforms *time* into *history*. Agamben recognises his debt to Claude Lévi-Strauss to whom he attributes what he calls an *exemplary formula*: "[W]hile rites transform events into structures, play transforms structures into events" (Agamben, p. 82).

Play is what a child might do in a session of psychoanalysis. But whether we are referring to a child or an adult, what is in question is the play of the signifier, produced as it is by the method of free association introduced by Freud. In psychoanalysis, the fact that play can destroy the structure of time is, at the same time, at the heart of its creative ability. For if play changes the calendar, or periodic time, it does this in a way that makes the structure of *time* accessible within psychoanalysis. So what we can read from Agamben's proposition is that through a child's play, that which pertains to the synchronic structure of time is transformed into a diachronic history. The structure of the infantile is able to be apprehended, through play, by being fictionalised into a lived experience.

This is how we can read Freud's initial proposition of a seduction hypothesis: the play in the session fabricates a history, or a succession of events, out of the synchronous structure of the signifier. Thus the play in the session, including the play of words, tends to historicise a structure, to give meaning to the atemporal structure of sex and death by constructing seduction as an historical occurrence. It is in this way that the *time* of infantile sexuality, otherwise inaccessible, is presented for us to work with in psychoanalysis.

If we are proposing that each analysis begins with a seduction hypothesis, we can also propose that the abandonment of the seduction hypothesis is the work that is required to be able to finish an analysis. This has already been examined in relation to Freud's self-analysis, as well as to the movement in Freud's theorisation provoked by what he described as his "continual disappointment" (Masson, 1985, p. 264) in his work with hysterical patients. So it is with each analysand. The proposition of a seduction hypothesis in an analysis, in the very demand for analysis, posits the cause of one's suffering as being due to an interference by an Other. In this way infantile sexuality is put forward as Other, as something or someone external to the subject.

The seduction hypothesis is posited in sexual terms, or given a sexual meaning. Seduction is a necessary hypothesis in order to account for, and to approach, the *impossible*, in a logical sense, of infantile sexuality. To abandon this position is to be able to grasp that this account is wanting. Hence the abandonment of the seduction hypothesis requires a loss of the very hypothesis upon which the supposed evidence of one's existence has hitherto been based.

History, time, and the event

In order to demonstrate the way in which the divisions between the different notions of time are foundational for our Western cultures, Agamben also examines a phrase from the pre-Socratic thinker Heraclitus—a thinker who was able to give voice to modes of thought inaccessible to Western culture following Socrates, Plato, and Aristotle. He renders Heraclitus' fragment as "history is a child playing" (Agamben, 1978b, p. 82) but in another version it is given as "lifetime is a child playing" (Robinson, 1987, pp. 36–37). In neither version, however, is the first word—*αἰών* or *aiōn* in the Greek—given its full weight as a temporal notion outside the history of the individual, a word from which the English word "aeon" is derived. Agamben notes that in Greek, *aiōn* refers to eternity, and *chrónos* to diachronic time. Thus we might read, in Heraclitus' phrase, that the child is able to put an atemporal structure into play in the manner in which we have referred to the seduction hypothesis above. What Agamben fails to point out, though, is that in this account, the child is not alone: there is someone, an Other, in front of whom the child is playing and who bears witness to this fact. For psychoanalysis it is specifically the dimension of the transference that allows an event to be produced from a ritual in play.

In this sense, play maintains a relation to the sacred, and Agamben states that play in fact derives from the realm of the sacred. What we are referring to here as the *sacred* is, as in the sacred texts, something that ultimately cannot be named but which bears a relation to truth. For psychoanalysis this unnameable, such as the name of God in the Bible, is effectively the *unbeknownst*, the unconscious. Agamben cites Benveniste who also proposes play as a structure: "It has its source in the sacred, of which it supplies a broken topsy-turvy image" (1978b, p. 78). In this, we might also hear an echo of Lacan's proposition that truth can only be half-said.

We have already proposed that the notion of *development*, as it is used in certain streams of psychoanalysis and other approaches to clinical practice, confuses and conflates the nineteenth-century notion of time as *process* with the *history* of the subject and that these two aspects of temporality are sutured together in this way. We could add, again drawing on Agamben's formulation, that this predominance of the notion of development that emerged in our Western cultures at the beginning of the twentieth century is an expression of a particularly Christian notion of time. In the Christian experience, time is of a finite duration and takes place between two specific events, those of the Creation and the Final Judgement. As Agamben puts forward, "In contrast with the directionless time of the classical world, this time has a direction and a purpose: it develops irreversibly from the Creation to the end, and has a central point of reference in the incarnation of Christ, which shapes its development as a progression from the initial fall to the final redemption" (1978a, p. 103).

It is through this purposeful direction of time that the unfolding of abilities and attributes are interpreted by reference to a developmental perspective. And since religion has lost the predominant place it had in the nineteenth century as a social and political reference point, this temporality is now described in a secular manner. Nonetheless it is just as pervasive. Such a notion of time maintains the very same structure if we replace Creation with the Big Bang, and Redemption with the end of the world conceptualised as an environmental catastrophe. It is such a finite and orderly notion of time that determines our very idea of history. Agamben proposes that, "[I]t is Christianity which has laid the foundation for an experience of historicity, rather than the ancient world" (1978a, pp. 103–104).

It is the conflation of the notion of the history of the subject with this developmental temporality that excludes the very notion of what we can call the *event*. The event, as we conceive of it, transcends our understanding and the notions of time and history. It is something that intrudes into and perturbs our orderly sense of progress and development. To employ Lacan's three registers, the *event* pertains neither to the imaginary consistency of a history of continuous development, nor to the symbolic milestones that provide a periodicity to time. Rather the *event* is the irruption of the real as it intrudes and perturbs.

Erik Porge stresses the etymology of *event* as *ex-venire*, something that comes from without, something that is experienced by the subject as irrupting from outside (2005, p. 202). The *event* is something radically Other to anything that makes sense. It is Otherness itself. For Freud such a moment might be experienced in the recounting of what he called the *navel of the dream*, that is, the point at which the associations are so dense that one cannot proceed any further. Freud also referred to "the prehistoric, unforgettable other person who is never equaled by anyone later" (Masson, 1985, p. 213). In other words, this event is prehistoric, outside human time, rather than being subject to the forgetfulness of history. Nonetheless its presence may be felt in the immediacy of the *now*, in the anguish of a moment of silence, or derealisation, in an analytic session. So if we can link the accidents of history to what Lacan called, following Aristotle, the *automaton* of repetition, the *event* then pertains to that which escapes from the history. Such an event may be experienced in a moment of truth in what Lacan also refers to as the *tuché* (1964), the intrusion of the real. Such an intrusion is emphasised by Lacan in his notion of the unconscious as *unebévue*, or *ablunder*, that is, as a singular *event*, and not a process.

Lacan proposes that the Oedipus complex is an event in so far as it must be something more than a myth:

> ... it is not a question of genesis, or of history, or of anything that resembles it, as it seems to be at certain points in Freud as it has been able to be enunciated by him, in other words an event. It is not a question of being an event that is represented to us as being prior to all history (the only event is that which is connoted in something that is enunciated). It is a question of structure. (1971–1972, p. 257)

That which is connoted as being *prehistoric* in Freud—attains the status of structure with Lacan. If this structure cannot be directly denoted in words, in language, it can nonetheless only be connoted through language. In one way or another, the subject attempts to pinpoint this structure through the only means available to him, that is, through the history by which he attempts to give an account of himself. Thus such a structure can only be discerned through the spoken word by virtue of which the subject endeavours to historicise the *event* as a seduction hypothesis.

Similarly, Lacan refers to the murder of the father of the primal horde, a myth invented by Freud, as yet another *event* (p. 259). It is by virtue of these two *events* that Lacan was able to derive his formulae of sexuation that gave a logical basis to what was articulated by Freud by way of myth. The Oedipus complex and the myth of the murder of the father of the primal horde together function as a type of *proton pseudos* for Freud. That is, they are the first falsity, in mythical form, through which a truth is able to be unveiled. These two events, effectively, are none other than those of sex and death, events that remain obscured for the child.

The seduction hypothesis and the fantasm of psychic reality

In *Totem and Taboo*, Freud speaks of the murder of the father of the primal horde as an historical event, or at least as a mythico-historical occurrence. But in concluding he notes that, "The mere hostile *impulse* against the father, the mere existence of a wishful *phantasy* of killing and devouring him, would have been enough to produce the moral reaction that created totemism and taboo" (1912–1913, pp. 159–160;

italics in original). Thus the psychical reality is literally a phantasy in Freud's words. Freud expresses a wish that the two "coincided at the beginning with factual reality: that primitive men actually *did* what all the evidence shows that they intended to do" (p. 161). We can propose that this is Freud's foundational fantasy, his proton pseudos.

Freud articulates here, in his own manner, the function of origin as the founding exception, which was later taken up by Lacan through the means of logic. Similarly, the story of Genesis in Jewish and Christian mythology indicates that the words of the serpent, as an exceptional *event*, mark the entry of language and sexuality for Mankind. This moment is the beginning of the history of Man as an incomplete and fallible being, through the eviction from the Garden of Eden. Freud also makes an analogy between the prehistory of the primal horde, and what we can call the clinical prehistory of the subject, in speaking about the childhood of neurotics: "Each of these excessively virtuous individuals passed through an evil period in his infancy" (p. 161). In each case this "infancy" functions as a founding exception in the structure of the subject in this description. Thus the *infantile*, through the retroactive logic of the *Nachträglichkeit*, is a necessary construction of an exceptional event.

For Freud, the subject in analysis, in being confronted with the inadequacy of language to give an account of his or her suffering, falls back upon a phantasy through the seduction hypothesis. In Freud's attempts to situate a logical position for the subject, however, he hits bedrock, the "bedrock" (1937c, p. 252) of castration. With Lacan we find a logical position for what is posited historically as being outside, or as exception to, the present. Here it is not a question of what existed or not—the supposed historical reality—but of what is constructed as an effect of language through the *Nachträglichkeit*. Thus it is more a question of what *ex-sists*, or stands outside the subject. This place outside language and history is what we have elaborated through reference to the notion of the *infantile*. This is the exception that founds the history of each subject by fictionalising it.

With Agamben and Lévi-Strauss, we have said that rites transform events into structures, and, conversely, that play, the play of the signifier, has the creative ability that permits the subject to transform structure into events. In a session, the subject makes an historicised account out of his or her psychopathological structure. Hence the seduction hypothesis is the quintessential, but also fictionalised, historical event that is put forward in the form of a fantasm in each analysis, or even in each neurosis. We can go further to propose that seduction is a necessary hypothesis in order to account for, and to approach, the impossible structure of sex and death: the time of the *event*. This is the very function of the Oedipus complex which literally provides a mythologised account of the crossroads of death and sex.

The seduction hypothesis that each analysand must put forward is an historicised version of a structure. This structure is specifically that of desire which we have correlated with *time* as the synchronous structure of the signifier. In other words, the *history* is always a retrospective story, or fiction, which is the subject's endeavour to try to make sense of the accidents of history. The tension between this historicised event and the structure of desire is maintained by fantasy—or the fantasm—through which something of desire might be grasped. History and structure, then, are linked in a mythical manner in the discursive form of fantasy.

CHAPTER THREE

The fantasm: a transformational formula

The child is suspended between two primary temporal elements, those that we have designated as *history* and *time*. As a consequence, the question must be raised of what relation there might be between the two, and what might afford a mediation between them for the subject. Freud, in his correspondence with Fliess, put forward that one cannot distinguish between truth and fiction. If fiction is the necessarily fictional account of the history, then truth maintains a relation to structure, to *time*. For the unconscious, it also implies that there is no distinction between truth and fantasy, which is specifically what Freud put forward in his abandonment of the seduction hypothesis. Freud further proposed that the sexual fantasy invariably seizes upon the theme of the parents. It is specifically this fantasy—or the fantasm, in the way that Lacan came to elaborate it—that will be in question here.

In his brief paper of 1909 entitled "Family Romances", Freud describes what he refers to as one step of the liberation of the individual from the authority of his parents. Here he states that "small events in the child's life which make him feel dissatisfied afford him provocation for beginning to criticise his parents" (1909c, p. 237). In this way Freud gives expression to a dissatisfaction pertaining to

41

something that lacks for the child, a lack that is perceived as being in the parents. In this way the child's mother and father are no longer able to respond to the authority and knowledge that the child has invested in them, and to be what he expects of them. Here again we find that there is something missing from the history, something in regard to which the child cannot find an answer in those around him.

In the place of his parental authorities who are found to be wanting, Freud explains that the child, in his imagination, replaces these fallible beings by others who are, as a rule, of higher social standing. Hence the child imagines that he is the progeny of some member or other of the aristocracy. Similarly, many of us at one time dispensed with and replaced our parents by the fantasy of having been adopted. One patient with more contemporary fantasies imagined that he was the son of superior beings from a distant planet and thus thought himself to be imbued with special superhuman powers. Another patient, an adolescent boy, imagined that he was a *test-tube baby*, the result of donor gametes. He imagined that the donor parents were better than his own parents in that they would not have any conflict, nor argue.

Freud notes that by replacing his father with a superior counterpart, the child is not getting rid of him, but rather exulting him. He notes here, in a rather lyrical turn of phrase:

> Indeed the whole effort at replacing the real father by a superior one is only an expression of the child's longing for the happy, vanished days when his father seemed to him the noblest and strongest of men and his mother the dearest and loveliest of women. He is turning away from the father whom he knows to-day to the father in whom he believed in the earlier years of his childhood; and his fantasy is no more than an expression of a regret that those happy days have gone. (pp. 240–241)

Freud is careful here to differentiate such fantasies from the nature of the actual parents of the child's past and present. Hence he uses expressions such as "when his father seemed to him to be the noblest and strongest" and "in whom he believed". Thus it is not a question of returning to a better time, but rather making good that which was always lacking but overlooked by the child in his idealisation of his parents. We have spoken of how the notion of history is always imbued with a type of causality: an aetiology of one's suffering. In a similar way, the family romance is a type of theory of origins, but one that attempts to correct the perception of an inadequacy in one's actual mother and father, replacing them with less fallible versions.

This very act of longing and nostalgia erect an ideal in the place of that which fails. In other words, such fantasies pertain to a childhood of desire, a longing regarding the parents who only existed *once upon a time*. Freud describes the construction of these mythological beings as constituting "the neurotic's family romance" (p. 238). By necessity, the child must respond to what lacks for him in this fabrication of the mythical account of his or her history. It is here that we can locate the origin of fantasy, or of the fantasm, as a construction that is an attempt to make good what lacks. For Freud, this neurotic's family romance not only partakes in a mythology of one's past, it also gives us a key to understand the very nature of myths themselves.

Nonetheless, the family romance is only one aspect of the mythology that the child constructs regarding the past. It is a very particular aspect that leans heavily on an idealised notion of the parents and thus participates in what Lacan refers to as the imaginary register. Another aspect of the mythology of origins constructed by the child is what Freud calls the *infantile sexual theories*. Such theories also attempt to give an account of something that fails or lacks for the child, in this case his knowledge of sexuality. This concerns, for Freud, both the distinction between the sexes and also the riddle of where babies come from. For Freud the child is a scientist and researcher who develops theories that are posited in an endeavour to give an account of something that is missing and hitherto unknown or enigmatic.

The infantile sexual theories, and the fantasies that stem from these, are again a response to something that lacks. These theories are attempts at obtaining answers to questions regarding the child's own origins, questions that might be prompted by the actual birth of a sibling. Freud notes that the threat posed by such an arrival makes the child quite thoughtful and clear-sighted in his researches regarding these questions of origins. He tells us that these activities are not set in motion by purely theoretical interests, but rather by practical ones. And the missing pieces of knowledge therefore concern, in the first instance, the riddle of where babies come from. In reference to what we have previously elaborated, Freud notes that this enigma is the very same riddle that was propounded by the Theban Sphinx. The second and related question that arouses the child's interest and curiosity is specifically that regarding the existence of two sexes, and therefore the difference between the sexes.

The child's theories and subsequent fantasies, however, cannot be invented from nothing, *ex nihilo*. They can only be developed by the child from elements, words, sounds, or images that he or she already knows or has experienced in some way. In his correspondence with Fliess, Freud writes that, "The fantasies stem from things that have been *heard* but understood *subsequently*, and all their material is of course genuine" (Masson, 1985, p. 239). The things that have been heard—and Freud gives emphasis to what is heard and therefore to the voice—are subject to the retrospective revision and interpretation implied by the *Nachträglichkeit*. Freud goes on to elaborate upon the material that is used by the child to produce the infantile sexual theories that are part of the mythology of origins:

> For fantasies … are manufactured by means of things that are *heard*, and utilized *subsequently*, and thus combine things experienced and heard, past events (from the history of parents and ancestors), and things that have been seen by oneself. They are related to things heard, as dreams are related to things seen. In dreams, to be sure, we hear nothing; but we see. (p. 240; italics in original)

In "Analysis Terminable and Interminable", in discussing the question of *theory*, Freud notes that he almost substituted the word "phantasy-ing" for "theorizing" (1937c, p. 225). We can read this quasi-substitution as a return of the repressed, or a formation of the unconscious, to use Lacan's term. Thus, in reference to the infantile sexual theories, what is at stake in these theories is the very phantasy, or the fantasm, of the child. So then for each one of us a fantasm is produced in what we can call the approach to the object.

So if the individual's family romance leans predominantly on the side of the imaginary, the infantile sexual theories lean more towards the side of the symbolic through their emphasis on what is heard, in particular through language. Included in these theories, though, are elements which for Freud are derived not from the subject's own history or what he or she remembers of it, but rather from the history of the parents and ancestors. This aspect of the phylogenetic inheritance is something that we have referred to previously, with Freud, as the *prehistory*, in other words that which lies outside history. It is here once again that we can locate what we are elaborating through the use of Freud's term the *infantile factor*.

These things heard or seen, in reference to Freud's patients, include things that were discovered or constructed in the analysis. Such material that was produced in analysis, even if it drew upon different experiences, was never necessarily a memory as such. Here we need to reassert the notion of childhood as a construction. Our young patient who spoke of *when I was little* refers to a structural place outside the present: an Other scene. Of course this is spoken of in many other ways such as *when I was a baby*, or *when I was in mummy's tummy*. Such *times* are put forward as historical, but need to be taken as structural.

As we have noted, this hole in the history is referred to by Freud as *primal, ancient*, or *archaic*, and also as the so-called *constitutional factors*. This profusion of terms that is necessary to approach and to endeavour to effectively account for what is missing from the history, speaks of something difficult or impossible to grasp. If we need so many terms to try to get to grips with this, it is because none of them is adequate to be able to circumscribe what lacks in the history. This hole in the history is something that is structurally absent. We have referred to this, by means of the particular way that we have approached it here, as the atemporal structure of *time*.

Lévi-Strauss and myth

In *The Elementary Structures of Kinship*, first published in 1947, the ethnographer Claude Lévi-Strauss examined a very particular myth, that of the incest taboo. This was of interest to him since in his examination of these elementary structures of kinship, the prohibition of incest holds a very particular place. Lévi-Strauss was influenced by his reading of Freud, in particular Freud's work *Totem and Taboo*. If the incest taboo is of interest to the researcher in ethnography, it is because it was of interest to the child researcher to whom Freud referred. If the child seeks answers to the enigmas of sexuality, it is because his ignorance of this topic is an effect of the incest taboo, which is, then, a taboo on knowledge of sex.

Lévi-Strauss notes that: "The incest prohibition is at once on the threshold of culture, in culture, and in one sense, as we shall try to show, culture itself" (Lévi-Strauss, 1947a, p. 12). We can take this even further and state that what is referred to as *culture* is, in fact, ultimately *language*. Towards the end of this work Lévi-Strauss examines a whole panoply of forbidden acts that have in common something he refers to as an "immoderate use of language" (p. 495). These acts are considered, in the various societies that he studies, to be equivalent to the act of incest. This implies that any prohibition against such acts is, at the same time, an incest taboo. This is put forward by Lévi-Strauss in the following way: "These prohibitions are all thus reduced to a single common denominator: they all constitute a *misuse of language*, and on this ground they are grouped together with the incest prohibition, or with acts evocative of incest" (p. 495).

By virtue of the introduction of language, therefore, there is something introduced that is excluded from the set of language, and is hence considered to be prohibited. For Lévi-Strauss this introduction of language is effectively the point of differentiation of culture from nature. While recognising that there are many ways of speaking of nature—some of which we will come to examine—if *culture* here is equivalent to language, then we can define *nature* here as that which lies outside of the structure of language, the *real* in Lacan's terms (Plastow, 2011a).

We cannot go without citing Lévi-Strauss' famous formula from this text, that: "The prohibition of incest ... is the fundamental step because of which, by which, but above all in which, the transition from nature to culture is accomplished" (1947a, p. 24). If this step is, in fact, the prohibition of incest, then what interests us is the mythology produced by it in this transition to culture. The prohibition of incest also serves to cover over the fact of incest—and the structuring role it plays for the subject—such that it becomes obscured by the mythology. Even though, according to Giorgio Agamben, history ultimately assumes the role of a "thoroughgoing myth" (1978a, p. 106), it is only through history—by the mythology generated through language—that we are able to approach what lies outside it. This was the next step in Lévi-Strauss' itinerary, that of examining the nature of myth itself. We recall what Agamben called the exemplary formula of Claude Lévi-Strauss, that while rites transform events into structures, play transforms structures into events.

Lévi-Strauss himself paid tribute to Richard Wagner, going as far as to say that Wagner was the "undeniable originator of structural analysis of myth" (Wilcken, 2010, p. 282). Lévi-Strauss cites a verse from Wagner's opera *Parsifal* to this effect:

Du siehst, mein Sohn/zum Raum wird hier die Zeit.
    You see, my son/here time turns into space. (cited in Wilcken,
2010, p. 282)

Lévi-Strauss stated that this was "probably the most profound definition ever given of myth" (Wilcken, 2010, p. 282). Here again it is a question of a transformation, a transformation indeed of *time* into something
here called *space*. We also can recognise, in this transformative power of
myth, the way that play can transform *time* into *space*, and thus transform structures into events in the course of a session.

In 1955, Lévi-Strauss published a paper entitled "The Structural
Study of Myth", in which he laid the groundwork for the following
decades that were devoted to elaborating his notion of mythology
(p. 230). In this paper he rejected all previous approaches to myth that
were based around interpretations of the meaning of myths and those
of the elements of each myth. This included Jung's idea that a given
mythological pattern, in other words an *archetype*, possesses a certain
signification or meaning. For Lévi-Strauss, this amounted to "reducing mythology either to an idle play or to a coarse kind of speculation"
(1955a, p. 428). Furthermore, given that many myths existed in versions
that conveyed quite the opposite meaning to other versions, this type
of psychological interpretation always ended up with apparently con-
tradictory findings.

Lévi-Strauss concluded from these findings that the content,
or meaning, of a myth was contingent rather than central to it. Thus the
problematic became one of being able to overcome such contradiction
in order to discover what was more fundamental and coherent in
mythology. As we know, the contents of the unconscious for Freud are
"exempt from mutual contradiction" (1915e, p. 186). This exemption can
be considered to follow from Lacan's aphorism that the unconscious
is structured as a language, in so far as myth is constituted in and by
language. Lévi-Strauss, to deal with the conundrum of contradiction,
found support from the linguistics of Ferdinand de Saussure, and the
differentiation of *langue* (language) and *parole* (speech) in his approach to
mythology. Lévi-Strauss proposes that "myth *is* language: to be known,
myth has to be told; it is a part of human speech" (1955a, p. 430).

Lévi-Strauss drew upon the distinction that Saussure made between
the signifier and the signified. Lacan further clarified that it was the

signifier that was determining in speech and language. Lévi-Strauss turned his attention away from the speculative meaning of myths, towards the symbolic elements, that he called mythemes, which constitute each and every myth. From the perspective of Lacan's elaboration of Saussure's structural linguistics, Lévi-Strauss moved from an emphasis on the signified, or meaning, towards a recognition of the function of signifiers in myth. It was these signifiers that he termed mythemes.

If there is meaning to be found in mythology, according to Lévi-Strauss, it is not to be found in the individual mythemes and their meaning, but rather in the way that these are combined in order to form a myth, and to *transform* prior myths that have been handed down (Plastow, 2000b, p. 26). It is this transformative power that allows myth to re-construe previously existing elements into a new form that permits an evolution of mythology that is able to take into account the current circumstances in which a society finds itself. Lévi-Strauss, like Freud, produced a logical model that is capable of overcoming contradiction. For Lévi-Strauss this kind of logic is just as rigorous as that of modern science.

Whilst in *The Elementary Structures of Kinship* Lévi-Strauss draws upon the incest taboo that Freud writes of in *Totem and Taboo*, strikingly, in "The Structural Study of Myth" Lévi-Strauss analyses variants of the Oedipus myth that Freud had earlier brought to light. Hence in these two fundamental works, Lévi-Strauss tackles what Lacan refers to as the two great myths of Freud. We can relate each of these myths to the temporal elements we have discerned. The Oedipus myth is that which concerns the child in relation to his mother and father and therefore pertains to what we have called *history*. It is in this myth that there is the elaboration of a rule, a rule that has a symbolic content: that of the prohibition of incest. Freud took up this myth from Sophocles' *Oedipus Rex*, amongst other sources. In other words, the Oedipus myth was already in existence and Freud took it up and utilised it in psychoanalysis.

However, this myth is also underwritten by the myth of *Totem and Taboo*, that of the murder of the father of the primal horde, which Freud elaborated much later than that of the Oedipus myth. The myth of *Totem and Taboo* is one that did not exist prior to Freud; thus he was obliged to invent it. Later it was taken up by Lévi-Strauss and others. The myth of the murder of the father of the primal horde refers to events *outside history* and therefore pertains to what we have elaborated regarding the notion of *time*. Arising from the Oedipus myth is the prohibition of incest. But Oedipus committed two crimes: the first was the murder of his father that led to the possibility of the incest with his mother. That is, the question of the prohibition of incest is also logically underpinned by that of the murder of the father in the Oedipus myth. Hence Oedipus' murder of his father is the very point of articulation of the two myths (Plastow, 2005).

Anna Freud, in her paper "The Analysis of Children and their Upbringing" in *Introduction to the Technique of the Analysis of Children*, also refers to ethnology, but in a rather different way (1927a, p. 39). She writes of the situation of the psychoanalysts of adults, who seek to understand the prehistory of their patients. She writes that they might search for an easy route to this prehistory by imagining that in the analysis of children there is something to be learned about the prehistory of adults. She raises this question when discussing the difficulty of gaining an understanding of the processes of the first two years of life through the analysis of adults. She compares this to the situation of an ethnologist who might seek in vain for "a short cut to prehistory in studying a primitive people instead of a cultured race" (p. 39).

Anna Freud states that the analyses of children are no more able to elucidate this prehistory—which, for her, pertains to the events of the first two years of life—than the analyses of adults. The limit point of history, for her, is the beginning of the child's faculty of speech. In this way, Anna Freud also refers to such a prehistory as a type of hole in the history, something that lacks in both the accounts of the adult as well as the child. The notion of a preverbal period is a common assumption in those who are not able to pinpoint the hole in the history. We accord an important place in this present work to this notion of a hole that makes each and every history incomplete. Anna Freud puts forward that "the analysis of children offers no advantage over that of adults but is in fact less able to extract unconscious material" (p. 39).

She compares this material to the myths and sagas that she claims exist in a cultured race but not in a primitive people. These myths are equivalent, in analysis, to the "reaction-formations and cover-memories which are only constructed in the course of the latency period, and from which the later analysis can extract the material condensed in them" (p. 39). Here she links myth and saga to such formations in the child. It is surprising that Anna Freud considered that so-called primitive peoples were devoid of myths and sagas. This is clearly in stark contrast to the elaborate myths that Lévi-Strauss studied in traditional societies.

Nevertheless, for Anna Freud the limit point that bars access to such a "prehistory" is the infant's lack of language, beyond which, for Anna Freud—unlike for Melanie Klein—it is not possible to go. Nonetheless, what we can draw from Anna Freud is that it is myth, or what we might call the *fantasm*, that provides a link between history and prehistoric, between the symbolic of language and the real that lies outside language.

Lacan and the individual myth of the neurotic

The title of Jacques Lacan's paper "The Neurotic's Individual Myth" (1978a), is evidently a reference to Freud's notion of "the neurotic's family romance". Furthermore, by speaking of "individual myth", Lacan makes use of a term that was introduced by Lévi-Strauss in a paper entitled "The Effectiveness of Symbols", first published in 1949. Lévi-Strauss states that, "In one case [psychoanalysis], the patient constructs an individual myth with elements drawn from his past; in the other case [shamanism], the patient receives from the outside a social myth ..." (1949, p. 199).

Lacan's paper, however, is a very significant elaboration of Freud's theorisation, through his analysis of Freud's case of the Rat Man. Lacan articulates the subject's debt to the prehistory of his family, that is, the family mythology, as a "constellation" under which he is born:

> The constellation—why not? in the sense astrologers use it—the original constellation that presided over the birth of the subject, over his destiny, and I would almost say his prehistory, specifically the fundamental family relationships which structured his parents' union, happens to have a very precise relation, perhaps definable by a transformational formula, with what appears to be the most contingent, the most phantasmatic, the most paradoxically morbid in his case ... (1978a, p. 410)

This notion of a "constellation", we can say, prefigures Lacan's later topological developments in which there are elements that retain a fixed relation to each other. This notion of a constellation, moreover, is itself an implicit reference to the paper by Lévi-Strauss, in which he asserts that, "Many psychoanalysts would refuse to admit that the psychic constellations which reappear in the patient's conscious could constitute a myth" (1949, p. 202). For Lévi-Strauss this myth refers to psychological, historical, and social situations which in themselves are moulded by an underlying structure. Thus: "In relation to the event or anecdote, these structures—or, more accurately, these structural laws—are truly atemporal" (p. 202). It is specifically via the myth that Lacan intends to arrive at the atemporal structure of desire, a structure that extends outside the contingencies of the history of the subject.

For Lacan it is a "phantasmic scenario" (1978a, p. 414), which resembles a little play or a chronicle, that is a manifestation of what he calls the individual myth of the neurotic. As noted in the citation from Lacan, this myth is a type of transformational formula. And just as for Claude Lévi-Strauss, this myth, which we can here call a *fantasm*, is what allows a contradiction to be overcome. We can discern this from the following citation in which Lacan is again referring to Freud's case of the Rat Man: "The conflict *rich woman/poor woman* was reproduced exactly in the subject's life when his father urged him to marry a rich woman, and it was then that the neurosis proper had its onset" (p. 411). The contradiction implied by this conflict unmasks the Rat Man's obsessional neurosis and his phantasmic relation to the object of desire. This relation is also deployed through the Rat Man's transference to Freud. Lacan notes that "myth and fantasy reunite here"; in other words, the neurotic's individual myth, in another moment, manifests as the fantasm within the transference to the analyst.

Lacan further clarifies his notion of myth in this paper. "Myth", he puts forward, "is what provides a discursive form for something that cannot be transmitted through the definition of truth" (p. 407). A little further on he notes that, "It is in this sense that one can say that the concretisation in analytic theory of intersubjective relationship, that is, the oedipus complex, has the value of a myth" (p. 407). It has the value of myth because speech can only express truth in a mythical modality. We note here that truth is an effect of speech. For Lacan it is possible to recognise a secret force in myth, a force he attributed to the power of the signifier in his seminar on *La Relation d'Objet* [*The Object Relation*]. This is the power, Lacan says, that makes man capable of introducing the signifier into the natural order:

> ... on the one hand, the power that he has to manipulate the signifier or to be manipulated by it, to be inserted into a signifier, and, on the other, the power that he has to incarnate the instance

of the signifier in a series of interventions which are not presented
from the outset as gratuitous activities, I mean to say, to accomplish
the pure and simple introduction of the signifying instrument into
the chain of natural things. (1956–1957, pp. 254–255, translated for
this edition)

Here the signifier stands between man and nature, or rather, between
the subject and the real. Lévi-Strauss writes in relation to the struggle between the moieties of the Bororo culture in Brazil, that "native
thought was trying to express the transition from unrestrained nature to
civilised society" (1955b, p. 317). Hence myth constitutes, in this sense,
the symbolic order as man's means of endeavouring to apprehend the
real. However, if Lacan, like Lévi-Strauss, draws upon Saussure's structural linguistics, he does so in differentiating the set of signifiers S2—or
knowledge—from the signifier that he designates as S1—or truth. As
Erik Porge notes: "The question of truth is absent from Lévi-Strauss'
texts on myths and thus it is Lacan's specific contribution to link truth
to myth" (2005, p. 48).

There is also a slippage in the translation of the term "discursive
form" (Lacan, 1978a, p. 407). In the French, Lacan says "formule discursive" (1978b, p. 292), that is, a "discursive formula". This notion of a
formula is much more precise and dynamic in regard to the question of
the fantasm. It is a discursive formula in so far as it is able to be articulated in speech, but also a transformational formula in that it provides an
articulation of the travails of the subject's history, in other words his
Oedipus complex, with the constellation of the prehistory under which
the subject was born. It is specifically through the discursive formula that
the subject can accede to truth in a mythical modality.

The construction of the fantasm

If we are able to speak of a transformational formula, it is only to the
extent that we construe this transformation as a relation between the
notions of history and time. In the child, as it is also in the adult, this
transformational or discursive formula is an invention. It is an invention that allows the child to overcome a logical contradiction between
his or her history, and that which lies outside this history. We have
noted that such an invention is built up in particular moments, through

the family romance, the infantile sexual theories, and through myth and the fantasm.

Erik Porge poses the question of whether any invention has the "role of intermediary, of liaison, between the real and the symbolic" (2005, p. 202). It is in this sense that we can say that the child's fantasm is an invention since it is exactly that which mediates between the real and the symbolic. It is at once the intermediary between these two but at the same time a barrier, preventing any immediate or unmediated access to what lies outside the history, that is, the structure of the subject determined as it is by sex and death.

Here we have to differentiate, as does Porge, between the notion of an *invention*, and that of the *event*. As Porge points out, both are derived from the Latin *venire, to come. In-venire* is *to come upon, to encounter, to find, to acquire or devise*. An *invention*, then, is something created or devised by the subject in order to respond to the *real*, to use Lacan's term. At the same time, this invention in some way *creates* this place outside history, this piece of the *real*. It is in this sense that Porge comes to say that "the invention is much closer to the notion of transformation, than that of creation *ex nihilo*" (p. 202). It is the subject that produces this invention, a subject confronted with the impossible situation of a logical contradiction. The subject responds with the invention of a myth or fantasm so as to overcome this predicament. It is in this sense that Freud *invented* the notion of fantasy in order to overcome the contradiction between what his hysterics recounted in their analyses and the truth that pertained to their desire. Porge asks whether such an invention can be approximated to "the invention of a transformation, of a transition, of a becoming" (p. 202).

Ex-venire, on the other hand, is *to come from, to emerge* or *result from, or to be produced*. Earlier we elaborated a notion of the *event* as being an intrusion into the orderly progress of a history, that is, an irruption of the elements of structure that are encountered as being imposed from without and often experienced as a trauma. The *event* is primarily an encounter, in one form or another, with sex and/or death. The *event* is something that is experienced as coming from outside and which intrudes upon the subject.

Nonetheless, we must differentiate the invention of the fantasm, which is constructed through a "montage" (Lacan, 1964, p. 169), from what is referred to as the invention of the object *a*. Porge (2005) dedicates a chapter to this invention of the object *a*. Jean Allouch (1998) similarly refers to the invention of the object *a* by Lacan. Porge refers to this object, designated by the letter *a*, as "a writing that comes not from the signifier but from elsewhere, it emerges from the analytic discourse" (2005, p. 209). If it comes from elsewhere it does not emerge from the history but precisely from the hole in the history, the place where the history is wanting.

Lacan's object *a* is of particular importance here. Any developmental model tends to construe the *cause of the suffering of the subject* as something to be sought in the past history. Such a cause is commonly construed as a trauma, sexual or otherwise. This is the point from which Freud began: by the supposition that his hysterical patients had been subject to an actual sexual seduction. Such seduction was generally attributed to the fathers of the patients, just as Freud attributed the same to his father in his self-analysis. But for Lacan, the object is not a concrete object like the breast, faeces, and phallus and so on, to be located in a developmental schema. While such an imaginary object might be located in the past, it is a *stand-in*—literally a *Gegenstand*, in Freud's German—for the object *a* as *object cause of desire* which is a structural, not an historical, referent. The object *a* is this structural referent that effects a hole in the history and through which desire is realised. The object *a* is not something readily grasped, but rather something to be apprehended, and indeed invented, through psychoanalysis itself. Thus, each subject may come to invent the object *a* through an analysis. The fantasm is that element of myth that allows the subject to approach the object, but is at the same time a barrier to it.

The *discursive formula* is what provides the specific articulation between history and structure, that is, the structure of the subject. In his recent work entitled *L'Infantile en Psychanalyse* (*The Infantile in Psychoanalysis*), Robert Lévy (2008) puts forward that the fantasy, or fantasm, is consequent upon the function of metaphor having already been constituted in the child. This in turn is coextensive with the possibility of repression occurring for that child. For Lévy, the consequences that follow for the child with a difficulty in the constitution of this discursive formula include specific types of symptoms that are often responsive to brief interventions with the child and the parents.

Erik Porge poses a question that is pertinent to our discussion here:

Why not forgo the term of fantasm, a received term and heavily laden with meaning, and substitute it with that of myth? This would result, it seems to me, in a reading of Freud that intersects with that of Lévi-Strauss (at least) and would prefigure a revision of the notion of fantasm that was born in 1957. (2005, p. 47)

Such a proposition is also consistent with Lacan's own proposals regarding the term *myth*, at least from earlier in his theorisation. In *Television*, he proposes: "That's what myth is, the attempt to give an epic form to what is operative through the structure" (1974, p. 34). However, as we have seen, Lacan replaces the more general term *myth* with the specific term *fantasm*—always preceded by the definite article: *the fantasm*—in which he draws upon Freud's term phantasy. Thus he elaborates upon the term *fantasm* and gives to this a greater specificity and theoretical rigour. Elsewhere I have given a more extensive account of the movement in Lacan's theorisation from the notion of *myth* to that of *the fantasm* (Plastow, 2000b). The fantasm, as opposed to myth, always evokes the historical and in particular the family structure, in which the desire of the subject is inscribed.

The "form-giving factor"

Nazir Hamad puts forward that certain children experience difficulty in their ability to apply themselves to schoolwork in so far as "this knowledge does not answer their question concerning the enigma of origins" (2007, p. 5). Here he is referring to his analytic work with children who have been adopted. Nonetheless, there remains for each and every subject, no matter how well known their history might or might not be, an enigma of origins to which he or she must respond. What we emphasise here is that this enigma will always remain. Whether the child is adopted or not, or has a family romance of being adopted or not, a hole in the history will always remain. Lévi-Strauss puts forward that "For the myth *form* takes precedence over the *content* of the narrative" (1949, p. 204).

Such a question regarding the enigma of origins is fundamental to all clinical practice with children. This question concerns the following: how does the subject give a place to an enigma, a structure that does not fit neatly into a personal history? Once again it is this stand-in, the discursive formula of the establishment of the fantasm, that might allow some articulation between these two critical dimensions.

In the Wolf Man case Freud endeavoured to give this question of origins a concrete form through the so-called primal scene. He notes:

> I should myself be glad to know whether the primal scene in my present patient's case was a phantasy or a real experience; but, taking other similar cases into account, I must admit that the answer to this question is not in fact a matter of very great importance. These scenes of observing parental intercourse, of being seduced in childhood, and of being threatened with castration are unquestionably an inherited endowment, a phylogenetic heritage … (1918b, p. 97)

Freud, to his credit, does not decide whether such events are phantasies or real experiences. He comes to the conclusion that "the answer to this question is not in fact a matter of very great importance". Elaborating upon Freud here, it is specifically at the point where there is a hole in the history, a hole that Freud refers to as the "phylogenetic heritage", that we can locate something of the *real*, to utilise this notion of Lacan's. It is the function of phantasy, or the *fantasm*, to cover over this hole and to be a stand-in for it. It does so by employing things seen and heard, as well as elements from experiences, traumatic or otherwise, re-construed through the effect of the *Nachträglichkeit*. In a letter to Karl Abraham in which he dispels the notion that sexual traumas are the specific aetiology of neurosis, Freud proposes that "[T]he compelling thing is that these traumas become the *form-giving factor* in the symptomatology of neurosis" (Falzeder, 2002, p. 2; italics in original). Freud goes on to say that the strong sexual impressions experienced by the child but which he is not mentally equipped to cope with, "later exercise more powerful effects as a retrospective reaction [*nachträglich*] and as *memories* than they did when they were real impressions" (Falzeder, 2002, p. 3). It is the fantasm, constructed retrospectively from such traumas and other elements, that gives form to the formlessness of the hole in the history.

It is specifically the fantasm that is the form-giving factor which allows a *discursive formula* to be produced, a formula that is able to provide an articulation between the history and what lacks in that history. We have given the term *the hole in the history* to this lack, a lack or enigma that structures the subject. This hole in the history is also a hole in language in so far as, for any subject, not all can be said: there is a limit to what is able to be articulated. This hole has its origin at the crossroads of sexuality and death, both marked by a fundamental lack. Freud has to maintain a tension between two elements: here the ontogenetic and the phylogenetic, which is also a tension between the historical and the pre-historical. By not being able to logically establish the hole in language and thus the hole in the history, Freud is obliged to put his emphasis upon the notion of phantasy rather than the hole that is obscured by the fantasm. With Lacan we are able to better circumscribe the hole in the history through his notion of the real, the real which punches a hole in language.

PART II

PSYCHOANALYSIS AS A CHILD AND ITS PROTAGONISTS

CHAPTER FOUR

The illegitimate beginnings of the field of psychoanalysis of the child

From its very outset, the field of psychoanalysis of the child was an affair of female psychoanalysts. The names of Melanie Klein and Anna Freud are those which most usually spring to mind. Here we will also give particular prominence to the woman who might be considered to be the first analyst of children but whose history is less well known: Hermine Hug-Hellmuth.

Sigmund Freud himself designated psychoanalysis of the child as the sphere of female psychoanalysts. In the 34th of his *New Introductory Lectures on Psycho-Analysis* entitled "Explanations, Applications and Orientations", Freud states the following: "It has automatically happened that child-analysis has become the domain of women analysts, and no doubt this will remain true" (1933a, p. 148).

What is curious here is that Freud describes this phenomenon as happening "automatically" and therefore without any prior thought or consideration, and in a repeated manner. He goes even further, proposing that this will continue to happen along the same lines. In clinical practice we might consider that actions which occur *automatically* are the very ones that occur *symptomatically* as a type of repetition compulsion. What needs to be questioned here is what it is that underwrites Freud's delimitation of the field of psychoanalysis of the child as being the preserved domain of women. Such a designation presents itself, in the first instance, as a symptom of this field.

In this particular paper, in referring to children, Freud places great emphasis, as does his daughter Anna, upon what he refers to as the educational aspects of psychoanalysis. In introducing this topic, he remarks that he is referring to "the application of psychoanalysis to education, to the upbringing of the next generation" (p. 146). In the *Standard Edition* a note alerts us to the fact that the term that Freud uses for "education" in German is *Erziehung* which has a much wider meaning than the word *education* in English and includes the sense of *upbringing* (p. 147). But even the word education in English is derived from the Latin *educere* whose primary meanings are *to draw out* or *to lead out*, and, by extension, to bring up or rear children in so far as they are led out of the darkness, that is, out of ignorance. In stressing the place of women as the analysts of children, Freud is also alluding to that other role that is allocated to women as those who bring up children: the place of the mother. This conflation of the place of the analyst with that of the parent, and more particularly that of the mother, must open up for us a fundamental question regarding the origins of psychoanalysis of the child.

We see this same conflation repeated in the common practice of the early analysts of children who analysed their own children and family members. The woman who was the first to practise the psychoanalysis of the child, Hermine Hug-Hellmuth, although having no children of her own, studied and wrote papers on the dreams and symptoms of her nephew Rolf (1912). Whether Hug-Hellmuth undertook any direct psychoanalytic work with Rolf is not clear. Bergès and Balbo nonetheless asserted that she "attempted to analyse her own nephew" (1994a, p. 108). The following is MacLean and Rappen's conclusion of this question:

> Many psychoanalytic observations of Rolf appeared in Hug-Hellmuth's papers; and this probably led to the opinion over the years that an actual analysis took place. This would not have been unusual. In those early experimental days, there were many examples of parents analysing their children. (1991, p. 8)

As we shall see, whatever transpired between Hug-Hellmuth and Rolf, whether in their family relations or as a result of Hug-Hellmuth's psychoanalytic interventions, it would end in tragic consequences. The question of whether there was an "actual analysis" or not is a spurious one since what is at play is the conflation of family and psychoanalytic relations that underpins the origins of psychoanalysis of the child.

Prominent among the early analysts of children, Melanie Klein analysed her own children (MacLean & Rappen, 1991, p. 8). We could also extend our questioning to analysts who developed relationships—and no doubt continue to do so—with their patients in which there again is an inmixing of analytical and affective relations. A case in point is that of Carl Jung with his young patient Sabina Spielrein, who later became an analyst of children. In the foundational case of Little Hans, the analyst was nominally the father. Nonetheless, Freud regularly supervised the father's work with Hans, and also took up the place of symbolic third for Hans.

But first and foremost was Freud's analysis of his daughter Anna. It was to Anna Freud that Freud relegated the field of psychoanalysis of the child: "I am glad that I am at least able to say that my daughter, Anna Freud, has made this study her life-work and has in that way compensated for my neglect" (1933a, p. 147). This is a curious statement from the father of psychoanalysis, given that it was this very father who allotted child psychoanalysis to his own child whom he had analysed. Freud asserts in this declaration, furthermore, that the place of the child is to make good the lack that the parents perceive in themselves. In Freud's case we can say that the "neglect" on his part is enacted symptomatically with his daughter. As we will come to see, the insight that the function of the child is to make good the lack in the parent was one that was first able to be articulated by Hug-Hellmuth.

Freud's comment also implies that the work of psychoanalysis is able to be passed on through family connections. Thus from his proclamation, we could say that it is Anna Freud who is the legitimate inheritor of this field. Moreover, it is a legacy that is left, not to *my colleague* or *co-worker*, but rather to "my daughter". Thus the inheritance, in Freud's own words, is bequeathed to Anna Freud on the basis of family relations. This is another significant aspect of this confounding of family relations with those of psychoanalysis, something which as we know was also to occur with Jacques Lacan in relation to his daughter Judith and son-in-law Jacques Alain Miller. This is something we are endeavouring to put into question here: can psychoanalysis function as a family affair?

As late as 1935, as noted by Bergès and Balbo (1994a, p. 107), Freud was asked by Edoardo Weiss whether it would be possible to take on his own son in a training analysis. Freud replied with some caution, but nonetheless did not advise against it:

> Concerning the analysis of your hopeful son, that is certainly a ticklish business. With the younger, promising brother it might be done more easily. With one's own daughter I succeeded well. There are special difficulties and doubts with a son.
>
> Not that I really would warn you against a danger; obviously everything depends upon the two people and their relationship to each other. You know the difficulties. It would not surprise me if you were successful in spite of them. (Weiss, 1970, p. 81)

Bergès and Balbo conclude that Freud never diverged from his view that the analysis of "one's own" child was possible. And Anna Freud, having been analysed by her father, maintained that, in analysis, the child's relations were to the parents who "are still real and present as love-objects". Hence for her, "[T]he child is not, like the adult, ready to produce a new edition of its love-relationships" (1927a, p. 34). In other words, a child cannot produce a transference to the analyst. Melanie Klein, who, as we have noted, analysed her own children, put forward that the transference of a child to the analyst is always possible. This of course raises the question of the differentiation of the parent from the analyst. Donald Winnicott took up Freud's inaugural position: parents are excellent therapists for their children so long as they are able to give an account of it to an analyst in the place of symbolic third who acts as a circuit-breaker for the transference. This is exemplified in the analysis of the Piggle (Bergès & Balbo, 1994a, p. 108).

In turn-of-the-century Vienna, as in many other places, there was also another division in regard to professional formation. Most early analysts were medical practitioners, and therefore, at that time, male. On the other hand, while women were educators in the home, in their professional lives they also were often educators, or teachers, in kindergartens and schools. But for women embarking upon the analysis of children there was a difference: the training of women in psychoanalysis introduced them to a place previously reserved for men and thereby offered the possibility of their emancipation. The division of roles in the homes of the first men and women to practise psychoanalysis was reflected in their professional lives with men being medically trained analysts, and women by necessity being lay analysts. This produced a difference in their approaches to clinical practice with the child. In the "Introductory Lecture" to which we have referred, Freud alludes to the psychoanalysis of the child as one of the "non-medical applications of analysis" (1933a, p. 146).

From the very beginnings of the clinical practice of psychoanalysis of the child, the analyst was placed right in the centre of the family drama. This division in the professional formation of men and women introduced the family drama as a real phenomenon, and not just as a symbolic one as proposed by the Oedipus myth. And, like the transgressions of the Oedipus myth in symbolic form, these family dramas occurred as transgressions of relationships between parents and children in the various ways in which the sons, daughters, nephews, and nieces became objects of observation for psychoanalytic research on infantile sexuality, as well as analysands of their own mothers, fathers, and in one case, aunt. Such an emphasis on analyses occurring with families opens the question of the transference between a child, his parents, and the analyst. It also raises the question of the relation of psychoanalysis to the contiguous disciplines of pedagogy and education on the one hand, in addition to the clinical disciplines of medicine, psychiatry, and psychology on the other.

A field of psychoanalysis of the child?

Is it possible to say that the child, rigorously defined, is a separate entity for psychoanalysis? This is also a question of whether the child can be an *analysand* in his own right, as an adult analysand is considered to be. Freud, once again in defence of his daughter Anna's approach, wrote to Joan Riviere that, "Ferenczi wittily remarked that, if Mrs. Klein is right, then children really no longer exist" (Hughes, 1992, p. 277). If this anecdote is recounted ironically, it is nonetheless to be taken seriously. Does a *child* exist for psychoanalysis? After all, a child might well be considered to be a *dependent*, but what adult is entirely independent, independent of otherness, of the Other? Similarly, if we are to examine fundamentals, we must pose the question of whether there is any theoretical ground to say that there can be a separate field of psychoanalysis of the child.

In their *Dictionary of Psychoanalysis*, Elisabeth Roudinesco and Michel Plon assert that, in general, there does not exist a special field of psychoanalysis of the child, and the requirements to become an analyst of children do not differ from those for becoming an analyst of adults (1997, p. 828). We can find exceptions to this, but by and large the field of psychoanalysis of the child has remained outside all of the erudite fields that are specified as pertaining to the child. The latter usually have the prefix "ped-" or "paed-", or reference to the word *child* is attached to the name of the field, such as paediatrics, pedagogy, child psychology, and child psychiatry—or *pédopsychiatrie* as it is known in France. Roudinesco and Plon stress that not only are these fields born from medicine, but that there is also a division within psychoanalysis. In France and other Latin countries there is an emphasis on psychology and psychiatry, whilst in Protestant countries there is a greater emphasis on *pedagogy* or education, and therefore upon lay analysis. We could say that Britain straddled these two positions with, on the one hand the British Psychoanalytical Society and a tendency towards the medicalisation of analysis, and, on the other, the approach of Anna Freud and Dorothy Burlingham with lay analysis.

Oskar Pfister attempted to define a field of pedagogical psychoanalysis by designating it as *pédanalyse* (Roudinesco & Plon, 1997, p. 796), but it is noteworthy that neither the field that he attempted to create in this way, nor the term, have survived. Nonetheless, from its very beginnings, this field has been divided on the one side as pertaining to medicine, and on the other as belonging to education or upbringing: *Erziehung*.

Freud's emphasis, to return once again to the "Introductory Lecture", is also to the application of psychoanalysis to pedagogy. Here he speaks of the way in which psychoanalysis concerns itself with the upbringing and education of the next generation. Freud states that "The difficulty of childhood lies in the fact that in a short space of time a child has to appropriate the results of a cultural evolution which stretches over thousands of years" (1933a, p. 147). Freud, in this moment, endeavours to make the *prehistoric* period—or what we have referred to as the *infantile*—reducible to an actual period in the child's life. He includes in this two principal tasks: "… the acquisition of control over his instincts [drives] and adaptation to society—or at least the first beginnings of these two" (p. 147). Of course it is difficult to separate these two factors, as the ability to respond to the drives must in some way occur through language, the major component of what he refers to as the "adaptation to society". This "adaptation" must be mediated by language, and hence by its limitations, to which the child must ultimately come to terms.

When Freud writes of the three impossible professions in "Analysis Terminable and Interminable", the word he uses for *education* in German is once again *"das Erziehen"*, a noun derived from the infinitive form of *Erziehung* (1937c, p. 93). The scope of this term, as we have noted, includes the raising of children. Freud underlines what effectively is the impossibility of education: the fact that in the adaptation to society, education must inhibit, forbid, and suppress, whilst at the same time recognising that it is this same suppression of the drives that is at play in the onset of neurotic illness. To this he adds what he refers to as the "accidental traumas of childhood" (1933a, p. 149), which are moments of the irruption of the drives via a concurrent *event* in the history of each subject, and, moreover, at any age.

In regard to the beginnings of the practice of psychoanalysis of the child, it was Freud himself, as articulated in the case history of Little Hans, who sounded the clarion call to promote, among his followers, the "observing in children at first hand and in all the freshness of life the sexual impulses and wishes which we dig out so laboriously in adults from among their own débris" (1909b, p. 6). There is an assumption that somehow, out of the mouths of babes, or rather, not even from their speech, but literally from "observing" them, it would be possible to directly garner some gleanings of the experiences which are later "exaggerated or distorted in the case of neurotics" (p. 5). This assumption implies that there would be a very different epistemological status accorded by Freud to the child if psychoanalysis were to proceed through observation.

Freud continues with his well-known call:

> With this end in view I have for many years been urging my pupils and my friends to collect observations of the sexual life of children—the existence of which has as a rule been cleverly overlooked or deliberately denied. Among the material which came into my possession as a result of these requests, the reports which I received at regular intervals about little Hans soon began to take a prominent place. (p. 6)

Thus, in one way, it was Sigmund Freud himself who initiated the psychoanalytic investigation of children, but upon the basis of supposedly confirming the material (p. 6) that had emerged from the analyses of adults, rather than for the treatment of childhood neuroses. This was not just any "material", but specifically what was considered to be that of *infantile* sexuality. Thus the "observations" of little Hans—of his behaviour, but also of his speech—took place initially to record his *normal* infantile sexuality. It was *fortuitous* then that Hans, during the course of these observations, developed a phobia that became the focus of the case history. Given this emphasis of confirming what was uncovered from the analyses of adults, it is perhaps in this sense that Freud is able to say at the end of the case history that, "Strictly speaking, I learnt nothing new from this analysis, nothing that I had not already been able to discover (though often less distinctly and more indirectly) from other patients analysed at a more advanced age" (p. 147). It was a disappointment for Freud that his call for infant observations revealed nothing new about infantile sexuality. The *infantile* always, necessarily, remained at a distance. But from this point of view, there is strictly no difference between the analysis of adults and that of children.

Even though little Hans' father was nominally in the place of his son's analyst, the transference was referred back to Freud and it was indeed Freud who took responsibility for it by intervening indirectly with the father and directly with Hans himself. Freud was effectively in the place of analyst, of symbolic third, as is evident from Hans' own words. For Lacan the transference is established by the positing of a subject—the analyst—who knows something regarding the patient's suffering: *le sujet supposé savoir*, the subject supposed of knowledge. For Hans, this is attested to by his references and letters to "the Professor" (p. 56). Thus Hans' transference, and of course that of his father, is ultimately, but clearly, to Freud.

But from Freud's point of view, there was a necessary conflation in Hans' father being in the place of analyst:

> It was only because the authority of a father and of a physician were united in a single person, and because in him both affectionate care and scientific interest were combined, that it was possible in this one instance to apply the method to a use to which it would not otherwise have lent itself. (p. 5)

Bergès and Balbo state, in regard to this proposition by Freud, that he "was not a man to think, conceive of or to put forward just any old thing" (1994a, p. 107), and hence we must give this statement serious consideration despite its apparently outdated notion of a parent analysing his child. Freud's proposition is that the transference of a child with the father is an optimal arrangement. We need, though, to add a caveat to this analysis of Freud's statement: this proposition is in the singular and refers not to *the* father in general, but to *a* father, to this particular father, "in this one instance".

In contemporary therapies, Bergès and Balbo note, particularly in those with infants and autistic children, a similar "parent(s)-child-psychoanalyst" (p. 108) triangle has been resurrected, as with Hans' father, Hans and Freud. They maintain, however, that such techniques have become a substitute for what is at stake in the transference which the analyst or therapist consequently "misapprehends [*méconnaît*]" (p. 109). Nonetheless, two things have been altered. The first is that the parent is no longer the *official* analyst of the child as the father was for Hans. The second is that, almost universally, the father has been replaced by the mother in such therapies, and that, in all the explanations that are put forward to claim that this is the way it has to be, "anything goes". They refer to these types of therapies as "mother treatments" (p. 109). All sorts of reasons are put forward to justify the fact that such treatments "end up with the irreplaceable mother, and, when the child is autistic, to the inevitable 'mother–child' conjunction, whose unary trait is evidently one of union" (p. 109).

In other words, in the history of the treatment of the child, there is an inexorable tendency towards this union of the mother–child *attachment*. Psychoanalysis works in the opposite direction to this: that of the installation of a law through the name of the father, to use Lacan's term. For this reason Bergès and Balbo, strikingly, put forward the following proposition: "Hence it is sound to maintain that, in the absence of another, of a new clinical and theoretical elaboration as rigorous and relevant as that of Freud's, the principles he put forward in 1909 remain valid, their prescriptive nature being strengthened by the multiple and less probing techniques invented since" (p. 109).

This is a proposition we can consider with the aid of a study of the work of Hermine Hug-Hellmuth, particularly in view of examining the basis upon which the field of the psychoanalysis of the child was founded.

Hermine Hug-Hellmuth and the beginnings of the psychoanalysis of the child

Hermine Hug-Hellmuth can be considered to be the first practising psychoanalyst of the child in her own right (MacLean, 1986, p. 586). Nonetheless, little is known of her, and much of her work has passed into obscurity or has simply not been translated from the German. MacLean and Rappen state that she wrote a will a few days before her death expressing a wish that no account of her life or work should appear (1991, p. xi). In doing so she presaged the scandalous circumstances of her death: scandalous, that is, for psychoanalysis. Nevertheless, injunctions such as the one she made in her will are rarely followed in the case of figures of such historical and theoretical interest. It seems that there was a more deliberate suppression of information. When George MacLean and Ulrich Rappen were researching their book regarding Hermine Hug-Hellmuth, they wrote requesting information from Anna Freud, who replied that they should "abide by this injunction" (p. xi). This raises questions regarding the claims as to who can legitimately be considered to be the founder of the psychoanalysis of the child. Here we will examine some other scandals and forms of illegitimacy in Hug-Hellmuth's life and work that may have contributed to her work being neglected.

Hug-Hellmuth in many ways epitomises the duality that is at the origins of the psychoanalysis of the child. Even though she was not a medical doctor, she was nonetheless one of the first women to obtain a doctorate degree—in her case in physics—from the University of Vienna. Her working life seems to have been divided into two distinct periods. Up until 1912, the year in which her first psychoanalytic publications appeared, she worked as a school teacher. After that time, it would seem, she devoted herself entirely to psychoanalysis. Thus in Hug-Hellmuth's working life there was already a division between education and psychoanalysis.

Both her personal and psychoanalytic lives were marked by scandals and also by questions of legitimacy. Even the name by which she became known is given differently by different sources and it is not clear how she acquired the ultimate form her name took. Her father, Hugo Hug, Ritter von Hugenstein, had previously fathered an illegitimate child whose name was initially Antonia Farmer. A military court refused an application by this titled aristocrat for his daughter to be recognised as legitimate. A number of years later he married Ludovika Achepohl who, following a stillbirth, gave birth to Hermine in 1871. Hermine's illegitimate half-sister seven years her elder, later, illicitly, reappeared in this family as a full sister named Antoine only two years older than her. Antoine later went by the name of Antoine Hug.

Antoine was another of the first female graduates from the University of Vienna. At the time she was finishing her doctorate in philosophy,

Hermine was beginning her studies there at the age of twenty-six. Curiously, Hermine signed her handwritten doctoral thesis "von Hugenstein", a name she never used in her later involvement with psychoanalysis. At the time of the collapse of the Habsburg Empire at the end of World War I, she changed her name as was officially requested of all nobility. Thus she gave up the title "von" and became Hug-Hellmuth or Hug.

In 1906, Antoine gave birth to an illegitimate son, Rudolf Otto Hug, who is commonly referred to as Rolf. Rolf is a diminutive of Rudolph which was also the father's given name. The fact that we know him by this familiar name is once again testimony to the manner in which the *familiar* is intimately caught up in the beginnings of psychoanalysis of the child. Rolf's father, whose name did not appear on the birth certificate, left for good when Rolf was two years of age. In 1915 Antoine died of tuberculosis—possibly the same illness from which Hermine's mother, who had been chronically ill during her daughter's childhood, died when Hermine was twelve years old. MacLean and Rappen write of the significant elements in the early lives of Hermine, Antoine, and Rolf, for whom they note that these early difficulties were seemingly repeated, in the following way: "Their lives [were] marred and distorted by illegitimacy, illness, and death" (1991, p. 19).

Not long after Antoine's death, Rolf's first guardian wrote, "Rolf will never become a useful member of society!" (p. 19). The fact that Antoine had not named Hermine as Rolf's guardian was testimony to the estrangement of the half-sisters. He had failed placements in families and schools and lived briefly with Hermine in 1918. In that year a new guardian was named for him: Dr. Victor Tausk. Tausk was already known to be a troubled man and in June the following year he committed suicide, another scandal for psychoanalysis. Following this, Isidor Sadger was named as Rolf's new guardian. No doubt Hug-Hellmuth had had a role in this as she had known Sadger since 1907, he having been first of all her doctor, then through psychoanalysis a friend and colleague, and also for some time her psychoanalyst.

Rolf routinely stole from Hermine and tried to get money out of her in different ways. In 1922 Hermine once again caught Rolf stealing from her: she had walked into the room as he was breaking into her desk. Following this incident Rolf attempted to kill himself by overdosing on alcohol. His father had died that same year in Graz, although Rolf was said to have been unaware of this. Hug-Hellmuth was afraid of Rolf and in a letter stated that she was afraid of being beaten by him. On one occasion she reported to Sadger that she was afraid that he would strangle her. In another letter she stated: "I will be killed anyway" (p. 42).

In her paper of 1924, "The Libidinal Structure of Family Life", Hug-Hellmuth dedicated a section to the illegitimate child. She wrote:

> The illegitimate child soon feels his special position into [which]
> a cruel society has cast him and his mother. At last when school
> begins he realises what it means not to know his father's name
> when the other children assure him of the humiliating truth that
> his embarrassed mother could not tell him. The boy's reaction is
> to unconsciously detest his mother and to secretly see her as a
> prostitute. Later, in his eyes all other women are prostitutes too.
> Because of his hatred for women, he will become a "lady killer"
> for whom all women are available, or he will simply hate women.
> (p. 270)

Rolf was indeed, literally, to shortly become a lady killer. In September 1924, upon his arrival in Vienna, Rolf went to Hermine's apartment and woke her while climbing in through an open window. A struggle ensued during which Rolf strangled her and then he took her money and a gold watch. Thus Hug-Hellmuth died at the hands of her nephew who had been the subject of many of her psychoanalytic papers, including this most recent one which indirectly refers to Rolf as a perverse young adult. We can consider her observations and studies of Rolf as an integral part of her formation as an analyst of the child. As we have noted, Hug-Hellmuth had also anticipated her own death in her will, seemingly attempting to "contain or diminish any scandal by invoking whatever censorship she could" (MacLean & Rappen, 1991, p. 43).

Professionally, another scandal arose around Hug-Hellmuth concerning a book that she had published in 1919 under the title of *A Young Girl's Diary*. Because it was published anonymously and "the editor"—Hug-Hellmuth—cites a note by Freud in the preface, the work is sometimes attributed to Freud. It was presented as an intimate journal of an anonymous teenage girl, describing her family and affective life. In addition, the girl discusses her developing sexuality, something of great interest to psychoanalysis at the time, and part of the response to Freud's clarion call. As in Hermine's own history, the death of the girl's mother was a major event. In the note cited in the preface, Freud wrote a glowing account that begins in the following way:

> This diary is a gem. Never before, I believe, has anything been written enabling us to see so clearly into the soul of a young girl, belonging to our social and cultural stratum, during the years of pubertal development. ... It is certainly incumbent on you to publish the diary. All students of my own writings will be grateful to you. (Freud, 1919, pp. 7–8)

The *Diary* was initially applauded for such insights, but then scandal ensued. The diary was declared to be a fraud by the prominent English psychologist Cyril Burt and in Germany by Karl and Charlotte Bühler. Claims were made that the *Diary* was written retrospectively by Hug-Hellmuth as a description of her own experiences and in the light of her psychoanalytic knowledge. Hug-Hellmuth wrote a response directly to Burt, as well as publishing a defence of its legitimacy in a special German edition of the *Diary* in 1923. We of course will never know the facts of the matter. Nonetheless MacLean and Rappen hypothesise that Hug-Hellmuth wrote the diary herself as an adult. It was published anonymously but given that Hug-Hellmuth was the only practising psychoanalyst of the child, it can only be assumed that everyone knew that she was "the editor" who signed the preface to the *Diary* (MacLean & Rappen, 1991, p. 27). In any case, there is a lingering illegitimacy that hangs over this work, as it does over many aspects of Hug-Hellmuth's life and work. MacLean and Rappen state that, "She could never admit either that she was the subject of the diary or that she was the adult author, just as she could never admit that she had an illegitimate half-sister" (p. 29).

Significantly, when it was published in 1919, the *Diary* came at a very significant time for Hug-Hellmuth and her primacy as the pioneer of psychoanalysis of the child. It appeared at a time at which Anna Freud had appeared on the psychoanalytic stage as an untrained but already powerful rival. MacLean and Rappen hypothesise that the publication and interest in the *Diary* would have been intended to enhance Hug-Hellmuth's stature in the eyes of Anna Freud's father (p. 29). It preceded Hug-Hellmuth's lectures on child psychoanalysis in Berlin by only a few months. It also came just before she presented her paper on the technique of psychoanalysis with children, the first ever paper on the technique of psychoanalysis of the child to be presented and published.

Psychoanalysis of the child: the bastard child of psychoanalysis

Hug-Hellmuth's paper, entitled "On the Technique of Child-Analysis", was a landmark paper in many ways. It was read before the Sixth International Psychoanalytical Congress at The Hague in September 1920 before, amongst others, Sigmund Freud. The paper begins from the position of the dichotomy between education on the one hand and psychoanalysis on the other, the same dichotomy articulated by Freud himself. For instance, she writes of the "*curative* and educative work of analysis" (1921, p. 287), but emphasises the former by italicising it. Nonetheless, at the beginning of this paper there is still a conflation of the two in her conceptualisation of the work with a child in psychoanalysis.

Towards the end of this rather circumlocutory paper, however, she arrived at a somewhat different position. She threw open a challenge to Sigmund Freud himself, as well as to Anna Freud who was also present when she read the paper. There she articulated what we can consider to be the foundational statement for the burgeoning field of child psychoanalysis. She proposes:

> I consider it impossible for anyone to analyse properly his own child. This is so not only because the child hardly ever reveals its deepest desires and thoughts, conscious or unconscious, to father and mother, but because in this case the analyst is often driven to re-construct too freely, and also because the narcissism of the parents would make it almost unbearable to hear from their own child the psycho-analytic revelations. (pp. 304–305)

The same statement also applies to whatever observations and work that Hug-Hellmuth engaged in with her nephew Rolf, and the tragic failure of these. Thus her proposition involves a type of renunciation and denunciation of the very practice that was at the origins of the psychoanalysis of the child. Her statement also proposes that this field is struck by a fundamental prohibition: that of the impossibility of being able to analyse one's own child.

Hug-Hellmuth's life and work were marked by questions of legitimacy: that of the illegitimacy of her half-sister that she never revealed, that of her half-sister's illegitimate son Rolf, as well the questions concerning the legitimacy of the book *A Young Girl's Diary*. However, from the basis of these illegitimate beginnings, Hug-Hellmuth was able to introduce the possibility of a legitimate practice of psychoanalysis of the child such that, with her statement, it was able to move away from being a family affair. The movement that I have described in her paper "On the Technique of Child-Analysis" is a type of resolution of the dilemma of the beginnings of the psychoanalysis of the child. It is precisely this that allows her to separate out the place of the analyst from that of the parents and educators of the child (Plastow, 2011b, p. 209).

Hermine Hug-Hellmuth was the forerunner of two divergent streams of psychoanalysis with children. The educative side of her work was taken up by Anna Freud, principally through the latter's assumption of a pedagogic stance in the treatment, as well as her emphasis upon the ego, or character, which later lent its weight to her prescriptive *developmental lines* and her elaboration of the defence mechanisms. The more properly analytical stream in Hug-Hellmuth's work was taken up by Melanie Klein, including Hug-Hellmuth's conceptualisation of the child's transference.

It is striking then that Hug-Hellmuth's work has virtually disappeared into oblivion. Her contribution remained essentially unrecognised by both Anna Freud and Melanie Klein, as well as by others who were, and are today, prominent in this field. Nonetheless her work with children preceded Klein's and Anna Freud's by many years. In the year 1912, Anna Freud was still at school when Hug-Hellmuth published six psychoanalytic papers. It was not until 1927 that Klein and Anna Freud began to publish their first important papers. This chronology, and the contributions made by Hermine Hug-Hellmuth, have been deliberately obscured. For instance, in the explanatory note by the Melanie Klein Trust in an appendix to Klein's work *The Psycho-Analysis of Children* we can read the following:

> *The Psycho-Analysis of Children* … is a classic text of child analysis. It sets out the psychoanalytic play technique Melanie Klein pioneered in Berlin in the early 1920s, at about the time that Dr. H. B. Hug-Hellmuth ('On the Technique of Child-Analysis', 1921) and Anna

Freud ('Introduction to the Technique of Child Analysis', 1927) founded a different line of development. (Klein, 1932, p. 283)

In addition, Anna Freud, who gave scant recognition to Hug-Hellmuth's developments in the field, took credit for Hermine's work herself. Indeed, as McLean and Rappen note, "Every concept outlined by Hug-Hellmuth in 1920, 1921, and 1924 is later described as a basic element of the child psychoanalytic technique of Anna Freud" (1991, p. 279). Anna Freud referred to these concepts as "my methods" in her book *Einführung in die Technik der Kinderanalyse* (*Introduction to the Technique of the Analysis of Children*) (1927b). Each of Hug-Hellmuth's two successors criticised aspects of her work that they identified with the rival. Hermine Hug-Hellmuth was thus caught up in a battle between her successors in their claims to be the legitimate pioneer of the psychoanalysis of the child. Furthermore, it also seems likely that if Anna Freud refused to participate in research on the life and work of Hug-Hellmuth, it was in order to promote the myth of her own primacy as a psychoanalyst of children.

If we are putting forward that the foundational moment of the psychoanalysis of the child is Hug-Hellmuth's statement that it is impossible for anyone to analyse his own child, what are we then to make of Freud's proposition that it was only because the authority of a father and of a physician were united in a single person that the analysis of little Hans was able to proceed? After all, Bergès and Balbo state that Freud's principles remain valid in the absence of any rigorous new clinical and theoretical elaboration. But we have already noted that since Freud's statement is in the singular, it applies uniquely to the situation with Hans, his father, and Freud.

The unity of the authority of the father and that of the physician, therefore, is precisely the point of departure of this case. But as Erik Porge points out, it is precisely at the moments of the dissociation of the *paternal authority* from the *medical authority*, for instance in Hans' visit to Freud, that the treatment was efficacious (1996b, p. 120). Furthermore, it has been hypothesised that part of the difficulty for Hans was the failure of the *paternal authority* to intervene in Hans' position as plaything of his mother's whims: the *jouissance of the mother*. So if the conflation of the paternal and medical authority is the starting point, it is only the separation of these that is able to be of use to Hans.

The analyst who is confronted with a child is also inevitably confronted by the history of the psychoanalysis of the child. Porge's thesis is that the conflation between the paternal and medical authorities that Freud mentions, is itself inspired by, and is a replication of another conflation. Specifically, it is a conflation of what Lacan later refers to as the name of the father (the paternal authority) and the subject supposed of knowledge (the medical authority, in other words, the transference). Such a conflation had occurred in Freud's transference to Fliess. Porge maintains that the myth of Freud's self-analysis in transference to Fliess, initiated by Didier Anzieu in 1959 and perpetuated by Octave Mannoni (1969), is at the heart of a fundamental difficulty for psychoanalysis.

As Freud suggests, this conflation was a necessary one for the establishment of the field of psychoanalysis of the child. Nonetheless, it is our task as the inheritors of this legacy to continue to tease apart these two strands that maintain a relation to each other, but one that has to be separated out from any family relation. In other words, if it was necessary in the case of Little Hans to conflate the paternal and the medical authorities, this foundational position was one that revealed its own impossibility. It needs to be stressed that neither Anna Freud nor Melanie Klein was able to recognise this very impossibility. Thus the seed that was sown by Hermine Hug-Hellmuth was ignored by her immediate successors, to the detriment of their theory and practice.

However, while the differentiation of the name of the father from the subject supposed of knowledge is essential in examining the history of the psychoanalysis of the child, it is also crucial in each and every psychoanalysis of a child.

Sigmund Freud, as we have noted, designated his daughter Anna as the pioneer of the field of psychoanalysis of the child, a field that he bequeathed to her. Accordingly, Anna Freud strove to perpetuate the myth that she was the founder of child psychoanalysis. But any mode of psychoanalysis that is formed in such a mould, will inevitably remain a childish form of psychoanalysis. In seeking to derive its legitimacy though family relations, this sort of psychoanalysis of the child is destined to remain a child: to not have an existence in its own right. It is only when the child is able to break free from its parental bonds, its *attachment* to the parental authority, that it might have its own life, and become established in its own name. Otherwise psychoanalysis of the child is destined to remain stuck in its conflation with education and upbringing, and inexorably ends up being a type of pedagogy. This is the usual fate of all the erudite fields regarding the child: to become a type of *ortho-paedics*—literally a straightening out or normalisation of the child—in the mould of all of the contemporary arrays of developmentalism.

It was Hermine Hug-Hellmuth, in her act of defiance of Freud's paternal authority, and her denunciation of the necessary initial step of the analysis of his own child, who was truly able to establish the field of psychoanalysis of the child. Any practice of psychoanalysis of the child that is worth its weight must be an illegitimate child, not the legitimate inheritor of a family legacy. Psychoanalysis of the child, following Hermine Hug-Hellmuth, is therefore the bastard child of psychoanalysis.

CHAPTER FIVE

The place of the parents: "the child does not come of his own accord"

In clinical practice with children, it is common to hear a clinician say that "the child presented with" certain symptoms. But in this type of case presentation, there is a fiction that is propagated, the fiction that it is the *child* who presents with his symptoms. Occasionally the child does articulate, in one way or another, to the mother or father, that he does wish to speak to a third party. Sometimes an adolescent might present without the parents, but often in this situation he is again referred by someone else, a teacher or counsellor, for instance. Usually, however, it is one of the parents, and in most cases the mother, who makes the phone call to refer the child for treatment. By saying that it is the child who presents for treatment, the place of the parents in regard to the treatment of the child is obscured in everyday clinical practice.

This predicament was well articulated, nonetheless, by Hermine Hug-Hellmuth who stated the following: "The child does not come of his own accord to the analyst, as the grown-up does, but owing to the wish of his parents and only then (and herein he resembles the grown-up) when all other means have proved futile" (1921, pp. 287–288). In making this apparently innocuous statement, Hug-Hellmuth opens up the question of the place of the parents in regard to a child's analysis, in a way that was original, but was subsequently lost. We will endeavour to elaborate upon this question, starting from Hermine Hug-Hellmuth's own contributions to this area, contributions that logically flowed from her foundational challenge to Freud's authority as the father of psychoanalysis.

Even this term the *parents* is one that perpetuates another type of fiction, that of the notion of the oneness of the mother and father, as if these two were fused in their relations to the child, their understanding of the child's difficulties, and their approach to the child's upbringing and education. It also begs the question of who the parents are in any particular case. There are now many combinations, such as single parents, blended families, or parents constituted by two sets of homosexual couples. Moreover, as well as parent-donors of sperm and eggs, there are surrogate mothers. We cannot assume to know in advance who might truly function as mother and father for the child, nor whom the child regards as his parents. This term the *parents*, then, is one that is used as a type of convenience or shorthand. But the convenience that it affords is outweighed by the illusions that it propagates. The *parents* can only be a provisional term that has no theoretical value in psychoanalysis.

This illusion is taken much further in clinical practice as well as in the ways in which clinicians inform the public through the media. For instance, there is a plethora of self-help books that promote the notion of *parenting*, which is presented as a set of tasks, or preformed knowledge or skills, that only need to be learned. The term *parents* already obscures the difference between a mother and a father, most notably that of sexual difference. The notion of *parenting* operationalises what it is to be a singular and sexed subject confronted with the upbringing of one's son or daughter, into a skill set.

If the already problematical notion of the *parents* becomes reduced to the cliché of *parenting*, parenting is in turn reified into a so-called *parenting-style*. Here we can quote from an article that appeared in a newspaper by the Australian author and cultural historian Maria Tumarkin: "In our culture, where the ideas of life and lifestyle are used interchangeably, and no one blinks, should we be surprised at the speed and ease with which parenting becomes parenting-style?" (2009, p. 20). The idea of parenting-style further reduces the particularities of the mother and the father into a supposed subtype of a generalised phenomenon. This can become a type of theory of hopelessness since the conception of a mother's or a father's struggle as a *style* not only takes it as something innate or fixed, but also as something that conveys these parents' *values* and way of life. These values are often promoted and reinforced by well-meaning therapists. Such a clinical conception makes it virtually impossible to hear the demands and complaints of the mother and father in the particularity of their own suffering, let alone those of the child concerned.

It is for these reasons, and others that we will endeavour to address, that the place of the parents in relation to the psychoanalysis of the child has always been a problematic one, and often one that is left entirely aside. In the previous chapter we strove to show one manner in which the place of the parents was critical for the very foundation of psychoanalysis of the child. Effectively then, the field of psychoanalysis of the child was born through the cut that was made by Hermine Hug-Hellmuth in the incestuous modality through which the first psychoanalysts analysed their own children, or nephew in the case of Hug-Hellmuth herself. Her declaration, however, was not heard—or was forgotten—by the analysts who followed her, through the suppression of her legacy. Here, as a basis to our elaboration, we will endeavour to rescue from oblivion—or from repression—some aspects of Hermine Hug-Hellmuth's conceptualisation of the place of the parents.

Melanie Klein, as is well known, analysed her own children. This produced such a serious conflict in her daughter Melitta, that when Melitta became a psychoanalyst herself, she changed her name to Melitta Schmideberg. This change of name was the necessary bastardisation of her family legacy that enabled her to become a psychoanalyst in her own name, a name that she had to forge anew. The change of name effectively produced a cut in the holophrase *parent-analyst*.

Similarly, the analyst might need to make a cut in the holophrase of the *parents*—which is also a *hollow phrase*—in order to hear the complaints of the mother and the father who bring the child for analysis. We cannot presume to know in advance that the complaint made by either or both of the parents regarding the child constitutes, in itself, a demand for treatment. Moreover, it follows even more strongly that we cannot know that there is any demand on the part of the child who, not infrequently, does not know about the referral until the last moment, and/ or is deceived as to its nature. Nonetheless it is necessary for the analyst to anticipate the child's demand through the listening that is able to be given.

Hug-Hellmuth and the demand of the parents

If Hermine Hug-Hellmuth gave psychoanalysis of the child a logical basis through her proclamation of the impossibility for anyone to properly analyse his own child, she took this further by clarifying the place of the parents in relation to the analysis. Hug-Hellmuth was quite specific about the demands of the parents in her paper, "On the Technique of Child-Analysis" (1921). She noted from her clinical practice that parents look upon psychoanalysis as the last resource when all other measures have failed, but nonetheless expect a miraculous cure. She notes that the parents' distrust of the treatment pertains to their sense of shame at having failed in regard to the child, as well as their anxiety about intimate family affairs being laid bare to the analyst. In making these observations, Hug-Hellmuth viewed the demands of the parents in a circumspect manner, not as something to be taken at face value, but rather as an aspect of their transference to the analyst to be worked with clinically.

She writes of their "demand for 'active therapy'" (p. 298) which is echoed in contemporary clinical practice by the frequent demand by parents—and offers by therapists—for *strategies*. She differentiates, moreover, the place of each of the parents. She states that it is the mothers who "nearly always show a desire to make use of 'active therapy'" (p. 303). Hug-Hellmuth also notes that it is difficult to convince them that their work lies in another direction, for them to "show the child during the treatment the greatest possible measure of patience and forbearance" (p. 303). She warns of the jealousy that might be experienced towards the analyst, especially by a mother, due to the child's transference to the person of the analyst. In her view, a mother in this situation feels deprived of her child's love.

Hug-Hellmuth notes that the child's analysis has to go through a process of re-crystallisation in which the child's old values are first destroyed. This *destructive* process requires tolerance on the part of the parents, and particularly the mother, of any outward deterioration in the child. This process puts the authority of the parents—something to which we previously referred as the *paternal function*—into question by the child's more violent rebellion against the parents' rules and regulations during this period. Here she refers specifically to the father: "Just as no father would think of sending his child to school when suffering from pneumonia, so no demands must be made for study from the child suffering psychically" (p. 303). Regardless of the *content* with which we may or may not agree, what is important here is the *form*—the fact that there *are* rules and regulations—which is circumscribed by Hug-Hellmuth.

Hug-Hellmuth became the third female member of the Vienna Psychoanalytic Society on 8 October 1913. The second female member was Sabina Spielrein who had, on 29 November 1911, presented part of her paper *"Die Destruktion als Ursache des Werdens"* (Destruction as the cause of coming into being) to the Society, a paper that was published the following year (1912a). While Hug-Hellmuth was not present when Spielrein presented in Vienna, she would have been familiar with Spielrein's work, which appears to have influenced her own. In that paper Spielrein proposes that, "coming into being proceeds from destruction" (1912b, p. 183). Such an assertion is echoed by Hug-Hellmuth's statement that in analysis there is a destruction of old values, followed by re-crystallisation. While this is true in the child's analysis, it is also true of Hug-Hellmuth's propositions regarding the parents.

On the same afternoon that Hug-Hellmuth presented her paper "On the Technique of Child-Analysis", at the International Psychoanalytical Congress at The Hague in 1920, Spielrein spoke on the topic of "The emergence and development of articulated speech". We have mentioned that Anna Freud was present at that congress, but we should note that Melanie Klein was there as well (Richebächer, 2005, p. 228). We will have occasion to return to Spielrein's writings in the final chapter.

In her paper, Hug-Hellmuth refers to the parents' wish for friendly relations with the analyst as "a legitimate demand on the part of the parents" (1921, p. 304) that furthers the treatment of the child. She conceives of this, once again, as an aspect of the transference of the mother and father, within which she proposes to work. The sole aim of this work is that of promoting the analysis of the child. Her emphasis is particularly on the negative transference of each of the parents towards the analyst, which is to be explained by their narcissism. The French analysts Bergès and Balbo, who elaborate upon Hug-Hellmuth's proposals, underline the particular emphasis that Hug-Hellmuth gives to this negative transference:

> … this author's genius is to have understood that it is of the utmost importance to start out from this transferential given, without too

many illusions, in other words taking stock of this, knowing that
this negativity will be a backdrop for the whole of the treatment,
and that the work of the transference is nothing in the end but a
work of mourning. (1994a, pp. 110–111)

Hug-Hellmuth's proposal is thus that the child does not come of his
own accord to the analyst, but comes, rather, owing to the demand of
the parents. In this manner, Hermine Hug-Hellmuth was able to formulate a circumscribed place for the parents in regard to the child's
treatment. She proposed working with the parents, specifically within
the transference of each, recognising that their transference is quite separate to that of the child. This is what enabled her to found a clinical
practice with the child, through being able to clarify the demand that
the parents make of the analyst in regard to their child. In this way she
enables the analyst to hear the demands of the parents, in order that the
analysis of the child might proceed.

The place of the parents in the history of child analysis

In 1909, Sigmund Freud had already outlined his view of the place of
the parents in regard to the child's analysis: "The therapy of a child's
nervous states will always have … one great difficulty: the parents'
neuroses, which will form a wall in front of the child's neurosis"
(Nunberg & Federn, 1967, p. 324). This was certainly an effect of his
experience with little Hans and Hans' parents. Freud's case history,
"Analysis of a Phobia in a Five-Year-Old Boy" (1909b), was, in fact,
published in that same year. Thus for Freud, the parents were literally
a barrier to the treatment of the child. Nonetheless, at the same time,
he saw the parents as potentially part of the solution: "One will avail
oneself of the help of a skillful nurse (in especially favourable circumstances, of the mother herself)" (p. 324). It is significant to note that
in Freud's time, much of the work of raising the child was done by a
nanny or "nurse", at least in middle-class families.

Anna Freud's first major publication, *Einführung in die Technik der
Kinderanalyse* (*Introduction to the Technique of the Analysis of Children*)
(1927b), was the one in which every major concept outlined by Hug-
Hellmuth was later described by Anna Freud as a basic element of
her child psychoanalytic technique. Even though this book does not
give Hug-Hellmuth due credit, much of it is devoted to a rivalry with
Melanie Klein, through a constant attempt to refute Klein's theses. But

with Anna Freud, the place of the analyst in regard to the parents is often obscured. She writes, for instance, of "two children who were being analysed by me" (1927a, p. 6), with no mention of the parents, as if the girls existed in a vacuum. And yet we know from other sources that these two girls—who were in fact her first patients—were the daughters of her well-known friend and colleague Dorothy Burlingham (Boukobza, 1993, p. 57). Indeed, Anna Freud was analyst for all of Burlingham's four children. From the beginning, Anna Freud already placed herself at the same level as the parents, particularly the mother in this instance. Consequently, she engages in a rivalry for the child's love, with those in *loco parentis*: "Thus I began a keen and sustained battle with the nurse for the child's affection" (1927a, p. 13). For her, the parental authority and that of the physician remain effectively fused. She states that after her initial period of preparing the child for analysis, a period she refers to as the "dressage" for analysis: "The position of authority … at this stage becomes essential" (p. 45). It becomes essential so that the analyst is at "liberty to guide the child" (p. 45). For this to occur, the child "must feel that the analyst's authority is even greater than [the parents']" (p. 45). Once again, we can conclude that what predominates for Anna Freud is her experience of her father and her analyst being one. This conflation of the parent and analyst reaches its apogee in her theoretical formulation when she proposes that, "The analysis of children … must for the present be confined to the children of analysts or of people who have been analysed" (p. 50).

Melanie Klein rarely referred to the parents, leaving us in some doubt as to their position in regard to the analysis of the child. However, in her book *The Psycho-Analysis of Children*, first published in 1932, she devoted a section to "the analyst's dealings with the parents of his patients" (p. 75). It is quite striking that Klein also reiterates many of the points made in Hug-Hellmuth's paper of 1921, giving scant acknowledgement of the paper or its author. Klein writes, for instance, of the difficulty for the parents of having their family life revealed to the analyst. She also writes of the mother's jealousy towards the (woman) analyst, which, she proposes, "is to a very large extent based upon the subject's [mother's] rivalry with her own mother-imago" (p. 75). Such a rivalry, for Klein, is "very noticeable in governesses and nurses, who are often anything but friendly in their attitude towards analysis" (pp. 75–76). That is, this rivalry with the analyst occurs in those who take the place of the mother.

Klein differs from Hug-Hellmuth, in that for her, the analyst's dealings with the parents are not, strictly speaking, part and parcel of the work of the analysis of the child. Due to this, she states that the parents "can therefore only be influenced by ordinary psychological means" (p. 75). This includes the responsibility for getting the child to come to the analysis in spite of the child's reluctance and difficulties. In other words, unlike Hug-Hellmuth, Klein does not consider that she is able to work within the transference of the parents. Hence her work with the parents takes on a practical aspect, principally that of getting them to refrain as much as possible from all interference with the child's analysis. On the other hand, she invites the parents to take up a similar place to that of the analyst, by getting them to encourage the child, "through questions or otherwise, to talk about its analysis or lending any kind of support to whatever resistances against the analysis it may give utterance to" (p. 76). Thus the parent conspires with the analyst, or is even an agent of the analyst, in intervening with the child outside the analytic sessions. For Klein, the analyst might also function as an agent of the parent towards the child's adaptation to his environment, by facilitating the realisation of the parents' wishes for the child to be carried out. For example, she proposes that, "It may also sometimes happen that after a successfully completed treatment, the child can be removed to other surroundings, for instance a boarding-school, a thing which had previously not been possible owing to its neurosis and lack of adaptability" (p. 78). Thus for Melanie Klein, in a slightly different way to that of Anna Freud, the conflation of parents and analyst, something we designated by the holophrase *parent-analyst*, remains intact.

Such a fusion and conflation of the parents with the analyst was shared by Donald Winnicott. This is exemplified in the case history of the Piggle, in which Winnicott uses his so-called "on demand" form of analysis. As with Anna Freud's comment that the analysis of the child should be confined to children of analysts or people who have been analysed, the parents of the Piggle were indeed "professional people who had knowledge of the psychotherapeutic field" (Winnicott, 1977, p. viii). The analysis consisted of infrequent meetings over two and a half years. In the intervals, the parents wrote to Winnicott and their letters also included drawings and messages from the Piggle to him. In her introduction to the book, Clare Winnicott cites a memo that Winnicott had left in order to comment on his way of working with the parents of the patient, "Share material with the parents—not family therapy—not casework—psychoanalysis *partagé* (shared). No breach of confidence on their part, and they didn't interfere" (p. viii). For Winnicott, therefore, the parents were literally co-analysts of the Piggle.

By way of contrast, Maud Mannoni states, "I have opposed the conception of psychoanalysis as 'corrective experience' that can be continued by the mother at home" (1967a, p. 196). In that way of working, she states: "There seems to be little concern about what is in play in the fantasy of the parents' desire" (p. 197). When the child is presented by the parents to the analyst for treatment, one approach—which was also that of Anna Freud—is to refer one of the parents, usually the mother, for his or her own analysis. Mannoni argued against such an approach: "In obliging parents to enter analysis themselves, the analyst fails to see that it is useless to analyse a mother for her own sake when her own sake is the child to such an extent that she expresses her presence through the child's symptom (a symptom that bears the imprint of her desire)" (p. 197). Maud Mannoni accepts the transference of the mother and father, and endeavours to work within these, in addition to that of the child. She works with the parents in order to address the "surroundings" of the child, specifying that "[T]he surroundings consist, above all, in the collective discourse in which the subject is trapped" (p. 195).

Mannoni not only receives the transference of each of the parents, but puts forward that the parents *must* bring their words to the child's analyst. She articulates this transference as occurring through discourse: "By listening to what the child and his parents say to us, we are enabled to orient ourselves in relation to their discourse" (p. 194). She puts forward that part of the difficulty, for the child, is to be trapped in a discourse: a discourse that is alienating and which impedes the child from assuming a place as subject. For Mannoni, if the presence of the parents is accepted by the psychoanalyst, not only does it prevent the disruption of the analysis by the parents, but it also allows for "the progressive disappearance of alienating speech in the discourse of the [child] subject, which is sometimes nothing other than that of the parent intervening in the place of the subject" (1964, p. 116, translated for this edition). Additionally, Mannoni separates out the place of the mother and father (p. 119), and notes the mourning that is required on the part of the parents, and particularly for the mother, of the place in which the child is maintained.

Mannoni's propositions regarding the place of the mother and father in relation to the analysis of the child are built upon the differentiation established by Jacques Lacan, of what we might call the functions of each of the parents for the subject, from the persons of the parents themselves. The notion of the imago of the mother and father, utilised by Hug-Hellmuth and later by Klein and others, remains restricted to a representation of each of the parents for the child, rather than a theorisation of how such positions may function for the child. Lacan's elaboration encompasses the very differentiation he makes between the *other* and the *Other*. Elsewhere he refers to the place of the *primordial Other* for the child, whose place may indeed in most cases be mediated by the mother, but is not contingent upon, or reducible to, the person of the mother herself. We might even call this place that of the *m/Other* to indicate the way in which the Other may be mediated by the mother. More specifically, particularly in his seminar *The Object Relation*, Lacan speaks at length of his notion of the desire of the mother—and later of the *mother's jouissance* of the child—as well as that of the *paternal function*. Neither of these is able to be reduced to the persons of the mother and father. Indeed, Lacan proposes that the symbolic father is the one that is nominated as such by the mother. Nonetheless, Lacan's differentiation of the places and functions of each of the parents for the subject does not preclude being able to speak of the actual parents who present a child for treatment, as he does in "Note on the Child" (Lacan, 1986b). In these ways, Lacan effects a cut in the holophrase, the *parents*.

More recently, in his book *The Infantile in Psychoanalysis*, Robert Lévy formulated the place of the parents in relation to the child's analysis through a logical formulation, "not without the parents" (2008, p. 80, translated for this edition). This formulation is built upon other logical aphorisms of Lacan, such as *a woman is not without being the phallus*, or *anguish is not without an object*. Accordingly Lévy states, "Therefore, no analysis of the infantile without the parents, and, for the analyst, the infantile is a 'passant' of the parents through its symptom" (p. 80). The *passant* is the one who, at the end of an analysis, undergoes the procedure invented by Lacan, designated as the *passe*, concerned with the end of analysis and the formation of analysts. In putting forward this proposition, Lévy is approximating the analysis of the child to the *passe*. He puts forward a definition of the *infantile*, however, that is different to what we are proposing here, referring to a period of childhood, roughly between two and five years of age, in which secondary repression has not yet been fully accomplished and in which analytic work with both the parents and the child can often lead to rapid resolution of symptoms. With Tine Nørregaard, I have addressed Lévy's notions regarding the so-called *infantile symptom* elsewhere (2011). Here, however, we might retain Lévy's proposition that the psychoanalysis of the infantile is *not without* the parents.

The work with the parents

If the parents bring the child to the analyst, it is often through a perception that there has been a disruption of a pre-established harmony, or that the child's difficulties represent a deviation from a harmonious situation that the parents, educators, or clinicians imagine should exist. Nonetheless, there is no harmonious state that exists in nature, except that of death. For Bergès and Balbo, this is the only starting point for our work with children: "All of the studies in neurological and psychological development, and even the most empirical and innate conceptualisations, through the diversity and quality of each of the researchers, in the end seem to oblige us to let go of our illusions of any pre-established or statistical harmony" (1994b, p. 5, translated for this edition). And even beyond relinquishing such an idea of harmony, they ask, "[I]s disharmony not the very principle that is required for development?" (p. 5).

The disharmonious predicament through which the child is presented to the analyst is often a conflictual situation between the parents, in which the child is secondarily concerned. Lacan articulates this in the following way: "The symptom may represent the truth of the family couple. This is the most complex case, but also the one that is most open to our intervention" (1986b, p. 7). In such a case there is work that may be done by the parents.

In regard to the child, however, the situation is more complex. Let us return here to Hermine Hug-Hellmuth, who elaborates upon the attitude of the parents in regard to the treatment of the child in the following way:

> In the case of the child … psycho-analysis is looked upon as the last resource, and the parents, who have found all other educational measures fail, have a good deal of mistrust even in psycho-analysis. In spite of this, they expect a "miraculous cure" which shall remedy in the course of days the mistakes of years. (1921, p. 302)

Here we encounter the negativity of the transference of the parents to the analyst, to which Bergès and Balbo refer. What Hug-Hellmuth underlines, which is an extremely pertinent observation regarding the parents, is their sense of failure. She continues in the following way: "The parents' criticism of the [child's] treatment is made more poignant owing to their painful consciousness, mingled with shame, anxiety and bitterness, of having failed in regard to their children's successful training" (p. 302).

It is this sense of failure that parents bring to the analyst but which often remains unspoken. It is further suppressed by any so-called *strengths-based* or *solution-focused* approaches that are currently so prevalent. When Freud writes of education—or raising children—as an impossible profession, it is precisely in the sense that each mother and father must necessarily fail in the child's upbringing. The very point of failure must be brought forward in the work with the parents.

Bergès and Balbo comment further on this sense of failure:

> [The parents] present themselves as guilty of having failed and they already know for a fact that any improvement in the health of their child will essentially be due to the analysis and that it will have little to do with them. As with their child, consequently it will all begin with a negative transference, and it is necessary to create the conditions which will allow this to be freely played out, then to be transformed. (1994a, pp. 113–114)

Here Bergès and Balbo refer to the *parents*, without unravelling what pertains to the mother and what to the father. The analyst must intervene within the transference that the mother and the father present him with, in a modality that is not an analysis of either of the parents, but rather an intervention that promotes the analysis of the child. Since it is the demand of the parents that brings the child to analysis in the first instance, it is always in reference to this demand that any analysis of a child is made possible. The analytic contract is, by necessity, negotiated with the parents. But in child analysis following Hermine Hug-Hellmuth, the analyst must be able to hear the demand of the mother and father, and negotiate this contract within their transference.

Bergès and Balbo, elaborating on the foundational positions of Hermine Hug-Hellmuth, are quite specific regarding what it is that is to be mourned on the part of the *parents*:

... the parents ask the analyst to identify with their own parental imagos. But their demand is also that he incorporate the imago of the child that is able to flatter the narcissism of the parents. Thus it is themselves, as they suppose themselves to have been as children, that they desire to re-find in the child: their child, in identifying with this ideal analytic imago in its turn, would be nothing but what they were in their childhood. Their narcissism thus pushes them to only accept the analysis of their child if, by this means, their own childhood returns in the child. The miracle that they expect from it is hence only a banal narcissistic return of the repressed ideal. (p. 114)

The narcissistic wound experienced by the parents is precisely the failure of which we have spoken. And it is only by being able to hear the place in which the parents hold the child, that the analyst may be able to permit a mourning of that place. This mourning on the part of the parents is what allows another space to open up for the child, a space that is not predetermined in such a fixed manner, and against which the child struggles with the resulting perception that an illusory harmony has been disturbed.

We emphasise that this work of mourning, this *Trauerarbeit* of which Freud spoke, occurs in particular moments, in response to particular interventions, or in the underlining of the signifiers already present in the discourse of mother and father. The mourning to which we are referring occurs in the acts of speech within the work with the parents, whether they are uttered as an intervention by the analyst, or by *ablunders* of the mother or the father in which something of the *unbeknownst* imposes itself.

The jouissance of the mother

Let us endeavour to tease apart from the *parents*, the part that pertains to the mother. For the mother the wound is not just a narcissistic one, but also a physical or carnal wound. It is the wound that is left from the child's body being ripped from her own. By intervening in the discourse of the parents, the analyst is able to effect a cut in what can be called the mother's knowledge of the child. But the mother's knowledge, in her necessarily incestuous relation to the child, is also a carnal knowledge. It is one aspect of her jouissance of the child, something we will elaborate here as the *jouissance of the mother*, regardless of the person within whom this might be located.

If we return for a moment to Hermine Hug-Hellmuth's paper of 1921, we note that in referring to the shame, anxiety, and bitterness of having failed, she goes on to remark that it is the mothers' attempt to make good this situation which underwrites their desire to use what she calls "active therapy". It is also the mothers, in Hug-Hellmuth's opinion, who experience intense jealousy towards the analyst concerning their children's treatment.

As well as manifesting through shame, anxiety, and bitterness, the sense of failure is often experienced as guilt. This guilt of the mother, particularly if unspoken, may easily turn into a feeling of being blamed for having failed in regard to the child. This guilt is one aspect of what we have referred to as the *mother's jouissance of the child*. But whether it is experienced as guilt or as blame, what is mediated by it is a type of aetiological formulation upon which we have previously remarked. In other words, the mother places herself as cause of the child's suffering, and therefore, ultimately, as cause of the child as subject. Such a formulation—whether it is that of the mother, or that of a clinician— needs to be teased apart in order that something might be done with it. It is this that must be handled with delicacy by the analyst, not seeking to reassure, nor to eliminate the sense of failure, but rather to allow it to emerge in order that it might be worked with.

The mother's relation to the child, as we have intimated, is one that is predicated on a lack of harmony: there is no *symbiosis* except in the imaginations of clinicians, only the disparity of *parasitism* of the child who is reliant upon the mother and not vice versa. The mother's jouissance of the child is a function of a relation that is marked by a foundational disparity. Lacan introduced the notion of transitivism in order to conceptualise the way in which the child, and his body, is brought into the symbolic order. Here we can understand transitivism as another of the modalities of the mother's jouissance of the child. We will briefly elaborate upon this in speaking of the place of the mother in relation to the child's analysis.

In its simplest form, transitivism corresponds to the situation in which one person is hurt, and another person suffers. One young child, for instance, hits another, but it is the child who has dealt the blow who cries. Bergès and Balbo refer to this simplest form as "one-way transitivism" which results in no more than identification. When utilised clinically with the clinician identifying with the patient, it produces inexorable "friendly practice based on the empathy of the therapist" (1998, p. 4). But in the case of a mother with her child, she makes the hypothesis of knowledge in her child. So if the young child knocks his leg, the mother experiences the pain in her body and says "Ouch", anticipating the child's knowledge of his suffering. It is precisely this that Bergès and Balbo refer to as "symbolic anticipation" (1994b, p. 6). But in this form of transitivism, the mother's knowledge of the child's suffering returns to her in the form of a demand from the child. In this case the child identifies, not with the mother, but rather with the discourse that she entertains with him.

This form of transitivism, through the mother's speech, ties the body image to both discourse and to the accident—the *tuché*—that intrudes upon the child's body. In other words, it provides a means by which the child might be able to knot the imaginary, symbolic, and the real, through the anticipated jouissance of a carnal experience.

Because of this, transitivism is also the mother's jouissance of the child's body, anticipated in her discourse. It is by virtue of this that the child gains access to the symbolic order: to speech, and ultimately to writing. But through her speech, the mother hypothesises the presence of a subject in her child. Literally, it is by virtue of this aspect of the mother's jouissance of the child that the child is able, in the first instance, to come to the place of subject. This aspect of the mother–child relation is something quite different to preconceptions of tender loving maternal care. In fact Bergès and Balbo describe the transitivism of the mother as a type of *forcing* (*forçage*) (1998, p. 3) of the child to come into the symbolic order.

Nonetheless, this transitivism must ultimately fail, that is, the child must reject the mother's discourse, in order to accede to the place of subject. The failure is built into transitivism since the mother can do no more than hypothesise regarding the child: hypotheses that must ultimately fail and which the child will come to disprove. This is one aspect of the mother's sense of failure that is in question here.

For the child's analysis to proceed, this position of the mother, the *jouissance of the mother* in regard to the child must, at least in part, be relinquished. The negativity of the mother's transference, of which Bergès and Balbo speak, is the pain of renouncing a quotient of her enjoyment, her jouissance of the child and his body. As we have intimated, the mourning of this position can occur through the analyst's intervention with the parents. Here we might be able to differentiate the mother's failure from the failure of the *parents*. The mother's failure, a necessary failure, is always then a failure at the level of her jouissance of the child. It is in this sense that we can say that the mother's failure is a *real failure*, a failure in the *real*. The mother's failure and its associated guilt are, in one sense, unspeakable. Nonetheless, the analyst's intervention must delimit her failure such that there occurs a cut in her jouissance of the child.

The call to the father

Tine Nørregaard Arroyo notes that an intervention in the parental couple "anticipates what is already functioning as Name of the Father for the child" (2012, p. 131). It is this anticipation of a paternal function that underwrites the analyst's intervention.

We commented earlier that the etymology of *invention* derives from the Latin *in-venire*, and the *event* from *ex-venire*. Hence to speak of an *intervention* is also to evoke the etymology of *inter-venire* which signifies *to break in upon, to put a stop to, to come between*. Literally, the intervention referred to above is one that breaks in upon, and comes between, the mother and the child, even if it is an intervention with the parental couple. It breaks in upon the necessarily incestuous position of mother and child, by evoking that which, as Nørregaard Arroyo writes, is already functioning as name of the father, or the paternal function, for the child. It is already functioning as it has already been anticipated in the mother's speech in her hypothesising, or symbolic anticipation. Bergès and Balbo refer to symbolic anticipation as something that occurs between the mother and child. Nonetheless, what we must emphasise here, is that in order to function, it requires the presence of a paternal function. Such a function may be, but is not necessarily, mediated by the physical presence of the actual father.

If a child remains fixed in the transitivism with his mother, with the Other, then there is, for the mother, "no longer any gap able to be tolerated between what she anticipates of ... her experience ... and the real ... experience which might be that of the child" (Bergès & Balbo, 1994b, p. 71). Such an absence of a gap might occur, for instance, in an autistic child. Here we can examine the intervention that might effect a gap between the mother's anticipation and the child's experience.

We have already referred to Freud's involvement in the case of Little Hans, whose analyst was nominally his father. In the last chapter we alluded to Freud's direct and well-known intervention when the boy's father took Hans to Freud's consulting rooms. As part of his intervention, Freud gave the boy a mythologised account of his pre-history: "Long before he was in the world … I had known that a little Hans would come who would be so fond of his mother that he would be bound to feel afraid of his father because of it." And Freud adds to this comment to Hans the following: "… and I had told his father this" (1909b, p. 42). With this comment, Freud appears to be endeavouring to hand back the baton of the transference to Hans' father, an ever failing attempt, since immediately following this consultation, Hans asks his father, "Does the Professor talk to God …?", clearly putting Freud in the position of the subject supposed of knowledge.

What interests us here specifically is not the effect of this interven-tion on Hans himself, but rather its effect upon Hans' father who was also present at the consultation. Of course Freud's account is a mythical one, a reiteration of the situation of Oedipus in relation to his mother and father. It articulates both the prohibition of incest as well as, indi-rectly, the fear of retribution at the hands of a vengeful father. In other words, the father holds a central place in Freud's intervention. Whether Freud's account is directed at Hans' father or not, it has an immediate effect upon him. It is the father who was first to respond, interrupting Freud's mythologised account by the following question to Hans: "But why do you think I'm angry with you?" (p. 42). It is very striking that Hans's father responds in such a manner, defending himself against the imagined accusation of being angry towards his son.

In any case, Freud's intervention had an effect on the father, calling into question his place as possessing the "authority of a father" and dissociating it from the authority of "a physician". To use the terms we have adopted here, we can say that Freud makes a cut in the holophrase *parent-analyst*. Further to this, Freud differentiates the place of the father as separate to that of the mother, thus also making a cut in the holo-phrase the *parents*. And it is the father's defensive reaction itself that indicates that Freud has touched upon something significant.

A few days after Freud's consultation with father and son, Hans one morning came to bed, to "coax" (p. 23) not with his mother, but rather with his father. When the father questions him as to his motives, Hans replies, "Why did you tell me I'm fond of *Mummy* and that's why I'm frightened, when I'm fond of *you*?" (p. 44). But this fondness cuts both ways and the whole of the case history is permeated by the father's fondness for Hans, which explains the father's defensive response to

Freud's implication that a father might be angry or spiteful. It is curious that Freud emphasises Hans' aggression in having quite unexpectedly butted his head against the father's stomach on the morning of the consultation. On the other hand he seems not to make anything of the fact that the father had forgotten this episode, including his response to it, which Freud minimises, saying, "He had given him as it were a reflex blow with his hand" (p. 42).

We can hypothesise that the father's forgetting and defensiveness is mediated by his *fondness* for Hans, something we might propose is a manifestation of the *jouissance of the mother*, located in the person of the father, and something to which Hans gives voice. And to take this further, we can suggest that is precisely the father's enjoyment of Hans, and his unwillingness to relinquish this, that detains him from taking up his place within the paternal function.

In *The Object Relation* seminar, Lacan proposes that little Hans' phobia is a "call for help" in regard to the difficult problem of the relations of the child with the mother. He states, moreover, that it is a "call for a symbolic element" since there was something failing in Hans' situation. Hans needed "an organization of the symbolic world that is called the father" (1956–1957, p. 58). In this way, through his cry for help, little Hans evoked his need for a paternal function, and invoked his father to that place.

If, as we have proposed, the failure of the mother is a *real failure*, then we can consider that the failure of the father is of a different order. The father's failure is a failure in the realm of the symbolic, the failure in the provision of an organisation of the symbolic world for the child. Hence the father's failure is a *symbolic failure*. But what we can also take from Lacan's comment is that it is precisely the child's difficulties that invoke the paternal function in this *call to the father*. Both the child's call and the response from the father—the paternal function—are necessary in the production of a symptom for the child.

The demand of the child

It is the parents, in the first instance, who bring the child for treatment. The analyst must negotiate the contractual arrangements for the analysis of the child with the parents. In the clarity of these arrangements, including that of the parents' own work with the analyst, the child might be able to formulate a demand of his own. Unlike the demand made by the mother and father in the name of the child, the child's demand is not necessarily present from the outset. In the preliminary sessions, therefore, it is a question of whether, and how, such a demand is able to be formulated. But as with the adult, the preliminary interviews with the child also allow a premise for the analysis to unfold.

We have evoked the failure of the parents, and teased apart the different modalities in which the mother and the father may fail. This failure is one that is inevitable. It is a logical consequence of the fact that educating, or raising, children is an impossible profession, as Freud put it. It is in the recognition of this failure that a door is opened for the mother and father to be able to present the child for analysis.

The child's difficulties—perhaps not yet crystallised into a symptom—can appear in the gap that has been left open. This gap opens in the failure of the mother's symbolic anticipation, and through the child's appeal to a paternal function to be able to operate and organise the child's symbolic world. Much has been said of the decline of the paternal function over the course of the last century, but against this we assert that the paternal function is *forever* failing: this is not a recent phenomenon, it is part and parcel of the structure of the paternal function. It is in the very nature of the paternal function to fail and to continually need to be propped up. Throughout the history of Man this has led to a profusion of rules and laws, in a continual, but always failing, endeavour to maintain a paternal function: a *name of the father*.

Nonetheless, something unassimilable remains for the child, a surplus that resists the effort to anticipate, as well as the endeavour to organise, his symbolic world. This something unassimilable may lead the child to suffer, even if we characterise this as the jouissance of the symptom. This surplus avails itself of the child's difficulties and struggles, in the child's call for help.

CHAPTER SIX

The leaking tap: the symptom of the child

In 1969, Jacques Lacan gave Jenny Aubry two handwritten notes in which he briefly articulated the place of the child's symptom in relation to the parents. These were later published in French as "*Deux notes sur l'enfant*" (Lacan, 1986a) and later conflated in the translation into English as the singular "Note on the Child". This "Note" opens by putting forward that "[T]he child's symptom is found to be in a position of answering to what is symptomatic in the family structure" (1986b, p. 7). This raises a question regarding whether the child's symptom is but a symptom of the family structure. In this case the child would have no existence in his own right, his symptom being only an effect of the family, of the family structure. However, if the symptom of the child produces some answer of his or her own to what is symptomatic in the family, then we could say that the child produces his or her own symptom. Thus we need to differentiate the position of the child who *is* a symptom of the family structure, from that of the child who *has* a symptom, in response to what is symptomatic or fails in that structure. Elsewhere, I have articulated that these two modes are structural positions and proposed that the child must, by necessity, move from one to another (Plastow, 2000b). It is the movement to this second position that will be of interest in this chapter.

In Freud's case of Little Hans, the moment of this switch from one position to another is clearly articulated. In Freud's written account it is in the movement between the first chapter, "Introduction", and the second chapter, "Case History of Analysis". The first chapter ends by the articulation, in a number of different ways, of the beginnings of Hans' enjoyment of his own body and in particular of his own penis, his masturbation and fantasies, and wishes for his penis to be touched by others. It is in this sense that Hans moves from the position of being the object of his mother's jouissance, to that of being subject to the enjoyment, or jouissance, of his own body. This movement, however, is marked by the sudden occurrence of both anguish and his phobia, articulated by Lacan in the following way:

> So what has changed, since nothing truly important, nothing criti-
> cal has occurred in little Hans' life? What has changed is that his
> own penis has started becoming something quite real, it starts to
> stir, he begins to masturbate, and the important element is not so
> much the fact that his mother intervenes at that moment. The gross
> fact of the case is that his penis is already becoming something real;
> from that moment onwards it is quite clear that we must ask our-
> selves if there is not a relation between this and what appears next,
> in other words, anguish. (1956–1957, p. 224)

We have described this change as a movement that occurs at a particular moment, or moments, in the child's life. In this movement there is a passage from one state to another, a passage which also evokes the movement which is at the heart of the structure invented by Lacan called the *passe*, in which there is notionally a passage from the position of analysand to that of analyst. In the previous chapter, with Robert Lévy, we proposed that the analysis of the child and his symptom must occur *not without* the parents. The *passe* is a passage to the position as analyst, a *passage* that can also be written in French as *pas-sage*, or *badly behaved*. This is an indication of the jouissance or enjoyment, in its broadest sense, of the child's symptom. I have referred to little Hans' masturbation as such a symptom (Plastow & Nørregaard Arroyo, 2011). In the case history Hans himself describes this, and consequent phobia and anguish, as his "nonsense" (Freud, 1909b, p. 31).

This *pas-sage*, or *badly behaved*, connotes something that is at odds with the parents' demands and expectations of the child, that is, the symptomatic place of the child for the parents. As with the *passe*, what is of interest here is the knowledge that can be transmitted: this is what remains "unassimilated" (Lacan, 1962–1963b, p. 349, translated for this edition) at the level of knowledge, and is taken up by the symptom of the child. It is *unassimilated* in that it is unable to be integrated into the subject's knowledge. For Freud, in his correspondence with Fliess, there remains a surplus that "does not permit the work of translation" (Masson, 1985, p. 208). What is not able to be assimilated or translated, may nonetheless be able to be transmitted through a *passe*.

To refer to the title of this chapter, we can say that what leaks out of the family mythology, what exceeds the family structure and is elaborated by the child, is what is unable to be assimilated, and which is then manifested in the symptom. Lacan, later in his teaching, in the paper known as the "Geneva Lecture on the Symptom", articulates the movement we are describing in the following way, in referring to Hans' encounter with his own erection:

> … this poor little Hans thinks of nothing else and incarnates it in the most external of all objects, namely in this horse that paws the ground, that kicks, rolls over and falls to the ground. This horse that comes and goes, that has a certain way of drawing a cart along the quay, is for him the most exemplary thing of everything that he is caught up in, but that he understands absolutely nothing of, owing to the fact, to be sure, that he has a certain type of mother and a certain type of father. His symptom is the expression, the meaning of this rejection. (1985, p. 15)

The symptom is the means by which the child is able to accede to his or her own truth, through an experience that exceeds the place reserved for the child by the mother and the father. This is an aspect of the symptom that is concerned at the same time with a leakage and with a surplus: a leakage at one point produces a surplus elsewhere. This loss is one that, at the level of the child's symptom, can be manifested as a loss of an object from the body, a loss which also produces a hole or a lack, in other words something missing.

Take for instance the common symptoms of enuresis and encopresis with their corresponding loss of the products of the body, or even of trichotillomania in which the object is the hair that is pulled from the body, or indeed of anorexia with its loss of gastric content and weight

(Plastow, 2005–2006). A hole can also be produced, for instance by the cutting of the body, or by piercings. And in an analysis, there might be a fall of an object connoted by the loss of something from the body, or something discarded by the subject, sometimes a piece of flesh referred to in a dream, by a slip of the tongue, or through associations. And often the fate of this piece of flesh is an inglorious one: it is discarded in order to be swept away, relegated to the status of rubbish or residue, something that one might prefer to be disposed of or to remain hidden.

In reference to this bodily loss, we can also consider that other loss from the child's burgeoning body, that of the sexual secretions, in both sexes, and of the loss of semen in nocturnal emissions and masturbation in the boy. In the book of Genesis in the Bible, this was the sin of Onan: that of spilling his seed upon the ground. Such leakage from this particular tap, as from any other tap, occurs under pressure, in this case the pressure of the drive.

For little Hans, the emphasis is on the potential loss of his *widdler*, articulated through his attempt at self-reassurance, by his words: "It's fixed in, of course" (Freud, 1909b, p. 34). And as for little Hans, the symptom is in some way associated with an anguish, an anguish associated with this loss of an object; an anguish, as Lacan notes, "precisely in so far as any object escapes [the subject]" (1962–1963b, p. 275). Here we will elaborate upon this question of the symptom in relation to the object, both through Freud's case of Little Hans and Lacan's reading of this, as well as Lacan's analysis of a case in an experimental situation as recounted by Jean Piaget.

First we need to say what it is that we are referring to as the symptom. Freud gives a definition in the text, "Inhibitions, Symptoms and Anxiety". The "anxiety" in this title once again translates *"Angst"* in the German, which I have rendered as *anguish* in English, also corresponding to the *angoisse* Lacan uses in French to elaborate upon the Freudian notion of *"Angst"*. *Anguish* is far preferable to the common translation by the term *anxiety*, which has become reduced to a psychiatric symptom, rather than an experience to which one is subject. In his paper, Freud gives the following definition of the symptom: "A symptom is a sign of, and a substitute for, an instinctual [drive] satisfaction which has remained in abeyance" (1926d, p. 90). Once more there is something that has been lost; the drive satisfaction is lacking and is substituted by something else in the form of the symptom. In Freud's definition then, the lack of satisfaction of the drive is taken up as the suffering of the symptom. But there is another element to this definition, that is, the "sign of" this drive satisfaction that is in abeyance. Hence this sign stands in for an excess, or a surplus, elsewhere.

Even though we have referred to some commonly occurring childhood symptoms, at least in the psychiatric use of the term, the notion of the symptom in psychoanalysis goes well beyond this. As good a definition as any other is the notion put forward by José Saramago in his novel, *The Year of the Death of Ricardo Reis*. In the section of this novel to which I am referring, Ricardo Reis responds to the young woman Marcenda who has spoken to him about her paralysed arm, a loss of function that followed the death of her mother. She had been told by the specialists she consulted, who have been unable to diagnose or treat her, that it is the consequence of heart disease. Ricardo Reis, also a doctor, says to her:

> … as far as I can judge, Marcenda, if you are suffering from heart disease, you are suffering from yourself … . We are all ill, with one malaise or another, a deep-rooted malaise that is inseparable from what we are and that somehow makes us what we are, you might even say that each one of us is his own illness, we are so little because of it, and yet we succeed in being so much because of it. (1984, pp. 106–107)

What is referred to here as an illness or malaise is specifically what in psychoanalysis we call the symptom. The symptom is as incurable as it is the most intimate part of our being, a symptom that is tied up both with our suffering and our particular modes of enjoyment. What is prominent in Saramago's description is also the fact that this malaise or symptom is not something that is limited to those suffering from mental disorders, rather it is a part of each one of us, an irreducible part of each subject. And the suffering and enjoyment that are part and parcel of the symptom are precisely what Lacan designated as *jouissance*. Lacan proposes that there is no difference between the literal and figurative uses of expressions pertaining to parts of the body (1962–1963b, p. 272). Consider, in regard to Marcenda in the citation from Saramago, the expression in English to suffer from a *broken heart*. Once again we are confronted with a loss, including a loss of function, of a part of the body.

Here we will further pursue the place of the symptom of the child by first examining the object that is lost, an object that Lacan designates as the object *a*: object *cause* of desire. In this way we will pursue the question of cause that is always evoked by the symptom. We will then examine the notion of the symptom through Piaget's experiment, and Lacan's reading of it, to propose the means by which the symptom is able to transmit something that goes beyond the objectivised experimental method.

The tap and the cause

Lacan's seminar X, *L'Angoisse*, has been rendered into English in at least one translation as *Anxiety* (Lacan, 1962–1963a), but I insist upon rendering it as *Anguish*. For this reason, and to follow Lacan's seminar to the letter, I will translate the passages here from the French version of the *Anguish* seminar. In this seminar Lacan asks: "What does the obsessional present to us in the pathognomonic form of his position? The obsession or compulsion, articulated for him or not in a motivation in his internal language: 'Check that the door is closed or not, the tap.'" Lacan goes on to say that, "It is this symptom, taken in its most exemplary form, which implies that in not following his line, if I may put it that way, anguish is evoked" (1962–1963b, p. 348).

What we would like to do here is to take this symptom as exemplary. In other words, the obsession presents us with something fundamental regarding the question of any symptom in this vacillation between an opening and a closing, or whether the tap has been left dripping or not, whether the light has been left on or off, or if the gas has been turned off or not. This form of the symptom is of course accompanied by anguish, an anguish that the subject attempts to attenuate by returning to check. But also, in its content, the obsession pertains to what might enter or exit from a door that is left ajar, or what might escape from the dripping tap, that is, the object. Once again, it is an object that could fall from a door, or orifice, of the body.

Lacan proposes here that the symptom is not constituted until the subject becomes aware of it and recognises it as such. The symptom also presents itself as something unassimilated or enigmatic that suggests to the individual that it has a cause. But it is the very notion of cause that is in question here. For the subject, and also for many clinicians, the cause of one's suffering is to be sought in the history and elaborated through an aetiological formulation. But as we have already proposed, the history is not able to account for the suffering incurred in the symptom. While the function of cause is linked to a part of the body that is irretrievably lost, it is also connected to the signifier. Again in the *Anguish* seminar, Lacan notes that:

> ... the carnal fragment that has been torn from us, it is this fragment in so far as it is this that circulates in the logical formalism in so far as it has already been elaborated by our work regarding the use of the signifier, it is this part of ourselves caught in the machine, forever irretrievable, this object as lost at different levels of bodily experience, it is this that is the support, the authentic substrate of all function as such of cause. (p. 271)

If this is a carnal fragment, a piece of the body—or a pound of flesh, to refer to Shakespeare's *The Merchant of Venice* (1598)—which also invokes the relation of the object to the notion of debt, we might ask: in which way is it part of the body? This question is not restricted to any one modality or register, but is answered by the manner in which Lacan ultimately comes to place this missing fragment as the object *a* in the centre of the Borromean knot, that is, as pertaining to the registers of the symbolic, the imaginary, and the real. Just as cause is invoked by the subject in relation to the missing fragment, so too does Lacan develop it in relation to a missing knowledge:

> Cause, therefore, always emerges in correlation with the fact that something is omitted in the consideration of knowledge [*connaissance*], something that is precisely desire, which animates the function of knowledge. Each time that cause is invoked, and in its most traditional register, this is in some way the shadow, the counterpart, of that which is the blind spot in the function of knowledge itself ... . The desire for knowledge with its consequences has been called into question, and always in so far as knowledge feels obliged to construe itself as last cause. (1962–1963b, pp. 273–274)

This desire for knowledge, or *connaissance*, is no doubt also a reference to the "instinct" or drive for knowledge that Freud (1905d, p. 194) invokes in the *Three Essays on the Theory of Sexuality*. Furthermore, this "last cause" invokes the notion of end, or finality, in relation to *connaissance*. That is, it is in relation to this conscious or familiar knowledge—not *savoir* or unconscious knowledge—that the notion of cause as finality is invoked. This common notion of cause was evoked by Lacan in referring to "a motivation in [the obsessional's] internal language" (1962–1963b, p. 348). Such a motivation pertains to the question of will or purpose. This is what Lacan refers to as the mental function of cause. Here, to put this in the context of the four types of cause described by Aristotle, we can invoke that of "final cause" as the means by which the subject—and generally, as we have said, the clinician—construes the notion of cause. It is interesting to refer to Aristotle, in his *Metaphysics*, where he proposed that: "The final cause is an end, and that sort of end which is not for the sake of something else, but for whose sake everything else is; so that if there is to be a last term of this sort, the process will not be infinite" (Barnes, 1984b, p. 1571, Ch 2, 994b lines 9–11).

Similarly for the subject, the notion of cause endeavours to put an end to the constant slippage of the question regarding the cause behind the cause, or an end to the child's persistent question *Why?* But the failure to produce a final explanation, paradoxically, leads to an even greater insistence on the notion of cause. Thus Lacan suggests that, "The less cause is able to be grasped, the more all seems to be caused, and, right to the last term, that which was called the sense of history" (1962–1963b, p. 352). We can take this sense of history as also pertaining to the sense of the history of the patient, the insistent endeavour to attribute cause and meaning to the history. A patient, whom I interviewed in a *Presentation of Patients* conducted in a psychiatry inpatient unit, stated, "It all started when I was four years old." This patient thus attributes cause, indeed the cause of his being, to the events of this particular moment in his history.

Furthermore, the dichotomy between the cause as unable to be grasped, and the sense that all is caused, is the very dichotomy between cause—as we understand it from psychoanalysis—and the common notion of cause which is effectively a type of determinism. This latter notion is also a type of teleology that attempts to attribute cause to all things. We note that teleology is derived from τέλος or *end*: the term used by Aristotle for the final cause. Thus we can say that the common notion of cause put forward by the subject is a type of deterministic teleology, one that endeavours to retrospectively impute a cause, either to history or to the body. Such a notion of cause is one that comes after the effect: that is, one attempts to explain any occurrence by imputing a cause. Such teleological thinking attempts to dispense with the *accident*, that which is not determined. And this accident includes both the "accidental factors" in the history to which Freud referred, as well as the accidents of the signifier, *ablunders*, that are produced in a session.

As we have attempted to emphasise, this teleological notion of cause is perfectly consistent with the one that is promulgated by objective science and by the media. Every archaeological discovery regarding prehistoric man is immediately attributed a *cause* by any expert consulted by the media, in the usual teleological explanation. On the other hand, the notion of cause, for psychoanalysis, is precisely what is lacking in the causal explanation of the symptom. It is this missing piece, the lacking piece of the body that continues to provoke the quest for a cause, despite all the available explanations. It is this dimension of cause, as enigmatic, that provokes anguish in the subject. This, we will see, is a very different notion of cause to that proposed by Piaget.

Piaget's tap

Here we will examine Jean Piaget's 1923 book, *The Language and Thought of the Child*, firstly a section from its beginning, to determine Piaget's aims, and then a section devoted to the study of how young children communicate with each other. We will also consider some of Lacan's comments on this latter section. In this way we will endeavour to determine how the *object as cause* to which the symptom is closely tied, comes to colour the experience of a particular child in a nominally objective experiment.

Like the early psychoanalysts of children, such as those we discussed, Jean Piaget also studied his own children. Piaget, though, despite having had a brief analysis with Sabina Spielrein in Geneva, was not an analyst, but a psychologist who endeavoured to circumscribe the cognitive development of the child along the lines of what Bergès and Balbo describe as an "ideal pedagogy" (1994b, p. 12). The latter was built upon what Édouard Claparède, the founder of the J. J. Rousseau Institute in Geneva in which Piaget conducted his studies, described as the two pillars of that institute: "the scientific study of the child and the training of teachers" (Claparède, 1923, p. xvi). Such an ideal pedagogy, from our perspective, could only be built upon the ego and its ideals, which we can also designate as illusions. Piaget approaches the child from a very different direction to the early analysts, but his approach in which there is an emphasis on the ego lends itself not just to the purposes of pedagogy, but to the very ideals of pedagogy. And this idealising function is that of the ego itself.

Nonetheless, whatever illusions might be promoted by such an approach, it cannot eliminate the unconscious even if it chooses to ignore or dismiss it. Thus Bergès and Balbo state that, even though it was not invited, "the transference came to the appointment" (1994b, p. 12) in Piaget's and other early psychologists' studies, including those of their own children and grandchildren. This was not part of Piaget's schema, despite his own study of and familiarity with psychoanalysis. However, it is precisely this uninvited transference that is of interest to us and which we will examine here in Piaget's work.

In his book, *The Language and Thought of the Child*, Piaget's opening enquiry is the following: "The question which we shall attempt to answer in this book may be stated as follows: What are the needs which a child tends to satisfy when he talks?" (1923, p. 1). Piaget's question is a teleological one: what is the purpose of speech? This question, placing speech in the realm of need, immediately eliminates the significance of desire. One of the difficulties of this approach of studying language as a means of communication is that Piaget assumes that the mode of the subject's thinking or speaking will conform to the linear cause and effect schema of objective science. It is this presupposition regarding the teleological nature of cause that excludes other possibilities.

Piaget, however, does not content himself with leaving the question there. He notes a little later on that, "If the function of language were merely to 'communicate', the phenomenon of verbalism would hardly admit of explanation." He goes on to add that, "... the very existence of such questions shows how complex are the functions of language, and how futile the attempt to reduce them all to one—that of communicating thought" (p. 2). It is all the more striking then that Piaget continues to put forward the notion that language exists in order to communicate, and that his experiments in this book are designed to illustrate the failures of communication. Rather, from the perspective of psychoanalysis, it demonstrates the failure of Piaget's conception of language.

Immediately afterwards, Piaget goes on to outline his developmental perspective, even if nominally calling upon Janet and psychoanalysis:

> The functional problem therefore exists for the adult. How much more urgently will it present itself in the case of defective persons, primitive races and young children. Janet, Freud, Ferenczi,

Jones, Spielrein, etc., have brought forward various theories on the language of savages, imbeciles, and young children, all of which are of the utmost significance for an investigation such as we propose to make of the child mind from the age of six. (pp. 2–3)

The developmental study of language inevitably becomes imbued with the prejudice of those who believe they possess a superior form of language. For this reason, studies of the origin and development of language have always focused on the child, the deaf, and languages such as those spoken by so-called *savages*, and *wild children* who have grown up without contact with adults. In this way, studies like those of Piaget focus on those who are perceived to be deficient in language, like the "imbeciles" referred to by Piaget. But as the semiologist François Rastier notes, "With children who have grown up in isolation, the deaf and Creoles, one implicitly re-finds the three major references of the positivist anthropology of the nineteenth century: the child, the defective and the savage" (2007, p. 89, translated for this edition). The difficulty that such an approach imposes on the clinical and experimental situation is that it prevents the examiner apprehending the language of the child in its particularity, pejoratively referred to by Piaget as "childish language" (1923, p. 90).

Piaget examines the development of language in the child and thus, in his case, effectively proposes that the beginnings, or origin, of language are to be found in the child. To put it in this way is to connect this to our examination of the notion of *cause*, since an origin is effectively a type of cause or genesis. Lacan noted that "[T]he implication of cause in the advent of the symptom … is literally a question" (1962–1963b, p. 353). That is, the symptom always raises a question about the cause, ultimately regarding the cause of the subject. This question does not have an answer, or rather, there is always an unbridgeable gap between the effect and the cause that is imputed, a gap that cannot be filled in by more history. It is this cause as gap that Lacan designated as object *a*, in so far as this *a* is "the remainder of the constitution of the subject in the place of the Other" (p. 353).

This is something we can also discern through Lacan's reading of Piaget's work, *The Language and Thought of the Child*. The main aspect of Piaget's study examined by Lacan is that concerned with the question of how children communicate to each other and understand each other. Piaget's thesis, as we might anticipate, is that the younger child communicates by utilising what he calls egocentric language and hence the child is effectively limited in what he or she can convey to, and understand from, the other. The particular experiment we will examine involves the examiner (Piaget) giving the child a diagram of a tube with a tap, and a basin underneath. He gives an operationalised explanation consisting of nine separate points to a child, designated as the *explainer*. This explanation involves the mechanism of the opening and closing of the tap, controlling the flow of water through a "canal" in the tap, which he also refers to as "the little hole, door, or passage" (1923, p. 84). The *explainer* must then repeat the explanation to another child, the *reproducer*, who in turn repeats it to the examiner. Of course, what the child repeats to another child is not the same as what he has apparently understood. We say *apparently*, because of the artificiality and limitations of establishing what has been understood by this operationalised method. The difficulty, we can say, is that what the child understands is something different to what Piaget understands.

This is precisely where we might locate Piaget's ideal pedagogy: the notion, or ideal, that a child—or any subject for that matter—should be able to repeat unaltered a so-called communication. The loss of communication is where Piaget locates the developmental deficiencies of the child. All species, of course, have different methods of communication: that of bees is among the best known. Leandro de Lajonquière cites research to demonstrate that all animals pass on a message unaltered, with one exception. To cite de Lajonquière, "Man is the only species that is unable to duplicate the content of a message without modifying it" (2013, p. 76, translated for this edition). This is related by de Lajonquière to the emergence of the field of speech and language, that is, the *signifying function*, in Man.

Piaget is interested in the supposed loss of knowledge in its transmission from one child to another. Again we have a situation similar in structure to that of Lacan's *passe*. And while for Piaget there is a loss from one step for another, he allows us to read some of the accounts put forward by the children in the experiment by citing what they report. The notion of the tap as *cause*, which is missing from Piaget's explanation, is reported by the *reproducer*, named Riv in Piaget's account: "Here … there's the pipe, and then it is opened, and then the water runs into the basin, and then there … it is shut, so the water doesn't run any more, then there's the little pipe … lying down, and then the basin's full of water. The water can't run out 'cos the little pipe is there, lying down, and that stops it" (1923, p. 91).

We can hear this evocation of cause, particularly in the "so" and the "'cos" in Riv's account. We can also hear a certain excitement connoted in Riv's account. Thus, as Lacan notes in his explication of the text, Riv puts his emphasis on the tap as something that opens and spurts forth, but can also be closed, that is, the dimension of the tap as cause. It is the movement of the tap that causes the water to flow or not. And, thanks to such a tap, one can fill a basin without it overflowing.

Strikingly, although the basin is prominent in the diagram used by Piaget to explain the function of the tap to the *explainer*, he does not mention it at all in the account of the picture that he gives to the child. Furthermore, the *explainer*, in this case a child named Schla, does not mention it either. Something is passed on in the explanation by one child to another that is not encompassed within Piaget's schema. Piaget states, and gives Schla's account as an example, "One of the chief causes of misunderstanding among children may be due to some personal trait in the explainer" (p. 89). For us, rather than being a cause of a supposed misunderstanding of a failure of a transmission of an already-known knowledge, this personal trait of the explainer is specifically what is able to be passed on from one child to another. It is the singular trait of the subject, the desire of the subject that might allow something to be passed on, which is of interest to psychoanalysis.

Since we began with the question of the obsessional symptom, locking of the door or turning off the tap, this is a question of fundamental importance in relation to the symptom. Lacan takes the implications of this question further:

> Why is it that Piaget completely misses the phenomenon that is produced, if it is not because he totally misrecognises that, in a tap as cause, for a child there are the desires that the tap provokes in him, in other words that, for example, it makes him want to do wee-wee or, like each time that one is in the presence of water, that one is, in relation to this water, a communicating vessel and it is not for nothing that, to speak to you of the libido, I used this metaphor of what happens between the subject and his specular image. (1962–1963b, pp. 358–359)

Cause here is specifically something carnal or corporeal, something whose orifice can open and shut. The notion of communicating vessels is, of course, also something quite carnal, something quite different to the idea of communication that Piaget had in mind. The phallic dimension of the tap is also linked by Lacan to the notion of the plumber, as something that can be unscrewed, removed, replaced, etc., that is, it is the –φ or symbolic phallus. Piaget's insistence on supposed finality of language as a means of communication leads him to ignore the dimension of desire. It is only the child who allows the strict determinism, that is, the teleology of the explanation that Piaget gives to the *explainer* to remain somewhat veiled—the child who failed at the level that Piaget calls understanding—to whom is revealed the essence of the function of the tap as *cause*. And the function of the tap as cause is precisely the concept of the tap that escapes Piaget's operationalised understanding of the tap. It is this child who is able to pass this on to the one who in the experiment, perhaps aptly given the phallic dimension of the tap, is named the *reproducer*.

Despite the limitations of Piaget's approach, it nonetheless allows us to see how the child, as subject of the experiment, produces something that is in excess of the experimental approach. The child, far from being the imperfect exponent of language that Piaget purports him to be, is caught up in language, as well as being carnally caught up in the vital flow of water from the tap. The child is able to articulate something of the notion of the tap for him, the fact that it excites him, and even makes him want to pass water, and to pass his experience on to the other child. This aspect of the child is not *officially* part of the picture; it is this child and his transference that were not invited to take part in the experiment. And it is this "personal trait" of the child that disturbs the smooth running of the predetermined notion of what it is for the child to understand. The personal trait bears the mark of the transference. But this *confounding variable* of the experiment, like a sort of silhouette outlined against the light of the official thesis, is able to show us something else. This something else is the drip that leaks from Piaget's tap, something that exceeds the ideal pedagogy of the child as a defective adult that is put forward here.

If the little pigs don't eat him ...

Lacan's allusion to the plumber who might come and fix the leaking tap, or even unscrew and replace it, is a reference to little Hans. Specifically it concerns Hans' fantasies regarding the plumber, including this final one: "The plumber came; and first he took away my behind with a pair of pincers, and then gave me another, and then the same with my widdler" (Freud, 1909b, p. 98). Here Hans invokes a type of intervention, in order to resolve the dilemma of his predicament, an intervention of what we can call, through Lacan, the *name of the father*. It is precisely this intervention—which includes a type of cutting—that allows Hans to take up a position as subject, not entirely subject to the desires and demands of his parents. In order for this to occur, a cut needs to be produced, a cut in the jouissance and knowledge of the Other for Hans, for the child. It is this cut that we have attempted to articulate here, by virtue of which the child is able to position himself through the symptom.

It is in this sense that we can say that one aspect of the symptom is that of an exogamic function, in so far as it allows for the possibility of realising something of his or her desire beyond the family. The cut referred to here is nothing but the incest taboo referred to by Freud, and later, in a societal sense, proposed by Claude Lévi-Strauss. Lévi-Strauss put forward that "The prohibition of incest is thus only the group's assertion that where relationships between the sexes are concerned, *a person cannot do just what he pleases*. The positive aspect of the prohibition is to initiate organization" (1947a, p. 43).

For little Hans, this organisation comes via the organ, in so far as the phallus refers to the phallic organ. But the organ here is also the organ of language and the name of the father that is mediated through language. Thus Lévi-Strauss concludes—and here I translate from the French to preserve the richness of the text that is lost in the published translation—that "[E]xogamy and language have the same fundamental function: the communication with others [*autrui*], and the integration of the group" (1947b, p. 565, translated for this edition).

This extends the notion of "communication" far beyond that utilised by Piaget, in which such communication is the realisation of desire within and then beyond the family. For the symptom, even if it has an exogamic function, derives, as we have seen, from an endogamic origin, that is, the original incestuous situation. Consider, for example, Louis Malle's film *Le Souffle au Coeur* (1971), in which the adolescent boy Laurent accedes to sexual relationships outside the family. But what is foundational in regard to this, as enacted in this film, is that Laurent accomplishes this through his incestuous relationship with his mother. It is precisely the encounter with this incestuous relation that allows him to go beyond it. We referred to Lacan's notion of the *passe* in relation to the child and we could say here that the child might allow a passage from the incestuous relation with the Other to the relations he or she will realise outside the family. It is in being able to take up a position in relation to the Other, for the child to be able to find his own enjoyment or jouissance in relation to the Other, which allows the possibility of being able to put his desire into play beyond the immediacy of the family.

Of course it is not specifically a question of the child going out beyond the family at any moment, but rather the possibility of being able to do this at some later stage. In commenting on Freud's paper "The Dissolution of the Oedipus Complex", Lacan proposes:

> I am not saying that he is already a little male, but that he can also become someone, he already has the deeds in his pocket, the matter in reserve, and when the time comes, if things go well, if the little pigs don't eat him, at the moment of puberty he will have his penis ready to go with its certificate—*Daddy is there, and, at the right time, conferred it upon me.* (1957–1958, p. 193, translated for this edition)

Thus the intervention of the name of the father, invoked here by the term "Daddy", is what is able to cut across the Other's enjoyment of the child, in order to allow the child access to the way in which he is subject to *jouissance* through his own body. And we must add once again that this access to jouissance is not specifically that of the child, it is that of the *subject*, whether a child or not. It is in this sense also that Lacan speaks of little Hans' "cure": "One thing that is certain is that the cure [*guérison*] arrives at the very moment in which castration as such is expressed in the clearest manner, in the form of an articulated history" (1956–1957, p. 228). That is, the critical moment that arrives in Hans' treatment is the one in which he is able to begin to situate himself, both in regard to the flow of language, as well as the flow of his bodily fluids.

PART III

DISCOURSES ON CHILDHOOD

CHAPTER SEVEN

The ages of the child

Freud feared that psychoanalysis would "find its last resting-place in a text-book of psychiatry" (1926e, p. 248), and it is true that psychoanalysis has found a resting place in psychiatry texts. It is not to be found, as Freud suggested, under the heading "Methods of Treatment", but rather as one of a myriad of developmental theories. Take, for instance, the following account from a psychiatry textbook: "Current thinking about the human life cycle has been shaped by a handful of highly influential sources. The dominant work on the subject remains the developmental scheme introduced by Freud in 1915" (Kaplan & Saddock, 1981, pp. 18–19). Throughout history there has been an inexorable tendency to think of the child in developmental terms and this is precisely what is being arguing against here. In this part, in examining a number of discourses by means of which the child has been conceptualised throughout history, we will pursue our question: *what is a child?* In this manner, we will endeavour to elucidate how we have come to conceive of the child today.

In this chapter we will investigate the way in which the child has been conceptualised by considering how he has been spoken of and written about through the ages. A change occurred following the Middle

Ages, at the beginning of the modern era. In his work *Centuries of Childhood*, Philippe Ariès (1960a) proposes that the notions of the child and childhood, with which we are familiar, are an invention of Western culture following the decline of feudal society. Ariès puts forward that the modern idea of the child is closely related to the emergence of the idea of the conjugal family. By being designated as a specific period, childhood comes to acquire its own significance both in family life and in social life beyond.

It is not a question here of the child or the family per se, but rather of the place that they are accorded in our thoughts, in our thinking. Ariès proposed that it is through the evolution of these ideas that the child has been inscribed as subject. In his account, the social rituals record and mark the events that occur from birth to death and then come to inscribe the idea of the child, childhood, and the family, with a symbolic value. Hence we will also trace the history of social legislation, with particular reference to the registering of births as a means by which the child is inscribed as having a separate existence. At the end of the seventeenth century, through the practice of recording baptisms and thus the name of the child, for the first time the child is granted status as subject by being a subject of the Church and subject to the Crown.

The Ages of Man

From ancient times, and throughout the mediaeval era, life was divided into a number of ages. Such a division into the *Ages of Man* constituted a logic that was universally understood in a way that we no longer comprehend today. According to Ariès:

> The "ages", "ages of life", or "ages of man" corresponded in our ancestors' minds to positive concepts, so well known, so often repeated and so commonplace that they passed from the realm of science to that of everyday experience. It is hard for us today to appreciate the importance which the concept of the "ages" had in ancient representations of the world. A man's "age" was a scientific category of the same order as weight or speed for our contemporaries; it formed part of a system of physical description and explanation which went back to the Ionian philosophers of the sixth century BC. (1960a, p. 19)

An early version of this system is significant in psychoanalysis: Oedipus' reply to the riddle of the Sphinx. The riddle was, in Appollodorus' account, "What is it that has one name that is four-footed, two-footed, and three-footed?" Oedipus was the only one to successfully answer this question. His reply was, "Man is the answer: for as an infant he goes upon four feet; in his prime upon two; and in old age he takes a stick as a third foot" (cited in Morford & Lenardon, 2007, p. 409). But this attempt to respond to the Sphinx's enigma of sexuality with the proposition of the three ages of life has proven problematical for psychoanalysis. Since the beginnings of psychoanalysis it has been difficult to speak of the *child* without such a reduction to developmental ages and stages.

We have remarked that in the *Three Essays on the Theory of Sexuality*, Freud writes of "The Phases of Development of the Sexual Organization" (Freud, 1905d, p. 197). In this, on the one hand, "sexual organization" makes a very structural reference. On the other hand, "the phases of development" makes no secret of a developmental trajectory. Again, Freud's genius was to maintain a tension between these two poles, resisting the temptation to resolve structure into a purely developmental theory as subsequently occurred with most psychoanalytic streams.

By mediaeval times, the life of Man had been divided up into distinct Ages. For theological reasons these were numbered as seven, like the seven planets, the seven deadly sins, or the seven liberal arts that Lacan refers to in Seminar XI, *The Four Fundamental Concepts of Psychoanalysis* (1964, p. 88). The account of these ages best known to us, and no doubt the best articulated, is that of Shakespeare in *As You Like it*. Here he evidently plays upon the polysemy of the signifier *stage*, not simply reducing it to a period of development:

> All the world's a stage,
> And all the men and women merely players.
> They have their exits and their entrances,
> And one man in his time plays many parts,
> His acts being seven ages. At first the infant,
> Mewling and puking in the nurse's arms.
> And then the whining schoolboy with his satchel
> And shining morning face, creeping like snail
> Unwillingly to school. And then the lover,
> Sighing like furnace, with a woeful ballad

Made to his mistress' eyebrow. Then a soldier,
Full of strange oaths, and bearded like the pard,
Jealous in honour, sudden, and quick in quarrel,
Seeking the bubble reputation
Even in the cannon's mouth. And then the justice,
In fair round belly with good capon lined,
With eyes severe and beard of formal cut,
Full of wise saws and modern instances;
And so he plays his part. The sixth age shifts
Into the lean and slippered pantaloon,
With spectacles on nose and pouch on side,
His youthful hose, well saved, a world too wide
For his shrunk shank, and his big, manly voice,
Turning again toward childish treble, pipes
And whistles in his sound. Last scene of all,
That ends this strange, eventful history,
Is second childishness and mere oblivion,
Sans teeth, sans eyes, sans taste, sans everything. (Shakespeare,
1600, p. 638, Act 2, Scene 7, lines 139–166)

What is remarkable here is that Shakespeare underlines the fictional character of such a life lived, in which these different developmental stages are mere roles that are played out upon the stage of life. In this rendering, such roles are arbitrary and may be reassigned according to any particular era. However, the repetitive division of life into these apparently clearly defined sections endeavours to give symbolic punctuation to the course of life, but through the device of such imaginary characters on the stage of life. In Ariès' words: "This division of life into periods had the same fixity as the cycle of Nature or the organisation of society. In spite of the constant evocation of old age and death, the ages of life remained good-natured, picturesque sketches, character silhouettes of a rather whimsical kind" (1960a, p. 25).

Shakespeare's account of the oblivion of the endpoint of life, the inexorable loss of death in which Man is "sans everything" is a little less picturesque. If the ages of life now seem antiquated to us, it may be that they have simply been replaced by yet other ages of life with which we are invited to identify. Some modern ages of life are less well articulated as a system, but may be just as influential upon us. As we have mentioned already, Ariès notes that the period that we call adolescence, effectively absent from the ages of life, has come to dominate our culture: "Thus our society has passed from a period which was ignorant of adolescence to a period in which adolescence is the favourite age. We now want to come to it early and linger in it as long as possible" (p. 30).

Ariès describes adolescence, as we know it, as a relatively recent phenomenon, with the prototype being Wagner's *Siegfried*. According to Ariès, the music of *Siegfried* expresses for the very first time a mixture of provisional purity, physical force, spontaneity, and joy of life that was to make the adolescent the hero of the twentieth century. Adolescence would gain its strength and become a generalised phenomenon in all countries that participated in the Great War. Ariès remarks that young people who returned from the Great War opposed the old guard *en masse*, following the debacle into which they had been led by the previous generations. And in the following citation I translate Ariès from the French myself as the verb *"refouler"*, at least in how we might read it from psychoanalysis—*to repress*— has disappeared from the English language version, being substituted by "encroached upon" (p. 30): "From then on, adolescence was extended: it repressed childhood which preceded it and maturity that followed" (1960b, p. 50, translated for this edition). From this translation of Ariès' text, we can propose that childhood is never lost, but rather, repressed.

Elsewhere I have considered the arbitrary notion of the term *adolescent* and its associated terms teen, teenage, teenager, teeny-bopper, etc. It is notable that these latter terms take up the signifier—*teen* in an age range that is defined by the vagaries of the names of a set of numbers in the English language. We may also note the means by which the cultural attributes of this group, whether by virtue of reference points in particular modes of appearance and dress, vocabulary and expressions, and taste for certain types of music, etc., go well beyond the age range demarcated by the term *teen* (Plastow, 2000a, p. 78). Thus children can now be *pre-adolescents* and adults of any age can identify with adolescent culture. And as Verhaeghe remarks: "Thirty-year-old teenagers and forty-year-old adolescents are by no means exceptional these days" (2011, p. 85).

The birth of the child and family

Our contemporary understanding of what constitutes a child, and the attribution of childhood as a phase of life distinct from all others, according to Ariès' thesis, is a relatively recent event in the evolution of Western culture. This development, for Ariès, was born out of the decline of mediaeval culture that continued to promote the ages of man as a scientific concept. In French, the title of his book translates literally as *The Child and Family Life under the Ancien Régime* (1960b), the latter referring to the political regime that was in force in France from the fifteenth century until the time of the Enlightenment. In the chapters that follow we will have occasion to take up the ideas of some Enlightenment thinkers regarding the emergence of the modern subject.

Ariès puts forward the following: "Medieval art until about the twelfth century did not know childhood or did not attempt to portray it. It is hard to believe that this neglect was due to incompetence or incapacity; it seems more probable that there was no place for childhood in the medieval world" (1960a, p. 33). He supports this argument by reference to modes of representation from the Middle Ages in which children are depicted in the exact same way as adults, albeit on a smaller scale. A depiction of the Gospel, in which Jesus speaks to young children, shows the Messiah surrounded by eight veritable men with none of the traits of children, except for their size. Ariès proposes that the refusal to accept the morphology of the child in art can be found in most archaic civilisations, with the exception of that of the ancient Greeks in which the realistic and even idealised representation of children, in their roundness and grace, is specific to Greek art. For mediaeval man, it would seem, childhood was a time of transition that quickly passed and was soon forgotten.

So, if we are to take up Ariès' thesis, how did we come from the Middle Ages in which there was no room for the representation of the child, to our modern conception of the child and the privileged place that he is accorded in our societies and in our photo albums, including in their electronic variety?

Ariès notes that in the thirteenth century, several types of children appeared in iconography, presaging the emergence of the modern representation of the child. Firstly, angels were represented with the appearance of very young men or adolescents. Such angels would become frequent in the fourteenth century, for instance in the early Renaissance paintings of Fra Angelico and Ghirlandajo. The second type of representation of the child and the model for the depiction of all small children in the history of art in the modern era is that of the child Jesus, the representation of the mystery of his conception and the culture of the Virgin Mary. The touching depiction of early childhood is tied, according to Ariès, to the mother's tenderness. A third type of child, appearing in the Gothic era, was that of the naked child, a type of depiction almost never made of the child Jesus. Curiously, the naked child, in the first instance, is a depiction of the soul made through the allegory of death. Thus the defunct exhales the soul through the mouth in many representations of the moment of death in mediaeval art. This soul is generally represented as a small naked child of an asexual appearance. And elsewhere the angel of the Annunciation delivers to the Virgin Mary a naked child, the soul of Jesus, which also penetrates her body through her mouth. Ariès refers to this moment as "the entry of the soul into the world" (1960a, p. 36).

This entry and exit of the soul of Man through the breath is of great interest in regard to the emergence of the modern subject. One of the words that is used to attempt to circumscribe the notion of the subject is still the ancient Greek word ψυχή, or *psyche*, which means, amongst other things, life, breath, and soul. The soul, through the German equivalent *Seele*, was also the means through which Freud spoke of what we are referring to here as the subject. This was of course sadly and mechanistically translated in the *Standard Edition* as the *psychic apparatus*. It is also curious that the soul of Man is represented as a child. It raises the question of whether we might still consider that the soul of man *is* a child, perhaps in the sense that the *cause* of one's own troubled soul, in the common developmental and aetiological notion, is to be found in one's childhood, that is, in one's early history as a child.

Gradually, over the centuries, from a religious iconography of the infant Jesus who was now depicted with the gracious, tender, and naive appearance of early childhood, a new lay iconography would emerge, one in which the child was to be depicted through a type of sentimental realism. Through this evolution, Ariès discerns two principal themes. The first is that in daily life, in previous eras, children were mixed with adults, rather than the contemporary tendency to separate the world of children—by virtue of kindergartens, play groups, schools, and so on—from the world of adults. Secondly what is presaged from the depiction of the child in a rather picturesque manner, is what he refers to as the modern sentiment of childhood.

Such a sentiment, Ariès argues, was not possible at a time when the survival of young children was much more doubtful. He refers to an account from the seventeenth century of a neighbour standing at the bedside of a woman who has just given birth, the mother of five "little brats". The neighbour calms the woman's fears in the following way: "Before they are old enough to bother you, you will have lost half of them, or perhaps all of them" (1960a, p. 38). Ariès notes that this strikes our contemporary sensibilities as a rather strange consolation. He puts forward that people could not allow themselves to become too attached to something that was regarded as a probable loss. Even in the eighteenth century, specifically in *Émile*, Jean-Jacques Rousseau was able to write, "Of all the children who are born, only a half, at most, come to adolescence; and it is probable that your pupil will not live to be a man" (1762a, p. 44).

We might also be shocked today to read Montaigne's observation, "I have lost two or three children in their infancy, not without regret, but without great sorrow" (Ariès, 1960a, p. 39). The apparent insensitivity of Roman or Chinese societies who practised the exposure of children is offensive to us. We forget that such exposure and infanticide were commonplace in Western nations throughout the Middle Ages. Ariès notes that infanticide was tolerated until the end of the seventeenth century. He proposes that, "A child's life at that time was considered with the same ambiguity as that of a foetus today, with the difference that infanticide was buried in silence whilst abortion is demanded out aloud" (1960b, p. 15).

The Church endeavoured to stamp out these age-old practices by vigorous condemnation, and states attempted to control them by coercive measures. It was for this reason that in the seventeenth century the first institutions for abandoned children were set up, such as the Foundlings' Hospital (*Hôpital des Enfants Trouvés*) that was established by St. Vincent de Paul in 1638 (Badinter, 1980a, p. 19). Exposure and infanticide still occasionally occur, particularly in countries where termination of pregnancy is illegal. In many European countries there are so-called *baby-boxes* in which it is possible for mothers to anonymously leave unwanted babies where there are facilities to ensure they are safe. This practice began as an effort to combat cases of infanticide or abandonment of unwanted infants. We could say that termination of pregnancy, as it is practised today, is also the anticipated, modern, and surgical mode of infanticide and exposure.

Another modern form of infanticide is that of child abuse, which in many cases leads to death. It is not unusual for a child to be killed by direct blows from its parents or step-parents. Such occurrences are often reported in the media, but each is perceived as an exceptional event. A recent newspaper article in France reporting upon child death, commented upon the frequency of the phenomenon, and the different means by which infanticide might be recognised. This article reported the findings of a study in which, over a period of five years, researchers had investigated child deaths of three French regions, representing a third of all births in France in that period. In only fifty per cent of cases of sudden infant death syndrome, a syndrome in which the diagnosis requires the exclusion of all other causes by autopsy, had an autopsy in fact been performed. In extrapolating the results of the investigation, a figure of "400 to 800 homicides of minors each year" (Dupont, 2013, p. 11), that is, approximately two children per day in France, died as a result of parental violence. There is no reason to believe that this is different in other countries.

Rather than understand exposure and infanticide as horrors to be relegated to a forgotten past, we can propose that our society is, in part, based upon these practices. We might forget, for instance, that the practice of exposure and infanticide is an integral part of the myth of Oedipus, and that of Moses, both foundational stories that underwrite our culture. Once again, exposure and infanticide in early childhood, like childhood itself, have not been eliminated, but rather, they have been repressed.

The new sentiment of childhood was coincidental with the changed demography that resulted from an increase in the survival of young infants and children, and with a gradual elevation of the status of women in society. It became manifested, not just in the depiction of children and families, but also in the expanded vocabulary of words that refer to young children, as well as the recording of children's jargon and idiosyncrasies of language. Hence "the discovery of childhood" (Ariès, 1960a, p. 33) in the sense that we understand it today, is an emergence of the modern representation of the child, his body, his manners, and his babbling. This new sentiment for the child was also a new sentiment between members of the family, most particularly of that between the mother and the child. Furthermore, as we will consider in the next chapter, it also coincided with a renewed interest in the education of children and specific pedagogical approaches that were directed at children of different ages. This led to a stratification and separation of children of specific ages from other children and indeed from adults.

Our modern categories

Regardless of the particular details, perhaps the most pertinent aspect of Ariès' work is the observation that the construction of the notions of the *child*, the *mother*, the *father*, and the *family* are dependent upon the thinking, the prejudices, and the contingencies of any particular era, including our own. This, we can say, is also the thesis of Élisabeth Badinter's book, first published in 1980, entitled *Mother Love: Myth and Reality: Motherhood in Modern History*. In this work Badinter disputes the existence of a so-called maternal instinct and demonstrates how the notion of maternal love, as we know it, is a construction of the past two centuries. This was not a new thesis, as Margarethe Hilferding, the first female member of the Vienna Psychoanalytic Society, had already proposed in 1911 that innate maternal love did not exist. That thesis was put forward in a presentation to the Vienna Society, entitled "On the basis of mother love" (Nunberg & Federn, 1974, pp. 112–125).

Like Ariès, Badinter dates the development of maternal love—in France at least—to the decline of the *Ancien Régime*, that is, the end of the eighteenth century. She opens her work in the following way:

> In 1780, Lieutenant Lenoir of the Paris police noted, not without some bitterness, that only 1,000 of the 21,000 babies born each year in Paris were being breast-fed by their mothers. Another thousand newborns, the children of privileged families, were being breast-fed by live-in wet nurses, while the rest were taken from their mothers and sent to wet nurses outside Paris. (1980a, p. xix)

Even if the long-term effects of these infants being brought up outside the home of their mothers and families are unclear, there are some indications of very immediate effects upon the infant. Badinter, for instance, recounts the story of one particular nonchalant wet-nurse, ironically called Marie Bienvenue (*Mary Welcome* in English!), who had thirty-one infants die in her care within the space of fourteen months (1980b, p. 12).

Such a removal of young infants *en masse* is unthinkable in today's era in which in many legislations it is particularly difficult to even remove a child who is at immediate risk from its mother. Badinter's conclusion is that the belief in the maternal instinct is a myth. Rather than any universal and necessary maternal conduct in a mother, she found, according to her study, an extreme variability of maternal sentiments, according to the culture and the era, as well as to the ambitions or frustrations in a particular mother. Thus maternal love is effectively contingent and cannot be taken for granted. Maternal love is, according to her title in French, *"en plus"* (1980b), something extra, evoking for us the surplus jouissance, the *plus de jouir* of Lacan.

Badinter's argument evokes the sterile debate that is always raised in such matters concerning the—false—opposition between nature and nurture, but more fundamentally the opposition that our culture has inherited from the Aristotelian schema between essence and appearance, potentiality and act, matter and form (Rastier, 2006). Such arguments these days are organised around a biological assumption, such as this *maternal instinct*, or other attributions like *genetics* or *brain chemistry*. These types of culturally prevalent ideas, such as the notion of the maternal instinct, or indeed the received wisdom regarding the child and the family, are taken as a sort of eternal truth. And, perhaps even more curiously, such ideas are extended by the preconceived idea, derived in part by the Enlightenment thinker Jean-Jacques Rousseau, that *nature is good*. Such goodness becomes a type of moralistic value that usurps the place of reasoned argument. Hence, paradoxically, the ideas of the Enlightenment are used to argue against the very achievements of the Enlightenment by closing down our ability to think and reason about such issues.

Similarly, Paul Verhaeghe notes that this opposition between potentiality and act is responsible for the Western pattern of thought since the time of Plato. In this mode of thinking, we are always in search of eternal ideas, constants that are independent of time, place, and person. He states that, "It is actually an almost automatic reflex to opt for the choice … of an unchanging human nature, the 'nothing new under the sun' theory" (1998, pp. 107–108). Thus the pre-Socratic idea of Heraclitus: "The sun is new each day" (Robinson, 1987, p. 13), belongs to some forgotten past. Nonetheless, we can still hear echoes of this mode of thought today, but from the poet rather than the philosopher or scientist. Here we cite a stanza from the poem "Là-bas, je ne sais où …" by Álvaro de Campos, one of Fernando Pessoa's semi-heteronyms:

> To leave!
> I will never return,
> I will never return because one never returns.

> The place to which one returns is always another,
> The *station* [*gare*] to which one returns is another.
> It is no longer the same people, nor the same light, nor the same
> philosophy. (Pessoa, n. d., p. 1041)

The preoccupation with the idea of sameness seems to attempt to create an identifiable and predictable world in which the fear of the unknown, or Otherness, is reduced to a minimum. For Plato, there are two basic categories: *tauton* (sameness) and *heteron* (difference), which cannot be reduced to each other. Nonetheless, Plato proposed that man always attempts to reduce *heteron* to *tauton*, difference to sameness. We draw from our investigations the conclusion that the modern conception of the *child* and *childhood* is a fact of discourse, and, as such, subject to ongoing change. The salient discourses are manifested primarily in speech and in popular culture. Nonetheless they are also underwritten by privileged texts such as the writings of Plato and Aristotle, sacred texts, most prominently the Bible, secular texts such as laws, and in literature—as demonstrated by Badinter (1980a, pp. 8–22).

We are not surprised then to find that both Ariès' and Badinter's works were subject to critiques that were vigorous and at times reactionary and retrogressive, as well as moralising. Thus in a book written *against* the work of Ariès, Riché and Alexandre-Bidon attempt to turn his theses to ridicule:

> Thus for centuries, men and women, teachers, whether lay, clerics or monks, were purported to have cared for children without speaking about them, to have considered them to be adults in miniature, and to have been happy to get them from childhood to adolescence by the means of methods that are called "mediaeval" to this day with disdain. (1994, p. 8, translated for this edition)

Similarly, Alexandre-Bidon and Lett write, "Let us briefly summarize the theses of the author [Ariès]: the child did not exist in the minds of the men and women of the Middle Ages" (1997, p. 9, translated for this edition). These authors seem to take umbrage at the theses of both Ariès and Badinter as they interpret these works as making a negative judgement on the people of the Middle Ages: "Mediaeval society, like ours currently, failed in a certain number of domains regarding the first ages of life" (p. 11), thus invoking the morality of a judgement. Furthermore they endeavour to discredit Badinter because she is a philosopher— rather than an historian, like them! They reject the *heteron* in favour of a *tauton*. They conclude their work, however, by reassuring themselves with the gross generalisation that "Mediaeval society as a whole felt concerned about the lives of children" (p. 250).

Both Badinter and Ariès, following the publication of their works, felt obliged to respond to some of the critiques that were levelled at them, each writing prefaces to new editions of their books. If we consider that the *child* and *childhood* are facts of discourse, then we might consider that a philosopher is indeed able to contribute to dispelling the attribution of what is considered to be an *instinct*. In other words, as Badinter puts forward, there is a need to question the presuppositions of biology, as well as those of history. She proposes that, "[L]ike the psychoanalysts, I think that there is no love without some desire." She continues, in response to her critics, in the re-edited French version of her book in 1981:

> Contrary to the animal kingdom which is immersed in nature and subject to determinism, humans—here woman, an historical being—are the only living creatures endowed with the faculty of being able to symbolise, which elevates them outside the strictly animal domain. This desiring being is always particular and different to all others. May biologists forgive me my audacity, but I am one of those who think that the woman's unconscious prevails over her hormonal processes. (1980b, p. 15, translated for this edition)

It is this dimension of desire, the dimension of the singular desire into which the child is born, that is absent from the normalisation and homogenisation implied in the assertion that "Mediaeval society as a whole felt concerned about the lives of children".

The silent history of the child

In the preface to the second French edition of his 1960 book, published in 1973, but absent in the earlier English translation, Ariès responds to the various critiques and manners in which his work was received since its first publication, particularly from the perspective of the psychologists:

> One can attempt a history of behaviour, in other words a psychological history, without oneself being a psychologist or a psychoanalyst ... The historian and the psychologist meet, but not always at the level of the methods which can be different, but at the level of the subject. (1960b, p. 10)

Here Ariès seems to intend *subject* in the sense of the subject matter of the study, but we can propose that this subject matter is precisely the subject in the sense of the *child as subject*. Thus we can read this text as an account of the locating, or *discovery* as Ariès puts it, of the subject in the child. We could even propose that this is the birth of the child as subject, at least as a Cartesian subject or *psyche* as we have put forward, which was a necessary precursor to the possibility of a psychoanalytic subject.

One of the criticisms of Ariès' theses came from the psychologist Besançon, who accused Ariès of "neglect of the curiosities of modern psychology". Here Ariès presents Besançon's critique:

> "The child is not just clothing, toys, school or even the sentiment of childhood [in other words the historical modalities that are able to be grasped empirically], it is also a person, a development, a history which psychologists attempt to reconstitute," in other words "a comparative term". (p. 10, Ariès' brackets)

For Ariès this comparative approach is one which functions poorly for the study of traditional societies, as it "adds nothing to the understanding of our world of today, because there are no new facts, not even about the previous era, because there is an anachronism, and the anachronism falsifies the comparison" (p. 11). He puts forward that in the study of a past era we must first be able to grasp the differences from our own era, before we have any chance of grasping the similarities.

Nonetheless, according to Ariès, there is a disparity between the idea of the family that has evolved over time, and what is actually recorded of this history of the family. In this gap lies what he refers to as the "silent history" of the child (1960a, p. 10, translated for this edition). He asks: "Is not this disparity between living ideas and legal structures one of the characteristics of our civilization?" (p. 10). Such an account of disparities, of difference, is one that is in marked contrast to the similarities that are privileged by the psychologists and sociologists who have studied the history of the child and the family. It is this that marks the originality of Ariès' study and its value to opening up the question of the place of the child.

Ariès poses the question, not just of how the concept of the child has changed since the Middle Ages, but also how the notion of the *family* has evolved. In the introduction to the English version of his book he underlines that:

> … it is not so much the family as a reality that is our subject here as the family as an idea … . The point is that the ideas entertained about these relations may be *dissimilar* at moments separated by lengthy periods of time. It is the history of the idea of the family which concerns us here, not the description of manners or the nature of law. (pp. 9–10, my italics)

Ariès refers to the belief, or the "idea" that the family constituted the ancient basis of our society, but that, from the eighteenth century onwards, it was thought to have been weakened by the advent of liberal individualism. Thus the nineteenth and twentieth centuries were, according to this belief, supposed to have been a time of decay of the family. Ariès, however, comes to the seemingly paradoxical conclusion that despite the increase in divorce rates and apparent decline in maternal and paternal authority, or even because of it, the institution of the family has never occupied so great a place in the human condition. We might recognise the place and status that the family currently occupies through the contemporary demands of homosexual couples to marry and have a family. Once again we find here a disparity between living ideas and legal and social structures.

The very idea, or ideal, of the modern family and society is the modality of a repression, a repression that is the foundation stone of the contemporary family. And it is in the "silent history" that we can locate the means by which the discourses of the child, the lost discourses of the child, have been repressed.

This is how Ariès refers to the *idea of the family*: a structure, which, by virtue of its function, becomes a social model for the upbringing of children. This conjugal family is hence also the place of the historical invention of childhood as a concept. The difference between the child in a feudal community, and the conjugal family, is one that is marked by the boundaries of private and shameful experiences—the conjugal family being a closed off private space—of sexuality, and segregations between different ages and stages of life. The experiences between children and adults in the Middle Ages, according to Ariès, consisted of a shared open space, where children interacted at the same level as adults and where the duration of childhood was only a minimal period of dependency and care. In the conjugal family, over time, the space for the child was inscribed by the distinction between reason and affect and the child was made exempt from various aspects of life because he or she was seen as a *creature of nature*, and thus of affect, not reason. The child became the non-civilised creature of nature without any control over feelings or bodily drives. In the next chapter we will examine the manner in which this in turn instituted him as an object of interest and knowledge in regard how to regulate such a *nature*.

Ariès approaches his study of the child through an examination, in the first instance, of differences rather than of similarities, a facet that brings his work closer to that of psychoanalysis. This difference is also the difference between the account of the parent and the account of the child, or to put it another way, the silence by which the parent, an Other, is no longer able speak for the child, to answer for the child. It is through this failure of language that the child is able to be born as subject, as subject of language, as subject of the unconscious. In this manner, the child as subject, like the modern subject, is born through repression. From psychoanalysis we can say that it is the law of the prohibition of incest that articulates a difference between the positions of the mother and the child; the prohibition of incest regulates jouissance as it stipulates that *at least one jouissance is forbidden*. But we have proposed that the incest taboo is repressed: incest is inscribed as something which is unthinkable. Later we will also have occasion to examine Foucault's hypothesis that the birth of the modern subject was the result of a repression from which the discourse of the subject as a sexual being was able to be written.

The baptism of the child

We have already noted the indifference towards young infants in the Middle Ages that shocks our contemporary sensibilities, an indifference that was due, at least in part, to the demography of the times in which babies were more likely to die than survive. Ariès notes that for a very long time people in the Basque country retained the custom of burying children who had died without baptism in their house or garden, much as we would today bury a family pet. Such children, we can surmise, were not yet true subjects. Certainly, in not being baptised, they were not yet subjects of the Church, nor of God.

Ariès notes that, at the end of the Middle Ages, "[T]he new taste for the portrait indicated that children were emerging from the anonymity in which their slender chance of survival had maintained them" (1960a, p. 40). This tendency indicates that the young infant was beginning to no longer be considered as an inevitable loss or a necessary wastage. Ariès notes that this new tendency did not eliminate the opposite attitude to which we have referred—that of Montaigne or the neighbour at the mother's bedside.

In Europe throughout the Middle Ages, society was almost unanimously Christian and every man and woman had to be baptised. Nonetheless, parents did not seem to be in a hurry to have their children baptised and neglected to do so in many cases. Ariès suggests that baptisms were held on certain fixed dates, such as twice a year on the eves of Easter and Whit Sunday. At that time there were no baptismal certificates or registers. Thus there was no immediate external constraint to have children baptised. Children were taken when the parents chose, and delays of several years were very common. At the time, baptisms were conducted in large vats in which the children, who were certainly no longer newborns, were immersed. According to Ariès, the parents would not be overly surprised or fussed if the child, while waiting to be baptised in these early tenuous years, happened to die.

Collective baptisms were abandoned as they imposed a delay in the administration of the sacrament. Similarly, the practice of immersion slowly ceased in favour of the modern practice of the symbolic sprinkling with holy water. Later, from the sixteenth century onwards, the establishment of church registers allowed baptisms to be controlled by the authorities of the local dioceses. Over time, there was more and more pressure from the Church for children to be baptised as soon as possible after birth. For this reason the ecclesiastical authorities permitted the practice of lay baptisms for sick or stillborn infants, by midwives for instance. In this way, for the first time, the child was recognised as a subject that had an ongoing existence, even when he was not expected to survive until adulthood. As Ariès puts forward, "Christianity ... respected the immortal soul in every child that had been baptized" (p. 39).

Ariès recounts that in the context of an increased demand for baptism as soon as possible after birth, there emerged a new series of miracles based around the notion of the resurrection of children who died without baptism. According to Jean-Pierre Lebrun, this possibility of the miracle of the child's resurrection in order to be baptised, also came about through popular resistance, towards the end of the Middle Ages, to the idea that a child who had died without baptism was excluded from heaven. This reform was also supported by eminent ecclesiastical personalities (Lebrun, 2007, p. 370). Such resurrections lasted just long enough for the child to receive the sacrament:

> Hence, under the pressure of the reformatory tendencies of the Church, all of this happened as though the child's soul was beginning to be discovered even before its body. As soon as the will of these men of letters was accepted, it was turned into folklore. (Ariès, 1960b, p. 18)

Once again, the child found a place as subject through the recognition of the existence of his soul.

From the ninth century onwards, children who had died without baptism were considered to be condemned to purgatory, a place that was invented specifically for this reason. From there, limbo was construed as a place to where such children would go, so that they would suffer only from not seeing God. Limbo is derived from the Latin *limbus* meaning border, *limbo* designating the edge of hell from which the children were saved (Lebrun, 2007, p. 370). The children of limbo are also on the border of being subjects, without quite being full subjects in the eyes of the Church.

We can consider the designation of limbo to also pertain, not just to being stranded at a certain age and stage, but rather to a certain structure in which one is not fully a subject. Such is the sense of Michel Tournier's novel *Friday* (1967a), whose original title in French is *Vendredi ou les Limbes du Pacifique* (*Friday or the Limbo of the Pacific*) (1967b), *Pacific* here referring to the Pacific Ocean in which Tournier's Robinson Crusoe is stranded. His existence there, however, is anything but pacific. This Crusoe is not fully a subject in so far as, through his isolation from others—and thereby from Otherness—he does not participate in the symbolic order. In Deleuze's analysis of this novel, it is precisely this exclusion from Otherness, from a third position outside the subject and the Other—outside the child and the mother we could say—from which he suffers. Deleuze cites the following moment from Tournier's novel as crucial:

> The thesis—the Robinson hypothesis—has a great advantage: the disappearance of the structure-Other is presented as the result of circumstances on the desert isle. To be sure, the structure continues to survive and function long after Robinson on the island encounters any actual terms or characters to actualize it. But there comes the moment when this is over: "Those lights have vanished from my consciousness. For a long time, fed by my fantasy, they continued to reach me. Now it is over, and the darkness has closed in." (1969, p. 348)

Tournier's Robinson Crusoe is held in limbo by virtue of not being able to sustain the position of Otherness through the lights of language. This structure underlines the place of limbo in which the child is stranded, unable to be fully recognised as a subject through baptism. Later, civil registration was to take the place that baptism had assumed during the Middle Ages, conferring the status of being subject to the Crown and the state upon the child.

But it was first through the process of baptism that the child was given a name, a name that placed him within a certain order and tradition, a name that always conformed to the religious custom, a name that was thus sanctified and sanctioned by the Church. In this tradition the name must conform to a certain code that is governed by law. Until quite recently in many Catholic countries it was not legally possible to give a child a name that was outside the code of religious names, mostly the names of saints. To have the name of a saint was to be part of an officially sanctioned cultural and linguistic code. This was the means of giving the child recognition as subject in the eyes of God, and thus the means of recognition that the child possessed a soul. Secondarily, the child became a citizen and thus subject of the state.

It is in being accorded a name that the child was brought into discourse and granted the status of subject. But this was also the means of giving the child recognition as subject of the Church or the state, that is, of the *Other*. By these means, the child was granted the status of subject, a subject of language and culture beyond the aegis of the parents. Henceforth this subject is not just a plaything or a possession of the parents, with the full rights of enjoyment that this might imply, and did imply, for instance, under Roman law. That is, it is through this recognition by the Other that the parents are effectively castrated, shown to be lacking. They are no longer able to be *all* for the child.

Infancy or in-fantasy?

If one conclusion can be drawn regarding the status of the child throughout history, it is that what we refer to as the *child* or *childhood* is a moveable feast. Our concept of what a child is, and the place that he or she occupies in regard to the *mother*, the *father*, and the *family*, as well as in society at large, is subject to ongoing change. The concept of the ages of man, and the evolution of the means by which we attempt to divide life up into categories, are presented to us as self-evident truths. Such divisions are imposed by the predominant notions of the era and the culture in which we live, without us even being aware of it. As Pujó writes: "The controversy of the historians puts into play the fact that the scope of certain words such as *child, adolescent, adult*, whose meaning is imposed on us by the evidence of the obvious, depends on their social, political, economical and ideological context" (1996, p. 57).

It is not pre-established notions of ages and stages that determine what we refer to as a *child* and *childhood*. We can say, moreover, that what we refer to as the *child* is by no means a natural concept, but rather, as we have seen, a fact of discourse, and subject to the changes undergone by all discourses. Nonetheless, discourses concerning the child are not lost, only forgotten and repressed. This is an aspect of what Ariès calls the "silent history" of the child in his account of the emergence of the notion of the child since the Middle Ages. In our endeavour to address our question, *what is a child?*, we firstly need to elucidate what has fallen silent.

If what is determinative for any notion of the child is discourse, we also need to indicate what it is that underwrites and mediates discourse. Discourse is mediated through language, through the structure of language, but also by the very limits of language, that is, what is not able to be articulated in language. And these limits of language, as Freud first indicated, are death and sexuality.

One of the discourses that has been repressed regarding the child is that concerning the question of exposure and infanticide, in other words, the question of the infant's death. The elevated death rate in infants in the Middle Ages could be included in this notion of infanticide. But infantile mortality remains high in many countries in contemporary times, including in sub-groups of our own countries such as indigenous populations. Thus there is a certain double standard regarding the intolerance towards infant deaths—we are able to ignore them in other populations. This is yet another mode of the repression of infantile death. The horror in contemporary times concerning the practices that we have included in our broad definition of infanticide indicates the degree to which we have repressed such notions. And yet, as we have elaborated here, exposure and infanticide are alive and well, albeit in covert forms. We then need to ask: what is it in particular, beyond our contemporary prejudices, that is invoked in the horror of infanticide?

In speaking once about these things, I made a slip of the tongue and said "in-fantasy", rather than "infanticide", condensing infanticide with the notion of infancy itself. As Lacan notes, the etymology of infant is the Latin *infans*, one who is without speech. And if one is without speech, then one is by necessity spoken for. So where then does infancy begin and infanticide end? If we take this slip seriously, we can propose that the child has an existence as subject only in so far as he is caught up in the fantasy, or to use Lacan's term, the fantasm, the fantasm of the Other. So far we have articulated the means by which the child is accorded a place in the Other of language through baptism and civil registration: the recognition that there is a soul; there is a subject residing in the child. But this recognition of the subject also has to be particularised by the mother and father of the child who have desired the child—or not—and given him life. It is the mother and father who initially speak for the child, even in order to give him a name.

In other words, the child can exist before he is born since he has already been given a name and attributed various ideals and aspirations, and occupies a particular place in the fantasm of each parent, in the speech of the mother and the father. The child in this manner can exist long before he is conceived and well before he is born. On the other hand, in the absence of being a child *in-fantasy*, the child might never have a true existence, despite the biological fact of his being. That is, the repressed notion of infanticide is precisely the reverse side, the repressed side, of the coin of the existence of the child by and through desire.

We are used to consider, in the common and idealised notion of a child, that he is *innocent*. And yet we could assert that the only innocents—as in the Massacre of the Innocents ordered by Herod that is recounted in the Gospel according to Matthew (2:16)—are those subject to infanticide, that is, those who, in our sense, are not desired. Once an infant is an infant *in-fantasy*, in the fantasm of the parents, he or she is stained by this original sin of the parents. This child is one who then must ultimately incur his own fantasy, desire, and of course symptom.

It is this *in-fantasy*, or the desire of the parents, that we can read in the French title of Badinter's book, *L'Amour en Plus*, love as well, or love in addition. In other words, love and desire must be an added ingredient, in addition to any biological and developmental definition of the child. And this is not just love *in general*, not the common notion that a child should come from a loving household, but rather a particularised love and desire of one or both of the child's parents. We recall that Badinter noted that this love is always singular: "This desiring being is always particular and different to all others" (1980b, p. 15). The enjoyment is always singular and cannot be collectivised into another common notion, that of the *parents*: the mother and the father glued together as a *holophrase*.

It is by virtue of this *en plus* that the child becomes infected with a piece of the enjoyment of either, or both, the mother and the father. This enjoyment is the jouissance of the primal scene that produced the child in the first place and to which he owes his existence. Later, the jouissance of the Other becomes the mother's or father's enjoyment of the child. It is this quotient of the Other's enjoyment that comes to stain the ideal of purity and naivety of the child. It is this stain that has also been called original sin, that is, the fall from Paradise. The child begins to have an existence when he is given the breath of life, the *psyche* which is breathed into him, by virtue of being a child *in-fantasy*. It is this particularised desire through which the child exists as a singular being.

CHAPTER EIGHT

The upbringing of the child: between nature and culture

In the prevailing notions of how we should raise and educate children in contemporary society, there are unspoken—and unthought—conceptions regarding the child and childhood. In order to examine these notions we must overcome the usual prejudice of assuming that the prevailing contemporary views, or our own, are the correct ones. We will endeavour to uncover some of these conceptions and their origins which we can, in part, date to the time of the Enlightenment. We will focus our discussions on the writings of Jean-Jacques Rousseau, specifically his 1762 book *Émile, or Treatise on Education* in order to evaluate its influence and effects today.

The end of the Middle Ages and the beginning of the Enlightenment marked the end of an age of innocence for children, given that prior to that time they were not fully recognised as subjects. In other words, the emergence of the child as subject is a moment of fall from Paradise, the moment in which the child becomes stained by what we have referred to as original sin. This original sin of the enjoyment, or jouissance, of the mother and father, leaves its mark upon the child and introduces the child into a world of fantasy and desire.

If the Enlightenment was a time of a fall from Paradise, however, it was also an historical moment in the creation of a new ideal of the child and of childhood, precisely the ideal of childhood as a paradise lost, to which we are urged to return. At this time, there was established a new type of mysticism—or rather, mythology—of the child as being close to nature, an idealised notion of nature unfettered by the trappings of civilisation and culture. Such an ideal of childhood would then be a paradise regained—or refound, to use Freud's word—but of course only refound in the retrospective nostalgia of the adult. In Rousseau's concept of childhood there is a return of a new type of paradise and consequently a return of the repressed, albeit in a different form. Rousseau specifically argued against the notion of original sin, stating, "There is no original perversity in the human heart" (1762b, p. 92).

In this way Rousseau introduces what can be called a sentiment of childhood, a sentiment that designates the child as subject, but at the same time casts a veil over the child with this very same sentimentality. And if Émile is no longer read so frequently by some, or is forgotten by others, its effect upon contemporary thought still prevails. This was already true in the century following the publication of Émile. De Lajonquière comments that, "The naturalists of the beginning of the nineteenth century were indebted to Émile's preceptor, but without knowing it" (2013, p. 121).

Similarly, in the many pedagogical doctrines that arise anew and influence the ways that children are raised by their mothers and fathers and educated by their schools, Rousseau's theses continue to remain influential, even if repressed and forgotten.

Rousseau's Émile

Émile, written in 1762, was considered very radical in its time, and still retains much of its rhetorical power. It is considered to be one of the greatest works of all time regarding education and upbringing. It has been extremely influential and has inspired many generations of pedagogues and educators. In fact it has been described as "one of the key works of our civilisation" (Burgelin, 1969, p. LXXXIX, translated for this edition). But like many of Rousseau's works it goes far beyond its nominal topic to address the questions of the nature of man, the family, society, and the state. As Harris notes, "There have been many reformers, but none more radical than Rousseau; for he advocates the overthrow of civilization and the return to a state of nature" (1892, p. viii). Rousseau's work *The Social Contract*, published in the same year (1762d), was considered to be one of the precipitants, together with the social upheavals of the time, that led to the French Revolution in which the old social order, the *Ancien Régime*, was upturned. Rousseau's writings were also, in a social sense, the beginning of modernity. Rousseau paid dearly for the radical nature of his propositions. He was persecuted following the publication of *Émile* and his books were banned both in his native Geneva and in France, where he was condemned by the archbishop of Paris. He was forced to flee, first to the Swiss canton of Neuchâtel and then to England, prior to returning to the continent— to live in France under an assumed name.

Another marker of *Émile*'s modernity is its turning away from the bookish approach of the Middle Ages and the regurgitation of established truths regarding upbringing and education, in order to nominally direct its attention to the child itself, rather than to the prevailing preconceived ideas regarding the child. This new approach is articulated in the author's preface to *Émile* in which he states from the outset, "We do not know childhood" (1962b, p. xlii). It is from this starting point of the abandonment of any preconceived knowledge, that Rousseau is able to set out to discover the child. He goes on to articulate the state of play inherited from the Middle Ages by speaking of the traditional wisdom: "The wisest men concentrate on what it is important for men to know without considering what children are in a condition to learn. They are always seeking the man in the child without thinking of what he is before being a man" (1762b, pp. 33–34).

What Rousseau is articulating here is the fact of repression in this forgotten past of childhood. His attempt to remedy this takes the form of a return to nature—a notion we must call into question here—based upon the notion that the child's nature was distorted and perverted by the type of upbringing, education, and socialisation he had received. Rousseau parted ways from some of his Enlightenment colleagues, notionally because of the insistence that he placed on the sensations, rather than thought and reason which were the stuff of the Enlightenment. Others rejected his writings because of his opposition to the civilisation and society which other Enlightenment thinkers sought to regenerate. Voltaire had the following satirical comment for Rousseau regarding his essay on the origin of inequality among men:

> I have received your new book against the human race, and I thank you for it. No one could paint in stronger colors the horrors of human society from which our ignorance and weakness promise themselves so many delights. Never has any one employed so much genius to make us into beasts. When one reads your book he is seized at once with a desire to go down on all-fours. (cited by Harris, 1892, p. viii)

The emphasis that Rousseau gives to sensation over reason is true in *Émile* in so far as the content of his writing is concerned. He is critical of the use of reason and language in the education of children. In response to his own rhetorical question regarding what pedagogues teach their pupils, he gives the following answer: "Words, more words, always words" (1762b, p. 108). Elsewhere he exhorts the reader, "Do not give your pupil any kind of verbal lessons; he ought to receive them only from experience" (p. 92). Rousseau believed that it might be possible to dispense with language, and that minds could be capable of communicating with each other in an unmediated and transparent way. As far as Rousseau's method is concerned, though, he was a quintessential Enlightenment thinker, an essayist who employed reason to put forward his own arguments—to the point of prejudice—and who argued against what he perceived to be the prevailing position.

Curiously though, Rousseau does not propose that Man is a being of sensation rather than one of reason. In fact this differentiation is one that he makes between the child and the adult man. He places children as being close to *things*, in other words, what he is referring to as *nature*: "The only habit useful to children is to subject themselves without difficulty to the necessity of things, and the only habit useful to men is to subject themselves without difficulty to reason. Every other habit is a vice" (p. 160).

If we are to follow Rousseau's logic, we must conclude that it is only the child, and not the adult, who is close to nature. In accordance with this, he also proposes that children, not being capable of judgement, have no real memory apart from that of sounds, forms, and sensations, but rarely a recollection of ideas (pp. 107–108). We might also conclude that it is only in the idea of the adult derived from retrospective nostalgia, an idea propagated by Rousseau, that childhood becomes an ideal veiled by forgetfulness. In this ideal, which verges on romanticism, the more sordid and less appealing aspects of childhood are obscured.

Nature and culture

Rousseau states his case quite clearly from the very beginning of *Émile*: "Everything is good as it comes from the hands of the Author of Nature; but everything degenerates in the hands of man" (1762a, p. 1). Here we can find an idea of nature, for Rousseau, as a type of established order that has been obscured and buried under the distorting influence of our society and civilisation. Perhaps this is not so far from the contemporary ideal of nature, for instance as promoted by the purveyors of *natural* products. But for Rousseau there is not only a nature to be refound, but there is an author of this nature, or, literally in the French, "the author of things" (1762c, p. 245). In other words there is a type of lay deity, or Other, who is the author of the unmediated idea of nature privileged by Rousseau. The Enlightenment occurred in the context of the weakening of the Church's grip upon society, but nonetheless a secular type of Otherness remains. We find something similar in economics, whereby Adam Smith in his work *The Wealth of Nations* of 1776 referred to the "invisible hand" that would direct the market place if only we could strip away our artificial regulations. Thus economic rationalists in recent times have utilised the "invisible hand" of Adam Smith for the purpose of "freeing up the market" and "unleashing market forces" (Edwards, 2002, p. 65). Rousseau similarly endeavours to liberate the child from what he sees as the artificial shackles of civilisation.

This "author of nature" also prescribes a natural order to a child's progress, a type of developmental theory that was no doubt a precursor to our contemporary notions of development, imbued as they are with the idea, or ideal, of the biological function of the organism. This is something he describes as a type of "education of nature", one of his modalities of education. In Rousseau's words: "The internal development of our faculties and our organs is the education of nature. The use that we are taught to make of this development is the education of men. And what we acquire from our own experience about the objects which affect us is the education of things" (1762b, p. 38).

Of these three such "educations", Rousseau states that only that of nature is entirely independent of ourselves. The education of men is effectively the one that he criticises, privileging "the education of things", once again the ideal upbringing through the unmediated contact with, and experience of, things. Here we see Rousseau's emphasis upon the child's sensations: "We are born with the use of our senses, and from our birth we are affected in various ways by the objects surrounding us" (p. 39). It is through our dispositions towards objects that Rousseau proposes to educate us, thus altering "what I call in us *nature*" (p. 39).

Rousseau also opposes his education of a child—as an education that makes a child into a man—to an education that makes a child into a citizen. The citizen, according to Rousseau, is the one who "no longer feels except within the whole" (p. 40). In other words, to be a citizen or to be a member of society is to be alienated from one's sensibility to nature. Furthermore, "Civil man is born, lives, and dies in slavery" (p. 42). If this is so, can *nature*, for Rousseau, be the source of free will? It would initially seem so since the reader is accosted by the following accusation: "You thwart them from their birth" (p. 43). Thus, for Rousseau, it is our very civilisation, and its mode of upbringing, that rob the child of his will.

Interestingly, in Rousseau, desire is something to be wrested from jouissance. He notes in this regard—and here I translate directly from the French to preserve Rousseau's expression, that: "Always more sufferings than enjoyments [*joüissances*]; this is the difference that is common to all" (1762c, p. 303, translated for this edition). Rousseau does not propose to spare the child from pain and suffering, but, on the contrary, it is through suffering, and through experiencing pain, that the child can come to learn. From this point on he proposes that "Every desire supposes privation, and all sensed privations are painful" (1762b, p. 80).

There is even a certain cruelty to the pain and suffering, however, which is allowed to be inflicted upon the child. Starobinski, an important commentator regarding Rousseau, has no hesitation in qualifying this as "sadism" (1971, p. 127). For instance, Rousseau asserts that "To suffer is the first thing he ought to learn and the thing he will most need to know" (1762b, p. 78). He follows this precept by prescribing Émile, for instance, an uncomfortable bed in which to sleep. In addition, he recommends waking him at odd times in order to accustom him to anything, including waking to a start. He also recommends dressing him in summer clothes and allowing him to go about bare-headed, whether it be in winter or in summer, during the day or at night. Rousseau thus proposes exposing Émile to extreme cold as well as the rays of the sun so that the child becomes hardened to them (pp. 127–128). In accordance with the naturalistic means that he proposes for the child's education and upbringing, he has the following advice: "He breaks the windows of his room; let the wind blow on him night and day without worrying about colds, for it is better that he have a cold than that he be crazy" (p. 100). And if the child is to again break windows, on this occasion Rousseau would have him locked up in a dark room without any windows and would ignore his cries and anger. It is striking that Rousseau's pedagogic stance takes precedence over the possibility of the child falling ill, and thus potentially, of his death.

But in Rousseau's notion of *desires*, it seems that it would be possible for them to be fulfilled. In his idea, unhappiness would consist in our desires being out of proportion to our faculties for fulfilling them: "A being endowed with senses whose faculties equaled his desires would be an absolutely happy being" (p. 80). But this ideally happy being is an equally elusive being. And Rousseau's means of creation of this being is through a return to childhood, to make childhood into something that never was and could never have been. This difficulty for Rousseau is that the origin of privation is to be found in the past, in one's origins, and his return is an endeavour to correct this. If we are to follow his example, then, we cannot locate and address privations and lack in the present, only in a forever elusive and imagined past. But to examine what motivates this notion, we need to examine more closely the manner in which Rousseau constructs his own past.

Rousseau's experiences

Starobinski comments in the introduction to his work that Rousseau himself was unwilling to separate his thought from his person. He states that, in reading Rousseau, "We must take him as he offers himself to us, in this fusion, and confusion, of existence and idea" (1957, p. xi). In other words, we cannot separate out Rousseau's autobiographical works from his treatises on education, culture, and society. In *Émile*, he refers repeatedly to his own childhood experiences and therefore this work is also an autobiographical one. Curiously, Starobinski proposes that this leads us to analyse his literary creation as if it were an imaginary action, and to analyse his behaviour as if it constituted a lived fiction. Thus Rousseau's own history, particularly as Rousseau himself recounts and writes it, is itself an integral part of his theses. If Lacan proposes that the only mode of truth is a fictional one, it is here that we can locate a truth in Rousseau's writing. Let us give some outlines of Rousseau's account of his own life, particularly from his *Confessions*, written in 1770 but not published until 1782, that are pertinent to our topic. It must be stressed that we are not attempting any form of psychobiography, but rather to grasp the manner in which Rousseau construes his own history and his motivations.

Rousseau's mother died nine days after giving birth to him, and moreover he specifies that it was he who was responsible for her death: "… I was born, a poor and sickly child, and cost my mother her life. So my birth was the first of my misfortunes" (1782a, p. 19). The theme of the tenuousness of life and ubiquitousness of infant death is raised by Rousseau himself: "I was almost born dead, and they had little hope of saving me" (p. 19). He was raised by his father, a watchmaker, initially in Geneva. It would seem that, despite not having known his mother, Rousseau attributes his literary interests to her, writing: "My mother had possessed some novels" (p. 19). Together with his father, he read these novels from an early age. His father would initiate their shared nostalgia for the lost mother, saying, "Jean-Jacques, let us talk of your mother," to which Rousseau would reply, "Very well, father, but we are sure to cry" (p. 19). In these attempts to retrieve his lost wife, Rousseau recounts, his father would say, "I am more of a child than you are" (p. 20).

This evokes the question of the father for Rousseau. Rousseau recounts that his father, after he left Geneva, took little part in the life of his son. In *Émile* Rousseau states that a father who understood the full price of a tutor would do without one and educate his son himself. And yet this is not what Rousseau did, nor what his father did in his case. The question of the father remains obscured for Rousseau, and is eclipsed by his idealisation and nostalgia for the mother.

Another episode recounted in the *Confessions* in regard to how Rousseau understood his own ideal of freedom and justice was that of his father's self-imposed exile from Geneva. Following a quarrel with a French captain in which the captain was injured, Rousseau's father left Geneva to avoid imprisonment, and Rousseau was placed under the guardianship of his uncle. However, this is presented as the father not giving way on a point of honour. In Rousseau's account, according to the law regarding such a dispute in Geneva at the time, both parties should have been imprisoned, not just Rousseau's father. Rousseau's later experience of having to flee Geneva interestingly reiterates this earlier experience of his father. It also forms part of his ongoing protest against what he considers to be the injustice of society and the law.

Despite his early and profound interest in literature, and his evident literary abilities, Rousseau insists that he was always a being of sensation rather than of thought. "I felt before I thought: which is the common lot of man, though more pronounced in my case than in another's" (p. 19). He describes the experience, as a child, of being punished by Mademoiselle Lambercier, the daughter of the minister with whom he and his cousin had been sent to board by his uncle. Through physical punishment, in the very pain and shame of the experience, he felt a mixture of sensuality, and a desire to re-experience it, "by the same hand" (p. 25). This was an experience that left a profound mark on Rousseau's affective and sensual life: "Who could have supposed that this childish punishment, received at the age of eight at the hands of a woman of thirty, would determine my tastes and desires, my passions, my very self for the rest of my life" (p. 26).

Nonetheless such tastes were to remain unspoken and unfulfilled with any member of the other sex, for want of daring to say what he wanted, or, in his words, "… being impossible … to be guessed at by the woman who could grant it. So I have spent my days in silent longing in the presence of those I most loved" (p. 27). In the first Neuchâtel manuscript version of his *Confessions*, Rousseau is even more explicit in regard to the structure of his forever unfulfilled wishes, stating, "I required another sort of voluptuousness" (1782b, p. 1243, translated for this edition). This other voluptuousness, this jouissance of the Other, remained forever elusive for Rousseau.

Another defining incident of childhood, and one which concerns the theme of this chapter and that of *Émile*, again involved Mademoiselle Lambercier. In this episode she accused Rousseau and his cousin of having broken one of her combs, and both were severely punished. But for Rousseau the critical aspect of this incident was that he was wrongly accused: "But I do most positively know that I was innocent" (1782a, p. 29). For Rousseau this effectively marks the termination of his childhood: "There ended the serenity of my childish life. From that moment I never again enjoyed pure happiness, and even to-day I am conscious that memory of childhood's delights stops short at that point" (p. 30).

The end of childhood then is the loss of innocence, real or imagined. Rousseau's notion that society is based upon a false order, or only an apparent order, is one that erodes any sense of justice for him, and his attempt to correct this is part of his endeavour to restore the imagined lost innocence of childhood. Rousseau's sense of persecution, real, imagined, or even delusional, only increased with the publication of both the *Social Contract* and *Émile* (Porge, 1996b, pp. 118–119).

Rousseau was sixteen years of age when he met Madame de Warens for the first time. He first came under her care and guidance, then later lived with her in her house. Finally he had found someone whom he could call a mother: "'Little one' was my name, hers was 'Mamma', and we always remained 'Little one' and 'Mamma'" (1782a, p. 106). Nonetheless, as well as his love and friendship for her, he initially also felt in her regard a sensation that he was unable to name, but which he described—and here I translate from the French so as to preserve the signifiers—as, "more voluptuous, more tender" (1782b, p. 104). Living in her house, he tells us that he "learned this dangerous supplement that deceives nature" (p. 109)—a "supplement" that disappears in the translation—in other words, masturbation. Later, at the age of twenty, Rousseau was taken by Madame de Warens as her lover. Rousseau stated, "I felt as if I had committed incest" (1782a, p. 189). Here he might locate the unnameable voluptuousness, as well as Rousseau's theme of the transgression of the law, a transgression he attempts to negate.

In a much later period of his life, following his return to France from England, Rousseau began a relationship with Therese le Vasseur, a seamstress whose family he also supported. He describes the beginning of this relationship in the following way: "What I needed, in short, was a successor to Mamma" (p. 310). Rousseau attempts to supplement, to correct, that which he takes as a deficiency: the mother he never knew.

According to the *Confessions*, Therese bore him a number of children but he convinced her to give each of them up, as the "sole means of saving her honour" (p. 322). "In due course it will be seen what vicissitudes this fatal conduct occasioned in my way of thinking and also in my destiny," Rousseau reports (p. 322). Here he is referring to the criticism to which he was subject as the author of *Émile*, for having given up his own children. But this conduct also evokes the other inevitably fatal consequences of Rousseau's conduct. Rousseau recounts that, at the table at which he was accustomed to eat at the time, there were many stories about deceived husbands, seduced women, clandestine births and that, in these anecdotes, he who gave the Foundlings' Hospital the greatest number of newborns was the most applauded. He claims that this cheerfully determined his resolve, "without the least scruple" (p. 322), to give up his own children to the Foundlings' Hospital, since it was the common custom of "fundamentally very decent people" (p. 322).

We have already mentioned that the Foundlings' Hospital, founded by Saint Vincent de Paul, was established in order to combat the exposure and infanticide of unwanted children. Nonetheless, more than seventy per cent of children admitted in the first months of life to that institution died before reaching one year of age (Gagnebin, Raymond, & Osmont, 1959, p. 1416). Here we see, from Rousseau's pen, the manner in which the infant death was repressed, differently, but just as effectively, as it is today.

In *Émile*, Rousseau says explicitly that he is unable to educate his own child: "'Who then will raise my child?' I already told you: you, yourself. 'I cannot'" (1762b, p. 49). Once again, he tells us himself that he was a poor educator, referring to a time when he was employed as a child's tutor: "In the past I made a sufficient trial of this calling to be certain that I am not proper for it" (p. 50). Rather than raising a child himself, Rousseau proposed to write: "I shall put my hand not to the work but to the pen; and instead of doing what is necessary, I shall endeavour to say it" (p. 50).

Rousseau describes, in *Émile*, the conditions required for him to educate a son. The primary condition is the following: "Émile is an orphan" (p. 52). We can then propose that Émile is precisely the orphan that he gave over to the Foundlings' Hospital, the unwanted child that he claimed he was unable to bring up. Moreover, he designates Émile as "my son" (p. 196). The writing of *Émile* is hence the supplement by which Rousseau makes up for what was impossible for him to do in his lived experience.

A dangerous supplement

If we stress the autobiographical elements in *Émile*, it is not in order to explicate Rousseau's theories by virtue of his own history, but rather to designate a certain mode of knowledge of childhood that he initiates. In his account, there is a very particular type of gaze upon the child, a gaze which idealises what is out of reach—not only for him, but for any subject who looks upon childhood retrospectively. In this way, the pain and the privations of childhood become a harmonious encounter with Mother Nature. For Freud, idealisation of the object is the very basis of perversion. In Rousseau we find a refusal of the childhood as experienced, a refusal of what is missing in it for him, a lack that is unable to be accommodated. Jean Starobinski articulates the nature of this "'veil' of separation" (1957, p. 11) that covers over the darkness of childhood for Jean-Jacques Rousseau:

> The temporal dimension that opens up behind the present moment is perceptible only because it is fleeing into inaccessibility. The mind turns back to an earlier world and sees that world, which once belonged to it, as lost forever. As the child's happiness slips away, the mind recognizes the boundless value of this now-forbidden joy. (p. 11)

This "now-forbidden joy"—the one he supplements with his own hand—is, at the same time, the quotient of joy that was never available, never accessible. The theme of lost innocence and of paradise regained veils the childhood that never was. But what was it that Rousseau endeavoured to retrieve and which struck a chord with generations of readers ever since? To have such an impact, *Émile* not only articulated an idealised sentiment of childhood with which its readers have identified across the centuries, but also proposed to remedy the lacks and deficiencies of childhood by a notional plenitude of nature.

Starobinski notes that it has been argued, by the psychoanalyst René Laforgue amongst others, that love triangles offered Rousseau the opportunity to relive the experience of being a guilty son hoping to restore a lost intimacy. But Starobinski remarks that in *Émile*, Rousseau attempts to overcome his deficiencies by assuming the place of teacher, of master, in sole possession of the knowledge of happiness. Rousseau indeed places himself in the imaginary position as master of jouissance (cf. Bergès & Balbo, 1994b, p. 34), but experiences joy only second-hand, through his imaginary others. Rather than remaining a guilty son, he endeavours to occupy the place of an impossibly omnipotent and omniscient father. Starobinski cites Rousseau from *Émile*, at the point at which he has made lovers of Émile and Sophie, both of whom he has raised:

> How many times, as I contemplate my work in them, I feel myself
> seized by a rapture that makes my heart palpitate! How many times
> I join their hands in mine while blessing providence and sighing
> ardently! How many kisses I give to these two hands which clasp
> each other! How many times have these hands felt the tears I shed
> on them! The young couple share my raptures and they too are
> moved. (1762b, p. 480)

Even in his rapture, Rousseau still remains outside the quotient of
enjoyment shared only by the lovers and never by him. In this strange
enjoyment there is, at the same time, an implicit renunciation of what
will never be his.

Nonetheless, there is also a discernable enjoyment of Émile's and
Sophie's tears at the time of their separation, pleasure at the tears he
causes to flow. We find Rousseau writing of a similar vicarious joy in
provoking the tears of others, in concert with his own tears, during the
performance of his opera *The Village Soothsayer*: "The pleasure of affecting so many pleasant people moved even me to tears .... And yet I am
sure that sexual passion counted for more at that moment than the van-
ity of an author … devoured, as I continually was, by the desire to catch
with my lips the delicious tears that I had evoked" (1782a, p. 353).

Starobinski comments that, through Rousseau's opera, "The maso-
chism of the spanking has turned into the gentle sadism of pastoral
tenderness" (1957, p. 176). But the unmediated enjoyment of contact of
a sexual nature with another being, a contact with the flesh, will never
be his. What *is* his is the fact of separation that he imaginarily produces,
making himself the master of proceedings. It is here that we can locate
the lost intimacy that remains forever inaccessible.

There remains for Rousseau, and for each and every one of us, only
the possibility of supplementing that which cannot be attained. He
speaks of Therese le Vasseur, and again I cite from the French in order
to retain this signifier "supplement": "When I was absolutely alone
my heart was empty, but all that was needed was another to fill it. …
I found in Therese the supplement that I needed" (1782b, p. 332).

"Supplement", then, is Rousseau's signifier for whatever endeavours to make good that which he never had, a signifier that persistently
disappears in the English language translations. We have already spoken of "this dangerous supplement", the manner in which Rousseau

speaks of masturbation, masturbation initiated in the house of the woman he called "Mamma". He goes on to qualify this supplement—and once again I translate literally in order to preserve Rousseau's words—in the following manner: "This vice that shame and timidity find so convenient has, moreover, a great attraction for lively imaginations; that of having at its disposal, so to speak, the whole [female] sex at will, and of making the beauty that tempts them serve their own pleasures without having to obtain its avowal" (p. 109). Rousseau operates on the level of a disavowal in his relations to imaginary objects. In this way his object, whether it be a "Mamma", or his notion of the child, is able to retain its idealised status, with no reference to its deficiencies or lacks.

One episode he recounts that draws out this relation to the object is his encounter in Italy with the courtesan Giulietta, or Zulietta in the Venetian dialect. Strikingly, Rousseau introduces this episode in the following way: "If there is a circumstance of my life and that clearly combs my nature, it is this one that I am about to recount" (1782b, p. 320). I translate this literally from the French, particularly for this word "combs". Not only does this circumstance, like a comb, brush up against his body, but it evokes that object he was wrongly accused of damaging: Mademoiselle Lambercier's comb. He describes his first meeting with Zulietta thus: "I entered a courtesan's room as if it were the sanctuary of love and beauty; in her person I felt I saw the divinity. ... 'This thing which is at my disposal', I said to myself, 'is Nature's masterpiece and love's. Its mind, its body, every part is perfect'" (1782a, p. 300).

As we have put forward in another context, the secular divinity to which Rousseau subscribes is his idealised notion of nature. After continuing to describe her charms in similarly exalted terms, there arrives a moment when he seeks to realise his passions, only to find a defect:

> But at the moment when I was ready to swoon over her bosom, which seemed to suffer the mouth and hand of a man for the first time, I perceived that she had a blind [borgne] breast. I beat my brow, looked closer; I thought I saw that this breast was not the same as the other. I started wondering how one could have a blind breast, and, persuaded that it must be due to some remarkable natural vice, I turned this idea over in my head and saw as clear as daylight that instead of the most charming person I could possibly

imagine, I held in my arms nothing but a type of monster, a reject
of nature, of men, and of love. (1782b, pp. 321–322)

The English translation takes away the specificity—and the
ambiguity—of this blind breast, by rendering it as "malformed" (1782a,
p. 301). We see here that nature, according to Rousseau, does not permit of any defects, with the proviso that we must once again qualify
these defects as real or imagined. This "blind breast" is for him, a sign
that allows him to see clearly, "as clear as daylight", the object in this
new light, that is, in Rousseau's interpretation. But for Rousseau, there
is no interpretation. As Starobinski puts forward, Rousseau's ideal of
immediacy demands that the meaning of the sign must be identical
with his perception of the object. Thus no interpretation is necessary
for Rousseau since the meaning of the sign is self-evident: "The gaze
that looks out upon the world elicits signs destined for it alone, which
disclose *its* world" (1957, p. 156, italics in the original).

Furthermore, we can suggest that the difficulty for Rousseau is precisely in the fact that the nipple is "blind", in other words that the nipple is unable to look back at him, to see him and thus to recognise him
and validate him as a mother should, at least in his ideal. Instead of the
return of the gaze, Rousseau encounters an intolerable absence from
which he takes flight. We are reminded of the last stanza of Hölderlin's
poem to Rousseau:

> In the first sign he sees the final meaning,
> And flies, this bold spirit, as eagles do
> Ahead of thunderstorms, to warn
> Of the gods' approach. (2008)

Rousseau attributes the defect to nature, his god, even if it is a reject
of this nature, or the effect of "natural vice". Rousseau flees from
this intimate encounter, and Zulietta, disdainful, sends him off with:
"*Zanetto, lascia le donne, e studia la matematica*" (Rousseau, 1782b, p. 302).
She says, in other words: "Little Johnny, leave women alone, and study
mathematics!"

Maud Mannoni recounts how the prevailing conceptions of childhood have led psychoanalysts to have a *blind* spot regarding the place
of the child in analysis: "Child psychoanalysis has repeatedly fallen
into traps of educationalist, social, or moral ideology. … We have seen

that since Freud's time a movement has grown to save analysis from the organic and pedagogic blind alleys where it was floundering" (1967a, p. 15). Rousseau's theses and the effect they have had upon our conceptualisation of the child have been prominent in the propagation of such ideologies—with their resulting dead ends—including amongst analysts.

Émile is an orphan

Rousseau's account of his own birth, that he was born almost dying, is itself imbued with a certain sentimentality whose purpose, we might propose, is to create an illusion. As we know very well, it was not Rousseau who died but his mother. Similarly, there is a certain deception, made at the points where Rousseau speaks of "honour". In his account, his father fled from Geneva, not in order to flee from the law but to uphold a point of honour. In Rousseau's version of events, taking flight from the law becomes honourable. And, when he recounts that he had to persuade Therese le Vasseur to give up their children in order "to save her honour", we detect more than a streak of cynicism. Similarly, when Rousseau proposes that the child has "no original perversity", this is a statement that gives an illusion of upholding the honour of the child. And yet such a claim is in itself a perverse statement, one which disavows the forbidden desires and joys of childhood, including those of his own childhood, forever relegating them to the field of the imaginary. This ideal of the child contributed to a repression regarding such original perversity in the child, prior to Freud's discovery of the polymorphous perversity of the child.

Rousseau's condition for bringing up a child is that, "Émile is an orphan. It is not important that he have a father and mother." He adds that, "He ought to honor his parents, but he owes obedience to no one but me" (1762a, p. 21). Hence the parents also retain their honour, but Rousseau makes himself the master of jouissance. In removing the child from the parents—as he did with his own children—Rousseau, by the same token, dislocates the child from the history and the sexuality that produced it. There is no longer any debt owing to the parents, only to Rousseau as the child's imaginary new father. We might be able to discern here a way in which Rousseau's pedagogic proposition is also one that is of interest to psychoanalysis. This question is one that concerns the place of the parents in relation to the child and therefore in relation to any possible psychoanalysis of the child. As we have remarked, a child, per se, cannot be an analysand, since an analysand must be a subject in his or her own right. Hug-Hellmuth's work with the parents was to enable the analysis of the child to proceed, for the mother and the father to undergo a mourning of the place in which each had held the child. This work is able to establish a place for the child as subject, such that the child might be able to take up a position as analysand.

An adult patient in analysis referred to herself in a session as "child-ish", denoting by this that she tended to adopt the opinions and attitudes of those around her, relying on the "endorsement" or "evaluation" of others to sustain her own opinions and activities. So then, to take her comment seriously, to be a child according to her definition is to not be able to define one's own stance. To no longer be a child would then be to take up a position, to make a mark such that one is no longer defined purely by virtue of the Other. This Other of course might be the parent, or any other: it defines a position in respect of Otherness.

Immanuel Kant said something similar in a paper entitled, "An answer to the question: What is enlightenment?", a question very perti-nent to our consideration of the evolution of the notion of the child and childhood at the time of the Enlightenment. Kant answers the rhetorical question of his title in the following way, "Enlightenment is the human being's emergence from his self-incurred minority" (1784, p. 17). Thus for Kant, the question of the Enlightenment itself is that of the emer-gence from a state of minority into that as a major: to be a subject in one's own right.

Kant further clarifies that minority, in other words, the state of being a child, "is inability to make use of one's own understanding without direction from another" (p. 17). For Kant then, to be a minor, or a child, is not at all a question of age, it is a question rather of the place that one takes up in regard to the Other. He notes that a great part of humankind, long after nature has emancipated them from the direction of others, nonetheless gladly remain minors for life. Moreover he puts forward that precepts and formulae are the ball and chain of an everlasting minority. We have seen in this chapter that Jean-Jacques Rousseau proposes to educate and raise the child by precepts, by making himself, at least in his writing, Émile's preceptor. His precepts, in fact, lead in the opposite direction: that of being the master of Émile's jouissance. Rousseau, in regard to the child, addresses us with the question: "Are you not the master of affecting him as you please? ... Doubtless he ought to do only what he wants; but he ought to want only what you want him to do. He ought not to make a step without your having foreseen it; he ought not to open his mouth without your knowing what he is going to say" (1762b, p. 120).

Such an approach ensures that the child remains a minor. The loss of innocence inherent in acceding to majority implies, according to Kant, the resolution and courage to use one's own understanding and knowledge, without direction from another. Thus it is only at the point at which the child becomes an orphan of the Other, that he might be able to accede to majority.

CHAPTER NINE

Condillac's statue: from the sentiment of childhood to the sensuality of the child

Rousseau fell out with his Enlightenment colleagues over the question of the senses, in positing the primacy of the senses over reason. Rousseau himself puts this in the following way: "The sensual man is the man of nature; the thoughtful man is a man of opinion; it is the latter who is dangerous" (1776, p. 808, translated for this edition). Rousseau has no hesitation in placing his judgement on the side of sensuality. Burgelin comments that "Rousseau thus understands himself as man of nature, but the opposition of thought and sensuality takes us back from the adult state to that of childhood" (1969, p. CL, translated for this edition). This is true in Rousseau's notion: it is the child who is deformed from a sensual being into a reflexive being by the ills of his education, upbringing, and society.

But is Rousseau's child truly a sensual being? Rousseau constructs an ideal of childhood, or what has been called a sentiment of childhood. Schiller defined Rousseau as the "sentimental" poet (Starobinski, 1957, p. 90). And if we consider Rousseau to be sentimental, then we need to differentiate this from the sensual. The sentimental after all is ultimately not a physical phenomenon or a phenomenon of the body, but rather an idea, or an ideal. This feeling or sentiment is thus a mental phenomenon, which we can write in the following way: *senti-mental*. We can even go so far as to say that the sentimental alienates us from the sensual. It obscures the sensual by supplementing it with a rosy ideal, the paradise lost to which we have referred. The sensual is certainly what Rousseau seeks, but which eludes him, causing him to constantly fall back upon the senti-mental and endeavouring to make up for this lack by the supplement that he describes. The sensual, we can surmise, is the element that refuses our apprehension of it. From the last chapter we can say that it is the element that exceeds the limits of language, language by which Rousseau, and we, attempt to grasp it.

We will examine this question of the sensual and sensibility through the work of a contemporary of Rousseau, Étienne Bonnot, Abbé de Condillac. In his work, *Treatise on the Sensations* (1754a), described as the finished and definitive exposition of his theories (Carr, 1930, p. xxii), Condillac makes use of the artifice of a fictional marble statue. This statue is imbued with the organic structure of the human body, but at the beginning of Condillac's study it is an insentient being. He allows this statue to have each of its senses awakened in turn. For Condillac, a sensation is an experience of the body of which the subject becomes aware, and which ultimately becomes consciousness itself. But for Condillac, the experience effectively tells us little of what is outside and which provokes the senses; rather, it tells us about the senses themselves. Geraldine Carr wrote in 1930, in her "Translator's Introduction" to the *Treatise on the Sensations*, that Condillac gave philosophy a new direction which ultimately led to the idealistic position of modern French philosophy, just as Locke may be said to have directed English philosophy towards a realistic, or empiricist, position (Carr, 1930, p. xxvii).

Hence if Condillac remains somewhat forgotten, he is nonetheless an interesting counterpoint to Jean-Jacques Rousseau from the time of the Enlightenment, and one who introduced an important theory of the senses and of language. His fiction of the statue also allows us to discern the manner in which developmental thought crept in to the conception of the child at that time and since. After all, Condillac's statue is most often interpreted in this manner: as a developmental model of a child who develops his faculties one after another (Quarfood, 1997). Here we dispute such a reductionist interpretation. If Condillac provides the best account of the senses from the time of the Enlightenment, he does so in order to demonstrate that sensation is the origin of thought and language. What we would also like to do here is to take up Condillac's work against its own grain, that is, starting from speech and thought, to discern the sensations and sensuality that lie on the other side of language.

Rousseau and Condillac

Condillac was some three years Rousseau's junior, being born in Grenoble in 1715. Curiously, Rousseau would appear to have met Condillac at the time that he was employed as a tutor to the two sons of Condillac's elder brother, M. de Mably, at Lyons in 1740. The two became lifelong friends and Rousseau gives himself credit for facilitating the publication of Condillac's first work, *Essay on the Origin of Human Knowledge*, in 1746. Rousseau also gives some acknowledgement to Condillac in *Émile*, but elsewhere in that work it is evident that he borrows heavily from Condillac's metaphysics without reference to him. Moreover, Condillac exerted a decisive influence on Rousseau's thought overall.

The question of the mediation effected by language between sensations and reason was an important theme at the time of the Enlightenment. To some extent it was a response to the Cartesian philosophy of the seventeenth century which established a sharp distinction between the soul and body, which consisted in rejecting perceptions and sense impressions as being outside the sphere of objective knowledge. That is, the sensation of pain that I feel through being burnt by a flame would be considered to be an objective quality of the fire. For Descartes, reason was primary: any knowledge of the essence of things had its origin in pure thought. Condillac's conceptualisation is almost the opposite of this. His conclusion is that sensation can teach us nothing of what is outside ourselves, but only about the senses themselves and the ideas that are generated from them. Furthermore, Condillac's philosophy of knowledge is organised around a reflection upon the nature of language. This was an important step for the understanding of man as a sentient being, and, we can argue, a movement that led towards the emergence of Freud's thought.

In his seminar *The Four Fundamental Concepts of Psychoanalysis*, Lacan refers to the encyclopaedist Diderot who was also an acquaintance of Rousseau (1964, p. 86). He specifically cites Diderot's "Letter on the Blind" (1749) in which he notes that Diderot demonstrates to what degree a blind man is capable of imagining, reconstructing, and speaking about everything that vision is able to reveal regarding space. In this way Diderot established that the imaginary order is a structure that is able to function, even for those who cannot see. Similarly, Condillac was able to begin to define the symbolic order, through the theory of language that he developed from the time of his very first work, *Essay on the Origin of Human Knowledge*. Despite the question of origins that are implicit in the title, Condillac is able to establish a structural approach to language. He differentiates different types of what he calls "signs", including those he refers to as nouns, or "names", which, in his understanding have "no particular foundation in nature" (1746, p. 135). These signifiers therefore have an arbitrary relation to the things they signify, prefiguring the notion that de Saussure later put forward. Condillac, moreover, speaks of "the absolute necessity of signs", which contributes towards the "progression of the operations of the mind" (pp. 328–329). For Condillac, the capacity for thought is secondary, then, to the function of speech. Even though Condillac is not exempt from the preoccupation of the time with the question of origins, he is not caught up, as is Rousseau, in the ideal of the natural man and his cry of nature that this man supposedly produces. This, as Jean Starobinski notes, is a myth of language.

The artifice of speaking of a statue was in keeping with the tastes and methods of the era of the Enlightenment (Carr, 1930, p. xxiii). There are also two texts in which Rousseau refers to a statue that are worthy of detaining our interest here. The first, an unfinished piece entitled "Fiction or Allegorical Fragment on the Revelation", remained unpublished during Rousseau's lifetime. It has received so little attention from English-speaking scholars that it has never been translated. Even though it aims to describe the revelation of a truth, it begins in a very heavily sensual manner, viz:

> It was on the occasion of a beautiful summer night that the first man who attempted to philosophise, surrendered himself to a profound and delicious reverie, and, guided by that involuntary enthusiasm that sometimes transports the soul out of its dwelling and makes it embrace the entire universe, so to speak, dared to raise his reflections towards the sanctuary of Nature and by thought penetrate as far as human wisdom is allowed to reach. (1738, p. 1044, translated for this edition)

Here we see the typical themes of Rousseau, beginning with a sort of delicious sensuality which he endeavours to regain. Rousseau makes himself both the first and the only man—the solitary man—to reach such heights, that is, the heights of nature unveiled through the "penetration" of his wisdom. Here "Nature" becomes a type of all-encompassing, or universal, wisdom. The sensuality of this scene evokes a type of encounter with Eden, replete with the tree of knowledge: nothing lacks here. Nonetheless, this account of the voluptuousness of nature must be articulated in a "so to speak", that is, through language. He continues:

> The heat having hardly fallen with the setting sun, the birds that had already withdrawn and not yet asleep were announcing with their languishing and voluptuous warbling the pleasure that they tasted by breathing a fresher air; an abundant and salutary dew was already reviving the greenery wilted by the heat of the sun, flowers were thrusting out the sweetest perfumes from every direction; the orchards and the woods in all their finery, through the dusk and the first moonbeams, formed a spectacle less lively and more touching than during the glare of the day. (p. 1044)

Here we bear witness to the voluptuousness that Rousseau had denied himself in his unending search for an ideal. The dreamer enters a mysterious temple that contains seven colossal statues, and then an eighth statue to which the whole edifice is dedicated and which remains shrouded in an "impenetrable veil" (p. 1049). This contrasts with the *penetrability* of knowledge in the first scene—also a type of forbidden carnal knowledge in its unrestrained sensuality. For Rousseau the theme of mystery is always charged with a negative value (Starobinski, 1957, p. 66). In Rousseau's text, a Christlike character appears, which for Rousseau is a type of revelation of truth, a truth that does not even require this character to speak. The question of the veil over the statue also reminds us of Lacan's discussion of the veiling of the phallus, effectively the veil over what lacks: something Rousseau would prefer not to know about. Rousseau constructs a myth to cover over what is missing.

The second text in which Rousseau refers to a statue is his short play *Pygmalion* that has, it would appear, also remained untranslated into English. In his version of this classical story, Pygmalion sculpts the beautiful form of Galatea. This ideal form, the object of his desire, turns out in Rousseau's account to be none other than the lost part of himself that he refinds in Galatea. In Starobinski's words:

> A miracle brings Galatea to life: the statue develops a sensibility, like the statue imagined by Condillac. But Galatea's existence does not begin with perception of the outside world. She does not become a "fragrance of roses." Her first sensuous [*sensible*] act is to touch her own body, an act that immediately yields "self-consciousness".
> (1971, p. 72)

Indeed, as we will see, the first act of Condillac's statue is to smell a rose, but Galatea's touching of her own body leads, in turn, to touching Pygmalion. At this point she says, "Ah, me again [*encore moi*]," to which Pygmalion replies, "Yes, dear and charming object: yes, worthy masterpiece of my hands, of my heart and of the Gods ... it is you, it is only you: I gave you all my being; I will live only through you". (Rousseau, 1771, p. 1231, translated for this edition). Hence Galatea's touching of her own body and then that of Pygmalion, is effectively a turning back upon oneself in a form of masturbation.

For Rousseau, this moment of revelation is, in the end, nothing other than an encounter with his own image, an encounter with his other half that provides him with an imaginary completeness. Strikingly, when Pygmalion unveils the statue of Galatea, he describes this moment in almost identical terms to Rousseau's account of his encounter with Zulietta, saying, "I believed I was touching the sanctuary of some Divinity" (p. 1226). The difference is that on this occasion there is no need to flee since there is no defect to be found: Galatea reflects his own idealised image back to himself.

Condillac's statue

What is the relation of the senses to language? This is something to which the whole of the *Treatise on the Sensations* is directed. Condillac begins with sensation and moves towards thought and language. For Condillac, it is through an apprehension of the senses, through the sense organs of the body, that language and thought ultimately spring. Condillac goes through each sensory modality one by one, in order to articulate the functions and the structure of thought and language. Here, though, we will endeavour to move in the other direction, to move from thought back to sensation, in order to understand something of Condillac's apprehension of the senses.

Condillac attributes the determining nature of whether the interest of the statue will be aroused by a particular sensation, to whether the sensation evokes pleasure or pain, to which it will react either by enjoyment (*jouissance*) or suffering (*souffrance*) (1754a, p. 4). And the statue endeavours to maintain a homeostasis, to try to avoid pain and to prolong pleasurable sensations. Here we have the first articulation of a pleasure principle, at least in the statue's attempt to avoid the over-arousal of pain. But it is through the discrimination between pleasure and pain that the first notion of difference is introduced. Condillac states that pleasure and pain are always the prime mover of the faculties. This makes Condillac quite Aristotelian, except that in this case the "prime mover" is not a greater Being, but rather jouissance. For the statue, desires and passions, judgements and thoughts, are ultimately nothing but sensations that have been differently transformed. In the first instance, for Condillac, the statue is not aware that pain can cease and become something else since it as yet has no idea of change, succession, or duration. It is in this way, through the apperception of difference, that the statue ultimately is able to form desires.

Hence the statue—a little like the polymorphous perversion of the child for Freud, or even the unmitigated enjoyment of the father of the primal horde—is initially only able to suffer and enjoy: the two aspects of jouissance. And like the primal father, it enjoys without being able to desire: here there is no change and no loss, since change and loss imply the possibility of desire. It is through a modification of the pain or enjoyment that the statue is able to desire. The enjoyment, or jouissance, is incarnated in the body. It is not, as in the Gospel According to St. John, the word made flesh, but rather, with Condillac, it is literally the flesh made word.

Thus the approach to the object, for Condillac, is primarily through the flesh. For this reason, in his writing, he privileges the sensation of touch by which the statue begins to discover what is outside itself. He refers to children, specifically to the enjoyment that they experience in movement. I utilise the French text here as the published translation eliminates the references to what is of most interest to us here, namely, the emergence of consciousness:

> The greatest happiness of children seems to consist in movement:
> even falls do not displease them. A blindfold would distress them
> less than a cord that would take away the use of their feet and
> hands. Effectively, it is to movement that they owe the most lively

consciousness they have of their existence. Sight, hearing, smell, and taste, seem to circumscribe it to one organ; but movement spreads it out to all parts and produces enjoyment [*jouir*] from the body in all its extension. (1754b, p. 193, translated for this edition)

Condillac starts with the jouissance of the body and it is from this enjoyment that consciousness emerges. For Condillac, from the pleasure derived from these sensations of the body, the statue is able to compare and judge the different sensations and this is where thought and language emerge. He introduces a temporal dimension into this experience, in this instance referring to the sensation of touch: "[T]he advantage, however, it enjoys is that pleasure is ever at hand, whilst pain is only felt at intervals" (1754a, p. 93). Thus the periodicity, so introduced, marks off and defines the pleasure and enjoyment that the statue experiences, thereby introducing the symbolic order. Moreover, the sensation, even when it has ceased to act upon the sense organ, is retained as an impression that remains stronger or weaker according to the amount of attention that it commands. This capacity to retain attention, then, is memory (p. 93). For Condillac, desire arises from this: "Since enjoyment [*jouissance*] is no longer limited to ideas represented in imagination, it extends beyond its own self to all objects within its reach; and desires, instead of concentrating our statue into its own states of being … continually draw it outside itself" (p. 93).

But for Condillac, unlike Rousseau's Pygmalion with his Galatea, the statue is drawn to the bodies of others, even if its first experience is that of its own body: "Its love for other bodies is the effect of self-love" (p. 93). And interestingly, Condillac's statue speaks in similar terms to Rousseau's Galatea in the touch of its own body: "It's me, it's me again [*C'est moi, c'est moi encore*]" (1754b, p. 188).

The *Treatise on the Sensations* was written in 1754, and Rousseau's *Pygmalion* was thought to be written around 1762, and therefore the former in some ways anticipates the latter. While Galatea moves towards an imaginary oneness, Condillac's statue is able to produce difference and thereby the possibility of desire. For instance, the statue firstly differentiates its own experience of heat, from heat itself: "It no longer will confuse itself with its modifications, it will no longer be warm and cold. It will feel warm in one part of its body and cold in another" (Condillac, 1754a, p. 88). And when the "me" or ego touches a foreign body, it experiences that its sensation has been modified but does not receive the same response from this foreign body as from its own body. Condillac writes, "As it has formed its body from [these responses], it similarly forms all other objects from them" (1754b, p. 189). These physical objects are imbued with the quality of "impenetrability" (1754a, p. 86), not Rousseau's mystical impenetrability, but the impenetrability of a body to the sensation of touch.

Condillac speaks of the child in this regard, and again I translate him myself, and in a literal fashion, in order to preserve Condillac's expression: "The first discovery that a child makes is that of his body. It is not he *properly speaking* who makes the discovery, it is nature that shows it to him already made" (1754b, p. 178, my italics). Here we can see that for Condillac, nature is no longer the idealised paradise that it is for Émile, but rather it is the place of the drive experienced by the child. But the child's apprehension of his experience of the body, like the statue's, must pass through this "properly speaking": the child must separate out what he is able to say, from the real of nature. For Condillac, thought and language ultimately arise from the sensations, but their origin is to be located in sensation. It is in this sense that Condillac states, "… nature begins entirely within us … our knowledge is entirely its work" (p. 178). And for Condillac, again a little like for Freud, this place that we could nominate as that of the drive is one that effectively cannot be represented: "There is in us a principle of our actions, which we feel but cannot define. We call it *force*" (1754a, p. 8). We can hear in this what Freud speaks of in regard to the "pressure" [*Drang*] of the drive (1915c, p. 122).

The place of cause, for Condillac, is also to be located in nature, and it is nature that provokes sensation. For the statue to go beyond the homeostasis of the pleasure principle, something must move the body. In the beginning of the discussion of the sensation of touch, Condillac asks, "I allow the statue the use of all its members: but what is the cause which induces it to move them?" (1754a, p. 84). He proposes that the cause cannot be any intention of moving them since the statue does not yet have any knowledge of them. He puts forward that it is nature that must begin: "It is to nature we must look for a beginning" (p. 84). For Condillac, nature is the prime mover, nature experienced as enjoyment or suffering. Moreover, for the statue—or the subject—the cause cannot be located in any one place: "It cannot differentiate between a cause which is within and a cause which is without" (p. 8). It cannot, moreover, at least initially, differentiate between the experience of a sensation or whether it merely recalls it.

Condillac's project is to endeavour to articulate the place of the subject that is born in this way through the sensations, a subject that he nominates as the *moi, ego,* or *self*. By the means that he describes of the sensations making themselves known to the statue, this subject then comes to invest itself in its own body. Condillac states, "The self [*moi*] of a child, concentrated in its soul, would never be able to regard the different parts of its body as so many parts of itself" (p. 82). It is through nature making his body known to him, not as modifications of his soul, but as modifications of the organs, that the ego, instead of being concentrated in the soul, comes to spread out and to be repeated in all the parts of the body. The experience of the *subject* for Condillac is first and foremost an experience of the body.

It is through what he calls this "artifice" (p. 83), that we come to believe we are able to find ourselves in our organs—or our bodies— which are, *properly speaking*, not ourselves. This artifice remains mysterious for the subject; it remains resistant to our comprehension and therefore outside the possibility of our knowing of it. The statue becomes aware that the parts of the body belong to it, but remains unable to understand this. I translate once again from the French to retain the emphasis he places on sensation: "I know that they belong to me, without being able to understand it: I see myself, I touch myself, in a word I feel myself, but I do not know what I am" (1754b, p. 415).

His own body, as well as the Other's body, remain impenetrable for Condillac's subject. Effectively they both remain a "foreign body" (1754a, p. 88) for the subject in so far as they are not able to be apprehended, *properly speaking*. Here we might locate in Condillac's thesis the question of the subject's apprehension of the body and its sensuality, whether it be one's own body or that of another. This is what we can call the real of sex, no longer reduced to an historical event, but rather as an atemporal structure. And in allocating a place for nature as incomprehensible for the subject, he retains a place for this real, which, from psychoanalysis, we might designate as the place of the drive. This is the usefulness of Condillac's artifice of the statue, since the statue is not a child, or a developmental model, but a hypothetical subject at any point along its trajectory. Through his conception of the statue, we can locate in Condillac's work the introduction of sensuality to the modern notion of the subject.

The libidinisation of the statue

Condillac introduces the idea of the appropriation of one's own body through the awakening of the senses and the perception of this. Hegel, in the *Philosophy of Right*, published in 1820, also spoke of the body—as well as the mind—as a question of possession: "The possession of the body and the mind, which is acquired by education, study and habit, is an inward property of the spirit" (p. 51). Thus it is the spirit, or soul, that must take possession of the body, as it takes possession of any object. Indeed, the body could be considered to be the first piece of private property. And for Hegel, it is the question of will that predominates here: there must be an inner act of will, and then comes the outer form of giving the object a predicate, or name. Interestingly, Hegel differentiates children and adults in this way: "Children often affirm this earlier act of will against the real possessing of a thing by others. But for adults such a will is not enough. The form of subjectivity must be removed by working itself out into something objective" (p. 57).

The mother and father take possession of the child by giving him a name. In this way they appropriate the child as an object that belongs to them. Later the child must struggle to take possession of his own body. Hegel delineates three ways in which one may take possession of an object: by marking, by use of the object, and by exercising one's will over the object by relinquishing it. We can certainly recognise all of these modes in the endeavour by the child to appropriate his body.

The contemporary mode of tattooing and piercing the body is one means by which the young person—or not so young person—endeavours to appropriate his body. Such markings are inscribed in defiance of the parent, or the Other, as an attempt to say, "It's my body, I can do what I like with it," a version of which is often articulated by the young person. Use of the body can also be considered, in the beginnings of sexual activity and drug use, as alien to the parents' possession of the child's body, and therefore part of the effort of the young person to appropriate it. And it is also interesting to consider how the subject might appropriate his or her body precisely in the relinquishment of ownership over it, by utilising it. Allowing one's body to be used for the sexual enjoyment of the other is such a means of taking ownership by relinquishing one's body, albeit temporarily, to the other's will.

More recently, Jean Périn raised the question of whether one actually possesses one's own body. He proposes that one only has—in the legal sense—jouissance of one's body, that is to say, usufruct or use of the body (1995). This is a useful proposition since it radicalises the question of the relation that the subject has to its body. After all, the rights that one has over one's body are indeed limited, even restricted by law. And the law also determines at what age the subject may be able to exercise these rights. The limits to such rights are evident when one considers that the law intervenes when it is reckoned that one is a danger to one-self, or to others. And one cannot legally do whatever one likes to one's body such as procuring a sex change, a late termination of pregnancy, or indeed to commit suicide or euthanasia, to mention a few possibilities, in any case without the intervention of the requisite authorities.

In his attempt to capture the corporeal origin of discourse, Condillac in some ways prefigures Freud, since the beginnings of psychoanaly-sis lie in the attempt of the patient, through speech—through the *prop-erly speaking*—to give an account of the disturbing sensuality or erotics of the body. This occurred from the beginning with the first hysterics to whom Freud and Breuer listened (Freud & Breuer, 1895d). Breuer was said to have fled from this experience, since his own sexuality was evoked, something he was unable to tolerate. And of course it was through Freud's *Three Essays on the Theory of Sexuality* and in his account of little Hans' fantasies and erotic life, that the child was first able to be apprehended as a sexual subject. We stress here the radical nature of the attribution of the erotics of the subject, something that goes beyond any psychological, developmental, or categorical grasp of the child.

And if the imaginary of the senses, elaborated by Diderot, began to be taken up in the symbolic of language by Condillac, what is inevita-bly missing is the real of the body, even if its place is designated as that of nature. It is the inability of the child, the parents, and the clinician to formulate the suffering of a child—to account for the ultimately inex-pressible erotics of the body, the real of sex—that frequently leads to suspicions of *sexual abuse* or any other *abuse* of the child in the absence of any material evidence of such. That is, what is invoked is some puta-tive external cause. There is trauma for each subject, including the child as subject, but the trauma is ultimately a confrontation with the real of sex, however encountered. The inexpressible—and unanalysed—erotics of the clinician, is part of this equation. To utilise Rousseau's term, this sensual is the "supplement" to the sensibility of Condillac: it is what is lacking in the account of the body by means of the senses.

The erotics of the child, and of the clinician, exceeds the discourse that endeavours, but ultimately fails, to circumscribe it.

Here we might attempt to differentiate what we can call *sensation*, from *sensuality*. Condillac's project is to locate the origin of thought and reason—or language and discourse—in the senses. Condillac begins with the perceptual organs, from which he extracts the thought processes from the functioning of the senses. He begins with the sense of smell, moves to the sense of hearing, then taste, vision, and finally touch and movement. He then elaborates upon how thought processes are derived from these senses. In this approach, he already begins with a categorisation of the senses and this eventually leads to a categorisation of the modes of thought that he describes.

But if there is something missing from this account it is the *sensuality*, or *sexuality*, of his hypothetical statue. Condillac imposes a sensorial organisation upon the body in order to introduce his conceptual notion of the subject. Such a discrete and categorical approach effects a type of domestication of the sensual, or sexual. This approach suffers from the obsessional aspect of any categorisation, like the common psychiatric diagnostic systems. Such a system effectively serves the function of repressing the erotics of the body. But the epidemic of hysteria and that of neurasthenia which preceded Freud's time belied the inadequacy of such a conception. In this way, Condillac's statue is doomed to remain a statue and not a being of flesh and blood. In common parlance if one says, "I am not a statue", this implies that one cannot remain unmoved by certain things.

Nonetheless, Condillac's innovation was to give prominence to the sensibility of the body. Like the "child playing" of whom Heraclitus once wrote, Condillac's hypothetical statue is not alone, it is not simply an empirical object of observation. It is Condillac, as *father* or *Other* of the statue, who effectively eroticises the awakening body of the statue. Through his writing he arouses the statue's senses, just as Rousseau's Pygmalion awakens the sensuality of his statue of Galatea. This eroticisation of the statue by Condillac through his writing prefigures Freud's description of the libidinisation of the child by the Other, such as we find in the following: "It was really the mother who by her activities over the child's bodily hygiene inevitably stimulated, and perhaps even roused for the first time, pleasurable sensations in [the girl's] genitals" (1933a, p. 120).

It is the Other, then, that eroticises the body of the child. And this erotics of the body includes this question of what is private property, specifically what are referred to, in addressing children, as their *private parts*. Thus it is also in this sense that what is deemed to be *private property* is also a question of jouissance. Jouissance, or enjoyment of the body, is a private affair.

Freud himself brought a marble statue to life, in his case the statue of Moses by Michelangelo in the church of San Pietro in Vincoli in Rome. Freud even described it, or what it had become for him, as a "love-child":

> My feeling for this piece of work is rather like that towards a love-child. For three lonely September weeks in 1913 I stood every day in the church in front of the statue, studied it, measured it, sketched it, until I captured the understanding for it which I ventured to express in the essay only anonymously. Only much later did I legitimize this non-analytical child. (cited in Jones, 1955, p. 367)

Freud was previously in Rome in September 1912, and he wrote to his wife Martha on that occasion, "I am visiting the Moses of San Pietro in Vincoli every day, and I will perhaps write something about it one day" (2002, p. 327, translated for this edition). But his love affair with the statue began well before that time. He was familiar with the plaster copy—of which he was critical—in the Vienna Academy of Art, but it was not until the occasion of his first journey to Rome in 1901 that he visited the original, writing the following laconic note in brackets on a postcard to Martha, *"Plötzlich durch Mich. verstanden"* (Jones, 1955, p. 365), which we might literally render as "Suddenly understood through Michelangelo". Freud was clearly moved by the statue, as he was by few other works of art. What matters here is less the content of his interpretation, but the fact that he felt driven from the very beginning by his own passion to understand and explain this marble statue, to put words to it. He writes of his understanding, like Condillac, as something emanating from the statue itself: "The stone image became more and more transfixed, an almost oppressively solemn calm emanated from it, and I was obliged to realize that something was represented here that could stay without change; that this Moses would remain sitting like this in his wrath for ever" (1914b, pp. 220–221).

Through his love of this work as well as the time he spent in its presence, Freud brought it to life. He spoke of it to Ernest Jones and others; he read everything he could find on the topic, and finally wrote his paper, "The Moses of Michelangelo", which was published in 1914. In this paper he describes the passions, and even the physical movements of Moses, which preceded the very moment in which he was sculpted by Michelangelo. Freud had continued to visit and spend time in the presence of the statue until it spoke to him. To use an expression in English, we could say that Freud really did get blood out of a stone. It is striking, though, that he initially had his paper published anonymously. Among other reasons, he cited the "shame at the evident amateurishness of the essay" (Jones, 1955, p. 366), but we might suspect that the reluctance to acknowledge his authorship was also due to shame and embarrassment regarding the disclosure of the passion through which this illegitimate "love-child" was conceived.

The conception of sensation

From Freud's efforts to apprehend the statue, we can propose that beyond whatever sentiment that the body of a statue or a living being might evoke, there is something that escapes our grasp, a missed encounter that Freud worked hard to circumscribe over his many years of visits to the statue of Moses. He endeavoured to put into words what he experienced when confronted by the statue, but even so, there is something unconvincing about his account. It is also this that was part of his embarrassment: the fact that not all could be revealed. In this love-child of Freud's, there was also an embarrassing *supplement* that could not be accounted for. It is this supplement or excess that marks the sensual and distinguishes it from the domesticated form of the sensible.

Condillac relegates this excess to the field of nature of which nothing more can be said. Such a notion of nature is beyond the grasp of a developmental, and thus historical, apprehension of the child. An orderly developmental and historical approach, like Condillac's, endeavours to categorise and order experiences. Such privileging of the senses, thought, and reason, over sensuality, is precisely the mode of the obsessional. Contemporary clinical practice with children also proposes a putative organic aetiology for problems that are presented as a difficulty of one or other of the senses. Hence in contemporary practice, diagnoses such as *central auditory processing disorder, sensory integration disorder, dyspraxia* or *developmental coordination disorder*, and so on, are made. Such *disorders* are perceived as a disturbance to the supposedly orderly and harmonious development that is expected in the child. The emphasis is clearly that there should be a well-processed integration, or Oneness of experience, an experience that is, however, inevitably fractured. Another contemporary modality of clinical practice is to privilege affects over the subject's speech. However, moving in the opposite direction to Condillac, it is precisely through speech, through the subject's words, that there lies the possibility of apprehending a little of the elusive sensuality of the body.

But Condillac's statue is not yet a sexual being. The developmental approach is indeed a continuation of Condillac's work, a type of obsessionalisation of experience in which the sensual is categorised into senses, and then converted into thought, which then remains cut off from the underlying sensuality that gave rise to it. There is a corresponding rendering into ages and stages. The apogee of this type of approach in psychoanalysis is Anna Freud's *Normality and Pathology in Childhood* (1965), in which there is multiplication of the categorisation of the child's development into a myriad of ages and stages that are characterised as *developmental lines*.

But to reinvoke the sensual is to underline the fact that the senses, and their corresponding reason and thought, are inadequate to account for the experience of the subject, and of course, for the symptom. The sensual describes what escapes from this account of the subject: that which ultimately cannot be accounted for. This is something that was missing in Condillac's account and absent in discourse generally until Freud first articulated the importance of the sexual. The sensual, or the sexual, lends itself to repression. Freud, though, allowed himself to be visited upon by the sensual, just as he also did not exclude it in his patients, young or old.

We can posit from this that it is specifically the manner in which we conceive of sensation, which determines our conception of the child.

CHAPTER TEN

A new discourse: the child as sexual subject

Up to this point, we have outlined what can be described as the birth of the child as subject. To some extent this has coincided with the emergence of a modern notion of the subject that has occurred since the twilight of the Middle Ages. Nonetheless, what is striking in the elaboration of this notion, which has been described as a *sentiment of the child*, is that such a conception is contingent upon the expurgation of any reference to sex and death in the discourses concerning the child. The contemporary notions—or, we might say, doctrines—that underwrite the various developmental and pedagogical approaches to the child, continue to view the child in the framework of a continuous development, reminiscent of the nineteenth-century ideal of progress which continues to shape our thinking in the twenty-first century. Thus the accidents of history, as Freud called them, are perceived as deviations from normative development and are to be corrected. This is what we have described as, literally, an *ortho-paedic* approach to childhood.

Infanticide itself has been repressed since the decline of the Middle Ages during which infant death, intentional or otherwise, was a fact of everyday life. In our modern conception, every child—and according to many, every foetus—has a right to life. If a foetus or infant dies, then blame is sought elsewhere, for instance in the blame of the obstetrician.

Similarly, when a child presents with sexual symptoms—or symptoms that evoke sex in the mind of the clinician—an external cause of sexuality is often sought through cries of sexual abuse. We have also evoked the way in which the sensuality and erotics of the child's body have been evicted from the clinical arena in favour of senses and affects. In these and many other ways, sex and death are posited as factors external to the child rather than something that is carried by, and confronted by, each subject. We can take a step further and say that to be a subject is to be subjected to sex and death. The question clinically is how this state of subjection might be appropriated by each child as a subject.

This chapter will endeavour to directly address these questions. To approach the way in which one might conceive of a child, it is necessary to raise the veil on sex and death in childhood. After all, the prevalent notion is that true subjects are *adults only*. The processes of development, upbringing, and education are designed to make of the child, or minor, a fully fledged adult, or major. To speak of the child as subject, we must bring forth what Philippe Ariès refers to as the silent history of the child. This will be addressed by first examining Michel Foucault's theses regarding the manner in which sexuality came into discourse in his *History of Sexuality*. The evolution described by Foucault in some ways paved the way for Freud's radical recognition of the child as a sexual subject. We will examine Freud's unveiling of infantile sexuality, as well as Lacan's contribution to—and extension of—Freud's discovery. Lacan posited that Freud created a new discourse, that of psychoanalysis. This is exactly what we put forward earlier, by reference to Michel Foucault's notion of a new *episteme*: Freud produced an epistemological rupture in discourse, through his discovery of the unconscious and recognition of infantile sexuality.

Foucault and the sex of the child

There is a myth that prevails, according to Michel Foucault, that prior to our modern era, sexual matters were dominated by a Victorian prudishness, or propriety, commonly considered to extend further back into history than the Victorian era. Against this view, he put forward testimony to the fact that at the beginning of the seventeenth century, a certain frankness was still common in regard to sexual practices.

Furthermore, Foucault's research indicates that codes were quite lax regarding the regulation of what was considered coarse, the obscene, and the indecent. There prevailed a tolerant familiarity in regard to what was regarded to be illicit. He also argues, as does Ariès, that there was far less segregation of ages and thus less differentiation of children from adults: "It was a time of direct gestures, shameless discourse, and open transgressions, when anatomies were shown and intermingled at will, and knowing children hung about amid the laughter of adults: it was a period when bodies 'made a display of themselves'" (1976, p. 3).

Such a glorious time of shameless sexuality smacks to us, from another angle, of an ideal of sexual liberation that is propagated by Foucault. But Lacan asserts that truth can only be half-said. So if the laughter of this display of bodies strikes us, in part, as a risible illusion, it also conveys a half-truth that is worth pursuing.

Foucault argues that in the period succeeding the Middle Ages, sexuality had moved out of open spaces and was carefully confined within the home where it came under the aegis of the modern notion of the family and its reproductive ends. Interestingly, this argument accords with the architectural evolution that Ariès also describes from the open and public spaces of mediaeval society, to the private and confined abodes of the modern family. And, as a consequence of this movement, the child was denied a sexuality: "Everybody knew, for example, that children had no sex" (p. 4). In a word, a regime that Foucault refers to as *repression* came into play. He puts forward that it had the following characteristics that repressed sex: it operated as a sentence for sex to disappear, as an injunction to silence it, as an affirmation of its non-existence, and an admission that there was nothing to see, to know, or to say about things sexual. Henceforth sex was restricted to certain circumscribed and clandestine locations such as the brothel and the mental asylum.

By the same movement, according to Foucault, the effect of this repression was to have "surreptitiously transferred the pleasures that are unspoken into the order of things that are counted" (p. 4). Here we can discern the beginnings of the scientific approach that endeavours to appropriate a phenomenon by first describing and categorising it—in an approach utilises the methodology first introduced by Linnaeus' botany—then counting and measuring it. This is the other side of Foucault's hypothesis: from the very repression of sexual practices, broadly speaking, there arose a discourse about sex, a particular mode of speaking of it. From this discourse there ultimately arose a particular modality of knowledge about sex. For Foucault, the object of this knowledge (*savoir*) was to "define the regime of power-knowledge-pleasure that sustains the discourse on human sexuality in our part of the world" (p. 11).

In his thesis, we can recognise Foucault's discussions of the manner in which a new gaze upon different aspects of our civilisation has led to a different type of knowledge, and ultimately, to the structuring of society in the modern era. Thus it also corresponds to the categorisation and medicalisation of the mad (*Madness and Civilization*, 1961), the development of medicine itself in the new gaze of the doctor upon the patient (*The Birth of the Clinic*, 1963), as well as the circumscribing and confinement of the criminal (*Discipline and Punish*, 1975). Foucault's theses are that this new modality of apprehending things led to the development of new discourses—"a veritable discursive explosion" (1976, p. 17), as he refers to it—that effected an upheaval in the practices of different fields, and in society at large.

Foucault puts forward that there is something specific in the sexual field that makes sex, and its effects, not as easily decipherable as other aspects of human existence. We could add, from psychoanalysis, that sex is structurally what is ultimately impossible to decipher. For Foucault, it is in the very nature of the mode of power that operates in our societies to be repressive. Such power is especially careful in repressing energies, pleasures, and modes of behaviour it finds useless and irregular. He argues that we should not be surprised if "the effects of liberation vis-à-vis this repressive power are so slow to manifest themselves" (p. 9). This is because, in his opinion, the effort to speak of sex and to accept it in its reality is so alien that it is likely to make little headway for some time. Perhaps we might not share Foucault's optimism that this can change at all, but rather, in this *repression*, we might discern a structural inability to speak of sex, even if at the same time we might be able to imagine it and have some words to connote it. In other words, for us there is a side to sex that is fundamentally unpronounceable and unspeakable. Here we mark sex, as Freud did, as being ultimately outside language.

Even if we have the impression, today, that we exercise much greater sexual freedom than in times past, speaking about sex nonetheless remains imbued with a type of taboo. To speak about sex is always to commit a type of transgression (p. 6). Sex can generally only be referred to obliquely, by an aside or a dirty joke for instance. We remain surprised when esteemed colleagues are found to be transgressing the bounds of decency or of professional ethics. Certain sexual activities are confined to circumscribed parts of the city, or relegated to XXX boutiques, or their products are delivered in plain brown paper wrapping. Sex tourism is also a booming industry, even if it remains rather covert. Foucault notes that alongside the repression of sex, there is a parallel discourse that promotes a longing for the garden of earthly delights, that in the imagined overcoming of the repression there exists the promise of a new day of sexual happiness.

Commerce, though, has no difficulty in exploiting this aspect of our society that remains under the wraps of the prevailing discourse. For Foucault the promise of the sexual liberation to come is perhaps what explains the "market value" (p. 7) of sex. This tendency, taken to an extreme, was vividly illustrated in the recent novel *Platform* (2001), by Michel Houellebecq, in which the generalisation and inundation of sexual commerce and tourism led to its own inevitable impasse and disastrous consequences. Thus sex, as a trauma that irrupts into the existence of each subject, remains something that exceeds, and indeed overflows, our imagined sexual liberation.

This illusion of sexual liberation is of course completely consistent with a certain medical sexual hygiene in which sexuality is dealt with in a scientific way by medicine: billboards can announce the preventive measures required to counteract the spread of AIDS and other sexually transmitted diseases, and condom dispensing machines can be found in any public toilet, and even on street corners in some countries. Foucault asserts that medicine made a forceful entry into the pleasures of the couple and created a pathology of what it considered to be incomplete sexual practices, that is, those not destined for the supposedly natural end of reproduction. It incorporated such pleasures "into notions of 'development' and instinctual 'disturbances'; and it undertook to manage them" (p. 41). In this we can hear the establishment of norms, including those of development, and the classification of deviations from such norms which are considered as *disorders* in our diagnostic manuals. Such notions today pervade the field of child psychology, psychiatry, and pedagogy, as well as being taken up by the law. Foucault spells this out in his own way:

> ... from childhood to old age, a norm of sexual development was
> defined and all the possible deviations were carefully described;

pedagogical controls and medical treatments were organized; around the least fantasies, moralists, but especially doctors, brandished the whole emphatic vocabulary of abomination. (p. 36)

Psychoanalysis of the child, after Freud, has also been subject to these very same normalising and pathologising tendencies. The discursive effects upon sex also pervade the manner in which names that refer to sexual anatomy—in English, but also in other European languages— have been lent Latin terms. Terms such as *penis, vagina, scrotum, vulva, testicles, uterus,* etc., afford a safe distance away from more immediate terms derived from Anglo-Saxon that have long been relegated to the obscene. We have already noted the way in which psychoanalysis was also sanitised by its translation, in the *Standard Edition*, into Latinised terms that effected a distance from the immediacy of Freud's language, "ego" for *Ich* (I), "psychic apparatus" for *Seele* (soul), and so on. It is precisely from this process that we endeavour to rescue the psychoanalysis of the child. Even when we hear the term *psychoanalysis of children*, we cannot fail to hear in this plural, a generalising and thus normalising tendency.

But in *The History of Sexuality*, Foucault specifically describes a mutation in the way that the child was viewed and treated. He puts forward that repression altered the relation of parents to their children, introducing, if not a complete silence regarding sexual matters, at least an arena of tact and discretion: "It is true that a longstanding 'freedom' of language between children and adults, or pupils and teachers, may have disappeared" (p. 27). This, once again, produced changes reflected in architecture, such as the division within schools and other institutions in terms of ages, stages, and sexes. This was tacit recognition, in its very suppression, that the sexuality of children did indeed exist and was in fact a public problem that had to be controlled. The child's sex was the object of the attentions of adults, in which Foucault describes the limited discourse on sex as a "discursive orthopaedics" (p. 29).

For Foucault, a type of perverse economy developed in which the transformation of sex into discourse became an attempt to expel from reality the forms of sexuality that were not amenable to the ends of reproduction. In this way, the sexuality of children was seen as one of the panoply of perversions that were contrary to nature. The manifestations of sex in children became unwanted intrusions that needed to be forcefully prevented, treated, and punished: "Educators and doctors combatted children's onanism like an epidemic that needed to be eradicated" (p. 42).

The suppression of childhood masturbation was part of a wider clampdown on sexuality. In her recent history of perversion, Élisabeth Roudinesco, in echoing Foucault, comments that: "It was … the hysterical woman, together with the homosexual man and the masturbating child who became the support for all sorts of fantasies centred on the fear that the family and the procreative order might be perverted" (2007, p. 69). We can add, strictly speaking, that such a societal negation of infantile sexuality is itself a perverse tendency. This tendency can also be discerned in the way in which the child is still perceived in the fetishised manner that Freud referred to as His Majesty the Baby. The child, in this manner, is idealised and presented hygienically as an innocent creature, stripped of his or her sexuality.

This is what Foucault refers to as an "extortion of truth" (1976, p. 97) which appears historically in specific places, in particular, in relation to the child's body. Initially this took the form of the sexuality of the child's body being problematised in the relationship between the doctor and the parents and educators, in the form of advice, recommendations, and warnings of future dangers. Ultimately, however, it was in the relationship of the psychiatrist to the child that the sexuality of the adults themselves was called into question. What remains in question, though, is the manner in which the sexuality of the parents or carers is deployed in relation to the child.

Foucault states that such relations of power-knowledge are not static forms but rather "matrices of transformations" (p. 99). Such matrices of transformations evoke for us the question of the *transformational formula* which earlier we linked to the fantasm. The question of how a particular child is viewed and treated is intimately tied to the question of the fantasm: that of the parent or educator in question. Such a fantasm is inevitably connected to the dominant discourses, as we have proposed here. Clinically, however, from psychoanalysis, we can only take sexuality—mediated through the fantasm—in the singularity of each one: in this case, that of each parent or each carer of the child.

Freud and infantile sexuality

Until the advent of Freud's new formulation, sexuality in children was perceived as an unwelcome intrusion that disturbed the prevailing public morality, as well as distorting the ideal of an orderly notion of child development. This is how Robert Lévy described Freud's recognition of infantile sexuality:

> Effectively, we had to wait for Freud so that psychoanalysis, via the dimension of infantile sexuality, could give recognition to the child as having his own existence by attributing a sexuality to him. Oddly, after the child had been denied a place in the society of the beginning of the twentieth century according to the equation: no sexuality/no subject, Freud, by lifting the fundamental repression on the child's sexuality, allowed the child to finally be recognised as subject. (2008, p. 21)

Much space has been devoted here to the question of the emergence of the child as subject in the modern era. It should be specified that what is in question, with Freud, is no longer the birth of the subject, but the recognition of the child as sexual subject. Through Michel Foucault, we can say that this recognition was, paradoxically, delayed by the very repression through which the child as subject was born. That is to say, the modern notion of the child has come about through the very repression of both sex and death in regard to the child and childhood. This notion of the child, which continues to prevail to this day, is a fetishised one that denies the child his sexuality. Such a notion was articulated by Freud in the following manner in *The Interpretation of Dreams*: "We think highly of the happiness of childhood because it is still innocent of sexual desires" (1900a, p. 130). Therefore, through Freud's recognition precisely of what had been repressed, in one movement he testified to the existence of infantile sexuality, as well as to that of the unconscious subject in the child. It is here that we can locate a radical shift in the history of childhood: with psychoanalysis, childhood lost its innocence.

In *The History of Sexuality*, Foucault notes that, "Until Freud at least, the discourse on sex—the discourse of scholars and theoreticians— never ceased to hide the thing it was speaking about" (1976, p. 53). The discourse regarding sex itself, not so different to what persists to this day, was part and parcel of its repression. It was precisely this prevailing academic discourse regarding sex that Freud dealt with in his *Three Essays on the Theory of Sexuality*. It was here Freud most emphatically elaborated his proposition that the child was a sexual being. But in doing so, he had to address the medicalised manner in which sexuality had been described at the end of the nineteenth century, and in particular the description of the sexual perversions as deviations from a supposed normality.

Hence from the very beginning of the *Three Essays on the Theory of Sexuality*, before introducing the topic of infantile sexuality, Freud examined the findings of the researchers of sexuality of the late nineteenth and early twentieth centuries. Thus he looked at the studies of Krafft-Ebbing, and Havelock Ellis, as well as others who are less well known today. In Freud's review of the literature of the time, he comes to the conclusion that "Not a single author has clearly recognised the regular existence of a sexual instinct [drive] in childhood" (1905d, p. 173). On the contrary, where there are occasional remarks regarding the supposedly precocious sexual activity in young children, these are always quoted as exceptional events and instances of depravity that are attributed to degeneracy.

Freud also needed to address the theories of degeneracy that were prominent in the nineteenth century and still influential at the time that he was writing. Specifically he gives mention to Magnan, and was obliged to argue that the notion of perversion, of which he wrote explicitly in the first of the *Essays*, needed to be separated out from degeneracy. One difficulty with the diagnosis of degeneracy, Freud argued—like today when troubles are attributed to *genetics* or a *chemical imbalance in the brain*—is that of being considered an innate quality. Such an attribution leads to a purely biological formulation which generally remains mysterious. This then leads, either to therapeutic nihilism, or to the administration of more and more medications, or in Freud's time, more physical treatments and recommendations. These sorts of attributions have the other effect of making the clinical history, and the accidents of history of which Freud spoke, irrelevant.

Freud took this much further, arguing that perversion must not be separated out into a pathological category, nor be allocated a putative biological or degenerate aetiology. Rather, he proposes that, "A certain degree of fetishism is … habitually present in normal love" (p. 154). This is a massive shift in thought whereby Freud took perversion out of its habitual confinement in the prison or mental asylum, to recognise its place in the structure of each subject. Using a certain degree of irony, he uses the terms of the nineteenth-century psychiatrists to agree that there is "something innate lying behind the perversions but that it is something innate in *everyone*" (p. 171). And rather than considering the child to be innocent, he proposed tracing this perversion back specifically to the sexual life of the child.

Freud recognised that each child, under the influence of seduction, could become polymorphously perverse and capable of being led into all types of sexual irregularities. However, once again he followed the logical implications and proposed that the disposition to perversion was "a general and fundamental human characteristic" (p. 191). For Freud this did not mean that all humans were perverts, phenomenologically speaking. Freud was referring to *perverse*, "in the widest sense of the word" such that the perverse tendency "could be expressed directly in phantasy and action" (p. 165). In this way Freud effectively introduced the finding that phantasy, the forerunner of Lacan's notion of the *fantasm*, is inherently perverse. Consequently, Freud is able to say that "neuroses are, so to say, the negative of perversions" (p. 165), in the sense that in neurotics, such perverse tendencies are encountered in the unconscious phantasy.

Interestingly, from here he is able to effectively describe the nature of the three fundamental psychoanalytic structures, derived from the three major categories of diagnosis for traditional psychiatry, structures upon which Lacan later elaborated. Freud writes in a footnote:

> The contents of the clearly conscious phantasies of perverts (which in favourable circumstances can be transformed into manifest behaviour), of the delusional fears of paranoics (which are projected in a hostile sense on to other people) and of the unconscious phantasies of hysterics (which psycho-analysis reveals behind their symptoms)—all of these coincide with one another even down to their details. (pp. 165–166)

Thus perversion in the pervert is enacted in manifest behaviour, that of the psychotic ("paranoics") is perceived as deriving from others in the outside world, and that of the neurotic ("hysterics") is repressed and manifested as his neurotic symptoms. Of course Freud later blurred, and effectively removed, the distinction between what he called neurotic and what he referred to as normal, leading to the conclusion, taken up by Lacan, that each of us pertains to one or more of the psychopathological structures. In this way, for psychoanalysis, the notion of *normal* was abolished.

Through the articulation of these structures in relation to phantasy, Freud located the trauma of sex as something that is mediated by the phantasy. Not only is the phantasy located differently for the subject according to the psychopathological structure in which the subject partakes, but it is different and particular to each subject. Sex, for Freud, is no longer the external trauma that is experienced by a child as articulated in his earlier seduction hypothesis, but rather, it is something innate to each one of us, in so far as each one of us experiences ourselves as being subject to sex.

The polymorphously perverse structure of the child allows, not simply some potential deviation, but rather for different sides of this perversity to be deployed in each subject in what Freud called the pregenital organisations. We insist that this must be read literally as "organisations", that is, a certain structure of each subject that is put in place from the polymorphous perversity. Lacan would later come to elaborate upon each element of this structure, not as a developmental phase or the manifestation of a partial drive, but rather as the subject's response to the partial objects: the oral, the anal, the scopic, and the invocatory (that pertaining to the voice) objects.

From an even earlier period in Freud's writings, specifically in a letter to Fliess of 31 May 1987, we find a passage that prefigures his much later works concerning the subject in relation to society, such as *Civilization and its Discontents, The Future of an Illusion, Moses and Monotheism,* etc. In regard to this same question of perversion, Freud proposes that the subject, to become a member of society, must forgo some part of his or her sexual perversity. He describes this in regard to what is considered to be *holy*:

> "Holy" is something based on the fact that human beings, for the benefit of the larger community, have sacrificed a portion of their sexual liberty and their liberty to indulge in perversions. The horror of incest (something impious) is based on the fact that, as a result of communal sexual life (even in childhood), the members of a family remain together permanently and become incapable of joining with strangers. Thus incest is antisocial—civilization consists in this progressive renunciation. (Masson, 1985, p. 252)

Freud articulates that, structurally speaking, for the subject in relation to society, or rather, the subject in relation to the Other, there is something missing: something is renounced. There remains a gap, which is precisely where we have located the *infantile*. This "holy" is thus also *holey*: it pertains to the hole in the history by virtue of which the subject gives testimony to the fact that there is always a piece missing, an enigma remains. This is articulated in this passage both as the incest taboo, as well as the question of renunciation by which there is always some part of jouissance that remains out of reach. The incest taboo is the piece missing in regard to the family—particularly in regard to the mother—and its renunciation is the equivalent piece that must be relinquished in relation to society.

It is in this later paper from 1927, *The Future of an Illusion*, that Freud speaks of another aspect of the child, in response to his question, "In what does the peculiar value of religious ideas lie?" (1927c, p. 15). It is worth noting that, for Freud, one aspect of the value of religious ideas is to protect us against "the painful riddle of death" (p. 16). Religious ideas are a type of fetishistic—and thus perverse—object, that endeavour to fill in for what is missing and unable to be explained.

Freud proposes that this is a central aspect of what he refers to as "our weakness and helplessness [*Hilflosigkeit*], which we thought to escape through the work of civilization" (p. 16). For Freud, this helplessness, this *Hilflosigkeit*, has an infantile prototype, that of the child in relation to his parents. He contends that "[M]an's helplessness remains and along with it his longing for his father, and the gods" (pp. 17–18). This longing defines a lack for the subject, a lack that is attributed to childhood, the lack that we have designated as the *infantile*. So the value of religious ideas, the *holy*, is once again to fill the void that is left by the *holey*, by the infantile.

Lacan and the fantasm

When Freud writes that neuroses are, so to say, the negative of perversions, it is striking that this assertion is underwritten by the "so to say", or *so to speak*. From Freud's early theorisation, the unconscious—including that of the child—was grasped by elaborations upon acts of speech. Even in the case of a child that he had published in 1909, that of little Hans, despite his being a preschool child, the analysis was essentially conducted through speech. Freud's early works regarding the unconscious were also works that analysed acts of speech. Lacan gave prominence to these works, particularly *The Interpretation of Dreams* (Freud, 1900a), *Jokes and Their Relation to the Unconscious* (Freud, 1905c), and *The Psychopathology of Everyday Life* (Freud, 1901b). Moreover, the family romance, the infantile sexual theories, and even the incest taboo, are ultimately structures that are articulated through speech. In particular, *The Psychopathology of Everyday Life* makes specific reference to the repression of sexuality and death.

Lacan took up the consequences of the fact that the unconscious, as unknown knowledge or *unbeknownst*, was manifested through such acts of speech, including the recounting of dreams, bungled actions, and other formations of the unconscious. Lacan elaborated his notion of the unconscious through the structural linguistics of Ferdinand de Saussure. This he did in such papers as "The Function and Field of Speech and Language in Psychoanalysis" (1966a) and "The Instance of the Letter in the Unconscious, or Reason since Freud" (1966b). Through this, Lacan enunciated his famous formula that *the unconscious is structured as a language*. But rather than follow Freud in saying that this discovery of the unconscious was a "revolution" as Freud says in "The Resistances to Psycho-analysis" (1925e), Lacan comes to say that it was a "subversion" in "the function, in the structure of knowledge" (1971–1972, p. 29). And for Lacan, this new status of knowledge is what has brought about a new discourse: the discourse of psychoanalysis.

We have remarked upon Freud's comment that it has automatically happened that child-analysis has become the domain of women analysts. The "automatically" of such an insistence—which remains unexplained—is the insistence of the signifier, an insistence to which Lacan alludes with the word "instance" (p. 31) in the title of his paper, "The Instance of the Letter in the Unconscious since Freud". This insistence, in its repetition, is that of the signifier, to which Lacan refers in his use of the Greek term *automaton*. It is this *automaton*, Lacan proposes, "by which we see ourselves governed by the pleasure principle" (1964, p. 54). But he goes on to note that Freud's research is in what lies beyond the pleasure principle, that is, the real, which Lacan designates here by use of the ancient Greek term *tuché*. This term conveys the notion that what we deal with in an analysis is something that occurs, "*as if by chance*" (p. 54), something that presents itself as a hitch or an obstacle to the analysis. The subject experiences it as being outside his control, and thus effectively being imposed upon him.

Lacan proposes here that Freud's true preoccupation in the function of phantasy, upon which we have been elaborating in this chapter, is precisely "the real, that lies behind the phantasy" (1964, p. 54). It is in the beyond of the pleasure principle, to refer to Freud's paper of that name, that Lacan comes to designate what he refers to as *jouissance*.

And jouissance is effectively always that of the body. Lacan notes that, "In order to enjoy [*jouir*], a body is needed" (1971–1972, p. 33). For this very reason, Lacan emphasised little Hans' enjoyment or jouissance of his body, dedicating a year of his seminar, early in his teaching, to the study of this case. There, Lacan remarks that he had noted that "[T]he phallus intervenes in another form—I am speaking of masturbation. It's always the same object, but it is presented in a quite different form due to the integration of sensations tied, at the very least, to turgescence, and, quite possibly, to something that could be qualified as orgasm" (1956–1957, p. 259).

But if there is a jouissance here, an enjoyment or suffering of the body, little Hans is not able to give an account of it, and therein resides his anguish. Lacan, in the "Geneva Lecture on the Symptom", points out that this enjoyment is not at all *auto-erotic*, in the sense that this experience for Hans is something that is experienced as imposed upon him, as a type of trauma. It is in so far as it is experienced as Other, that Hans, as Lacan says, "incarnates it in the most external of all objects, namely in this horse that paws the ground, that kicks, rolls over and falls to the ground" (1985, p. 15). Lacan goes on to say that:

> This horse that comes and goes, that has a certain way of draw-ing the cart along the quay, is for him the most exemplary thing of everything he is caught up in, but that he understands absolutely nothing of, owing to the fact, to be sure, that he has a certain type of mother and a certain type of father. His symptom is the expression, the meaning of this rejection. (p. 15)

So for little Hans this jouissance of the body is an impossible jouissance, one that is impossible to symbolise, to articulate, and which is the source of his anguish. Lacan in fact adds that: "The enjoyment [*jouissance*] that has resulted from this *Wiwimacher* [widdler] is alien to him—so much so that it is at the root of his phobia" (p. 16).

So it is precisely the dimension of jouissance, the enjoyment or suf-fering of the body, to which Lacan refers in his very condensed "Note on the Child" (1986b). Here he comments upon the manner in which a child is presented by the parents. As we have noted, he proposes there that the child's symptom is in a position of answering to what is sympto-matic in the family structure. Lacan is specifying the place that the child takes up for the parent, in particular in relation to the jouissance of the mother, and mediated by the function of the father. Should the media-tion of such a paternal function be absent, Lacan remarks, this leaves the child open to every kind of fantasmatic capture. Lacan proposes that in this position the child realises the object *a* in the mother's fantasm, and here has no other function than that of revealing the truth of this object.

This position, logically speaking, is the a priori position from which any child begins. Lacan refers here to the three psychopathological structures utilised by Freud. He notes that the child, in this position, "saturates the mode of lack in which (the mother's) desire is specified, whatever it's [*sic*] special structure—neurotic, perverse or psychotic" (p. 7). In regard to these three structures, he states that it is the somatic symptom—of the child—that gives the greatest possible guarantee of misrecognition (*méconnaissance*). The somatic symptom "may testify to guilt, serve as a fetish, or incarnate a primordial refusal" (p. 7), once again referring to the place that the child occupies for the Other, contingent upon the psychopathological structure of the mother.

To return for a moment to the "Geneva Lecture on the Symptom", let us consider the place of the child in relation to the parents. Lacan puts forward that parents mould the child by "the way in which a mode of speaking has been instilled in him", which, he continues, "can only bear the mark of the mode in which his parents have accepted him" (1985, p. 13). Here we might recognise the way in which the child becomes caught up in the mode of speech of each of the parents. It is by these means that the child enters discourse through a very specific entry point, that of the way in which the mother and the father desired the child in reference to the fantasm of each, to the modes of jouissance of each.

By this means, each child is conceived in a very particular relation to the Other, to Otherness, mediated through the speech of each of the parents. It is this particular "so to speak" into which the child is born and which is conveyed to him through the acts of speech of the mother and father. If we refer here to the discourses regarding the child, the mode of transmission of such discourses is, in the first instance, through the discourses of the mother and father, not the discourses they possess, but rather the discourses by which they themselves are possessed.

Raising children: an impossible profession

In "Analysis Terminable and Interminable", Freud put forward that there are three impossible professions: analysing, educating, and governing. He described each of these professions as having exacting demands upon its practitioners, and in which one can be sure in advance of achieving unsatisfying results. As we have noted, the word that he used for *educating* was *das Erziehen*, which can indeed be translated as education, but also encompasses the bringing up, or raising, of children.

Freud's insistence on "professions", though, is close to the insistence in contemporary clinical circles upon *tasks*. Such an insistence even construes the place of the mother and the father as *parenting tasks*. However, if we are to take Freud's proposition seriously, the task that each and every mother and father faces, in raising his or her child, is an impossible one. It is impossible to get it right, it is impossible to be the perfect parent or to raise the perfect child. Thus each parent must necessarily fail in this task. Furthermore, it is essential that the parent fails in this task for the child to be able to grow up. To put this in another way, if we are to speak of *tasks*, it is the task of the parent to fail the child, to be *not all* for the child. This of course does not prevent each generation from imagining that it can do a better job than the previous one, and endeavour to correct the perceived errors of its forefathers.

Lacan made these three impossible professions into his four discourses, by adding a fourth "impossible profession": that of the hysteric (1970). In changing the emphasis of Freud's impossible professions in this way, Lacan moved away from Freud's notions of professions, towards his concept of discourse. It is discourse then that is able to specify the logic that underpins the manner in which the modalities of the subject are determined. Lacan made Freud's impossible profession of educating or raising children into the discourse of the university. We might also locate the task of raising children in the discourse of the master, in so far as the master, derived from the Latin *magister*, also refers to the teacher or schoolmaster. In different moments, the parent additionally finds him- or herself within the discourse of the hysteric. What is new in Freud's invention of the unconscious, according to Lacan, is the discourse of the analyst. Lacan proposed that it is this discourse that specifies the very nature of the speaking being. Historically speaking, it is this last discourse that comes to complete the round of four discourses, thereby allowing the movement that makes possible a change of discourse, that is, a movement between the different discourses. Christian Fierens proposes that "Analysis is the science of these changes of discourse" (2002, p. 49). Such a movement also signifies that we may be able to locate the place that the child occupies within discourse, and therefore the change of place that is possible.

There is a movement from the emphasis that Freud places upon tasks and professions towards, with Lacan, the writing of the discourses. Thus, in the movement from Freud to Lacan we have been able to articulate the discourses that have historically determined both our notion of childhood, as well as the singular history of each and every child. If discourse operates within society, in part, by specifying the place of the Other, it is in so far as it also operates for the singular subject. Here we can endeavour to say more specifically what we are referring to as *discourse* in relation to the subject. Discourse, then, is what is able to specify—in being able to be written—the modalities of enjoyment, or jouissance, in which the particular subject is caught. The child—and perhaps this is a definition of a child—is determined and entrapped within the modalities of enjoyment of the mother and father, mediated, as we have seen, by their fantasms. To discover a means by which he or she is no longer subject to the fixity of the modalities of enjoyment through which he or she was determined, is the path to no longer remaining in the place of the child, to no longer be a minor.

Through our examination of the thesis of Philippe Ariès, in the decline of the Middle Ages there arose a new sentiment of the child, a sentiment in which the young child was depicted as gracious, tender, and naive. This new sentiment of the child—or new sentimentality regarding childhood—was elaborated upon by Jean-Jacques Rousseau in his work *Émile* through which the notion of childhood became glorified and the child transformed into a being close to nature, akin to the eighteenth-century ideal of the noble savage. Such discourses have fetishised the child by stripping him of his relation to sexuality and death. We can speak of a fetishisation in so far as the castration of the child—precisely his intimate relation to sexuality and death—becomes obscured and in its place is erected a nominally innocent and idealised image of childhood. Today it is only the adult, the major, who has the right to sexuality and death which have become defined as *adults only*, or X-rated. But even then, sexuality and death are restricted to certain codified representations, and confined to certain locations and age groups. Sexuality and death remain an *x*: an unknown or enigma.

In this way we can see that our modern notion of childhood has also been constructed as a period of waiting and a preparation for the adult form of life, or rather, an adult form of suffering from which we believe the child should be spared. Literally, childhood has become a type of limbo, deferring the moment at which one pays for original sin, in this case the original sin—the jouissance—of the mother and father who desired the child. With such a limbo the child is conceived of as being innocent and therefore free from sexuality, free from desire.

There is a similar position that is constructed for the subject in Michel Tournier's novel *Friday*. As we have already noted, this work is Tournier's version of Daniel Defoe's novel *Robinson Crusoe*. In the novel, Crusoe remains in limbo in so far as he is isolated from the full effects of language, and diverts his sexuality towards ends that are different to those of the neurotic. Limbo is the place reserved in Catholic doctrine for children who have died without having first been baptised. In other words, the children in limbo are those who have not yet fully attained their status as subjects.

Gilles Deleuze comments, regarding Tournier's novel, that the position that is structured for Crusoe in this account is indeed a perverse position. Deleuze poses the following question in reference to Freud: "If it is true that neurosis is the negative of perversion, would not perversion, for its part, be the *elemental* aspect of neurosis?" (1969, p. 343). Here it is not a question of whether the child is structurally perverse or not. It is rather that the child comes to occupy a perverse position for the parents, realising for them elements of each of their fantasms. In this position, the task that the child must realise for the parents is that of making good the perceived failures and shortcomings of their own childhoods, in other words, their own lost ideals. Hermine Hug-Hellmuth first pointed this out in 1921, and, for this very reason, implied that the work of the parents towards any possible psychoanalysis of a child would be marked by a mourning of that position. The fetishised position that the child has come to occupy detains him from taking up the effects of language, conveyed through the Other. For Tournier, the Other is mediated through the *others*, the others who are missing for Crusoe.

For Deleuze, the definition of Tournier's Crusoe is "the man without Others [*autrui*] on his island" (p. 344). Deleuze makes of these *others* a theoretical notion of *Others*, which Jean-Pierre Lebrun (2007, p. 383) relates to the intervention of the real father, the father incarnate to whom Lacan refers towards the end of his *Object Relation* seminar in his function of real presence: "In order that the castration complex be truthfully experienced, the real father has to truly play the game. He has to take up his function as castrating father, the father function in its concrete, empirical, and I was almost going to say, degenerate form" (1956–1957, p. 364). *The man without Others on his island* could also be a definition of a child for whom the place of Others does not function: the autistic subject. For Tournier's Crusoe, such a position leads him to turn towards ends that, to cite Deleuze, "represent a fantastic deviation from our world, under the influence of a transformed sexuality" (1969, p. 343).

The new sentiment of childhood also derived its impetus from Rousseau's proclamation that there is no original perversity in the human heart. This assertion is, at the same time, a refusal or disavowal of the original sin of the parents by virtue of which the child was engendered, the *en plus* or surplus that stains the ideal of purity of childhood. The original perversity comes to be repressed for the parents in construing the child as innocent. This perversity is enacted in the negation by society of the child's sexuality. And in Rousseau's world, in the world we have inherited, the child assumes the position of he who is expected to learn, to be taught about adult life during this period of waiting. The child then, for the adult, is the one who does not know, and who is the object of the adult's pedagogical mode of speech in which the adult teaches him what he is to be.

However, if what we refer to as the *child* is the place of he who is waiting upon the speech of the adult, the subject must emerge from this *child* at the point where the parents, once again, must necessarily fail. They necessarily fail to answer the child's questions, questions that ultimately concern the enigmas of sex and death. As Lacan said:

> The desire of the Other is apprehended by the subject in that which does not work, in the lacks in the discourse of the Other, and all the child's *whys* reveal not so much an avidity for the reason of things, as a testing of the adult, a *Why are you telling me this?*... which is the enigma of the adult's desire. (1964, p. 214)

For Ariès, the history of the child can be first grasped only by virtue of the differences from the discourses of our own time, if what we might apprehend is to be something other than an anachronism. For the child, it is only by virtue of a disparity, by a difference or distance between him and his parents—mediated by their failings and the lacks in their knowledge—that he might be able to constitute himself as subject.

PART IV

THE CHILD AND THE SUBJECT

CHAPTER ELEVEN

From the razing of the child to the advent of the subject

Maud Mannoni begins her book *The Child, His "Illness", and the Others*, in the original French version, in the following manner: "The psychoanalysis of children, is psychoanalysis" (1967b, p. 7, translated for this edition). For Mannoni there is no fundamental difference between the psychoanalysis of a child and that of an adult. Similarly, Freud commented at the end of his case history of Little Hans that strictly speaking, he learnt nothing new from that analysis, nothing that he had not already been able to discover from other patients analysed at a more advanced age. As we know, this case history arose from Freud urging his disciples to collect observations upon the sexual life of children. Freud initially posited the notion of the *infantile*, by these means, as something that might be found in a particular age or developmental stage, something that could be observed in the child. Through the analysis of this case, Freud is disabused of this notion. For psychoanalysis there can only be analysis of a subject, not of a child, adolescent, or adult. Those who, for instance, reify the specificity of so-called *play-therapy* or *play technique* in analysis are led astray by what is merely a technique, something that distracts from the fundamental method of psychoanalysis. In this work we have begun from a notion of the *infantile* as a time outside history. In this way the *infantile* functions as a structure that operates for each and every subject.

In the English translation of Mannoni's book referred to above, however, the very same first line is rendered in the following way: "The psychoanalysis of children is psychoanalysis in its purest form" (1967a, p. 3). Here, quite a different emphasis is placed upon Mannoni's statement. This "purest form" introduces some other notion of the psychoanalysis of children and implies there is something about it that is specific to, and different from, the psychoanalysis of adults. Moreover, there is something of what is called *the sentiment of childhood* itself that permeates this translation, something through which the child is pure, unadulterated, and untainted by the stench of sex and death. We could consider that this "purest form" is a familiar type of disavowal by which the child once again becomes fetishised into a perfectly wholesome and innocent creature.

This insistence upon the notion of "form" also reminds us of the way in which Lacan's "discursive formula" was trans-formed into "discursive form" in the translation, as we have previously remarked. In both of these translations we can perceive a type of reduction into a static *form*, a form which no doubt also pertains to an insistence upon the form as image. There is a privileging of form over substance, whereby a dynamic formula is replaced by an inert form. We have attempted to restore Lacan's discursive formula in this work, by reference to his notion of discourse, as well as that of the *formula*, the formula by virtue of which a formation might occur, the formation of the subject, or the formation of the analyst in psychoanalysis. This *discursive formula* has been given prominence by defining it as a structure that transforms the family myth into the individual fantasm. This fantasm is the subject's apprehension of the real, the real that underwrites the imaginary form as well as spoken language.

As we recall, Freud described a crucial moment in the itinerary of the subject when small events in the child's life, that make him feel dissatisfied, afford him provocation for beginning to criticise his parents. This is the moment, a logical moment, in which the subject is confronted by the lacks and failings of the Other, mediated through the *others* of the parents in the particular instance referred to by Freud. It is this specific moment that affords a point of formation through which the subject is able to emerge from the constraining and fixed form that we refer to as the *child*.

The de-formation from the child

The child is raised by the parents and further educated by others, an upbringing that induces certain modalities of enjoyment that are at risk of remaining static, as a fixed form. The child becomes determined by the prevailing discourses, notably the discourses of the mother and the father, through which each of their fantasms is inscribed. The parents have engendered, not only their child, but also his or her modalities of enjoyment. It is the original sin of the parents, the jouissance through which the child was engendered, that remains a type of surplus for the child. This surplus, or *en plus*, remains out of reach but at the same time determining for the child. It is the quotient of jouissance to which the child owes his existence but which risks taking on a static form, by virtue of which the child remains entrapped, or *attached*.

The discourses of each of the parents undoubtedly leave their mark upon the child. This, in part, is also the means of formation of the symptoms that bring the subject to the attention of the psychoanalyst. We have endeavoured to define discourse as the inscription of the modes of enjoyment, or jouissance, that can be effectively discerned only through speech, speech being the medium through which psychoanalysis operates. Moreover, what we have referred to as the fetishisation of the child contributes to the fixity of this position by negating the child's reference to sex and death.

But if this fetishisation of the child is a perversity that is perpetuated by our post-Enlightenment society, and mediated by each of us as parents, on the other hand it has the effect of denying the child his or her own perversity, his or her own relation to sex and death. Consequently, each child must discover his or her own *perversion*, just as little Hans did through his masturbation and whatever equivalents of orgasm he experienced. However, beyond the pleasure and pacification derived from this masturbation, Hans, like any subject, experiences something disturbing through his encounter with sex: it is something that is endured by the subject. That is, beyond the exercising of his self-stimulation, he is in turn enjoyed by sex. There is something that exceeds his so-called *self-soothing* or *affect-regulation*, as such activities are often referred to in clinical circles these days. Such terms are a further negation of the child's relation to sex in assuming that the child endeavours to return to an illusory prior harmonious state. To return to the terms of Lacan that we have already considered, there is anguish in the *tuché* that is experienced, an anguish that exceeds the *automaton* of the pacification of *self-soothing*.

Each child must discover his own *perversion*, a version of the child that is forbidden and negated by the parents. Such a perversion is a version of the surplus experienced by the child, a version of the original sin of the parents. To imagine a complete metamorphosis or transformation would be another fantasy, the fantasy of people *reinventing themselves*— as is repeated as a hollow phrase these days. But in discovering his perversion, by making it his own, the child is effecting what we can call a *de-formation* of the surplus that he has inherited through the original sin of the parents.

Such a version of the child is then the possibility of his *de-formation*, of emancipation from the self-imposed minority that Immanuel Kant attributed to his version of enlightenment. This is inevitably a lonely path for the subject, as it must by necessity occur outside any approval or validation from the Other, in particular from each of the parents. The child or adolescent at many points opposes, rejects, and rebels against the parents. While this might be a necessary preliminary step, it can only be a provisional position as it still takes its reference point in the word, or the will, of the parents. Therefore to be defiant towards the parents is only a small step from being compliant. In this position, the parents and their will become a contingency for the subject, a pretext for remaining in a fixed and static form. To remain compliant to, or defiant of, the position of the parents, is in fact to idealise this position by making sure it remains intact. This is also the position from which any subject, child or adult, may enter into analysis, that of blame of the other for one's predicament. I have proposed elsewhere, by citing Philip Larkin's now famous line, "They fuck you up, your mum and dad", that this is "the universal complaint of the neurotic, a position from which any analysis may begin" (Plastow, 2012b, pp. 75–76).

But the deformation required to accede to the place of subject is precisely the abandonment of this position in which the Other is the contingency or pretext for what is impossible to bear. Instead of idealising the position of the parents, the Other, or *Others*, the subject can deform it in order to appropriate it, to make it his own. So then, rather than finding others to be the cause of his suffering, the subject must leave a place for the impossible, for an enigma, and an absence, to remain alive. To return to the place from which we started this work, this *impossible* is also the riddle of the Sphinx: a riddle in regard to which Oedipus' developmental response of the three ages of man falls dramatically short. This shortfall is something that all developmental theories have in common in their attempt to respond to the enigma by virtue of an explanation in terms of different ages and stages. But the shortfall also leaves a leftover that remains unexplained, a surplus to the failure of the developmental explanation.

For *de-formation* to occur, the subject must destroy his reliance upon pre-formed notions of causality, and hence blame. The child's symptoms or struggles cannot be continually referred back to the parents or any others, perceived as cause of one's suffering. In this way, the place of cause must be emptied out. At the same time, however, this now empty place is the source of a surplus of jouissance, an excess that cannot be so easily grasped. This is the jouissance by virtue of which the child was conceived and from which he is excluded, but to which he nonetheless owes his existence. But if the child is able to *de-form* this jouissance he may be able to produce his or her own version, or perversion, of it. Thus he may be able to *leave* his own mark, in order to *live* his own mark. The child may become a subject by producing his own discourse, his own position in relation to jouissance.

Or, as de Lajonquière articulates in another way, the subject must conquer "a place of enunciation in his own name" (de Lajonquière, 2013, p. 152). To be a subject is to be in discourse with others, by being subjected to discourse beyond that of one's parents and teachers. In this way the child must destroy something. He must *break the mould* to come to the place of subject. Thus the subject can only arise out of destruction and not from development.

What is the place of the parents in this *de-formation*? Hermine Hug-Hellmuth proposed that from the outset, the transference of the parents is primarily negative. It is because of this that the work of the transference of the mother and father is effectively a work of mourning. It is a taking stock of the failure that is particular to each of them. To facilitate emancipation of the subject from the former position as *child*, each of the parents may give up something of their prior investment of the place that this child occupies for them. This place, for Bergès and Balbo, is effectively their wish to refind, in their child, an ideal of themselves as they imagine themselves to have been as children. For the child to de-form into a subject, such an ideal in which the child is caught must be destroyed. This is the essential task of *parenting*, if we are to take up this abusively used term. After all, *parenting* implies both an illusory oneness of the *parents*, as well as the place of the mother and father being reduced to the functionality of *tasks*. Thus the tasks of *parenting* are to be found in the very word parent: *par-ing* and *rent-ing*, that is, to produce cuts, smaller and bigger cuts, in the ideal in which the child is held captive.

Razing the child

If we have examined the question of *raising* children, from the perspective of psychoanalysis we cannot ignore its homophone, which is *razing* children, in other words, the annihilation of what we have referred to as the *child*. We have already elaborated upon the structural negation by the parents of the child in relation to sex and death. But as we have noted, for the child to truly take up a place of subject, it is necessary for his position as *child* to be razed. This question of raising children and the contiguous *razing* of them evokes Freud's paper on "Negation", and the discussion of this paper by the philosopher Jean Hyppolite included in Lacan's *Écrits*.

Hyppolite refers to a passage in Freud's paper in which Freud remarks that, "Negation is a way of taking cognizance of what is repressed; indeed it is already a lifting of the repression" (1925h, pp. 235–236). In other words, for Freud the negation of what is repressed is simultaneously an affirmation of this very same repressed material. Here the word "lifting", which we could easily replace with *raising*, translates the term that Freud uses in German, *Aufhebung*. Hyppolite comments that this is Hegel's dialectical word, a word that:

> ... means simultaneously to deny, to suppress, and to conserve, and fundamentally to lift [*soulever*]. In reality, it might be the *Aufhebung* of a stone, or equally the cancellation of my subscription to a newspaper. Freud tells us here: "negation is an *Aufhebung* of the repression, though not, of course, an acceptance of what is repressed". (1966, pp. 747–748)

This *Aufhebung*, the lifting or raising, we can also propose, is the *raising* of the child, which is simultaneously the *razing* of the child. Hyppolite goes on to refer to Hegel's master-slave dialectic, in which there is an appetite for destruction that takes hold of desire. We recall here that Hegel's master-slave dialectic is at the heart of Lacan's writing of the discourse of the master. For Hyppolite, Hegel's dialectic is conceptualised, "in a profoundly mythical rather than a psychological manner" (p. 748). Thus he reads Freud's text as affirming a "genesis, based on the destructive tendency, of the kind of negation whose true function is to engender intelligence and the very position of thought" (p. 749). In an analogous way, what we are endeavouring to assert here is that it is precisely in the razing of the notion of the *child*, that from it, the subject might be formed, or rather, de-formed.

For there to be a subject, it is not sufficient to raise a child. The same *child*, in so far as he is the expression of an ideal through the very negation of his sexuality and the kernel of his death, must also be razed. In his paper, Freud writes that, "Affirmation—as a substitute for uniting—belongs to Eros; negation—the successor to expulsion—belongs to the instinct of destruction" (1925h, p. 239). For the child, the affirmation and Eros pertain to the loving way—not exempt from the erotics of the jouissance through which the child was conceived—in which the child is *raised* by his mother and father. On the other hand, negation and expulsion, the side of the *razing* of the child, belong to the "instinct of destruction". The latter is, of course, a poor translation of the term used by Freud, *Destruktionstrieb* (p. 239), in which it is a question of the destruction *drive*, rather than any instinct.

It was Sabina Spielrein who first referred to the drive in relation to destruction, in her 1912 paper, "Destruction as the cause of coming into being". Here she posits destruction as a fundamental component of the sexual drive. She states that "death is necessary for the advent of life" (1912b, p. 166). In reference to the discussion on negation, Spielrein had already noted—in *The Interpretation of Dreams*—that "Freud has also shown that linguistics recognizes 'an antithetical sense of primal words'" (p. 173). This then explains why we overlook the death drive, which, according to Spielrein, is already existent within the sexual drive.

In *The Four Fundamental Concepts of Psychoanalysis*, Lacan recounts that, "Not so long ago, a little girl said to me sweetly that it was about time somebody began to look after her so that she might seem lovable to herself" (1964, p. 257). He goes on to speak about how this alienation of the identification in another's gaze and love—the gaze of the Other—becomes supplanted by "an identification of a strangely different kind, and which is introduced by the process of separation" (p. 257). He ties this separation of the subject, a separation from the position of the *child*—here in the form of "a little girl"—to the apprehension of the object. This object, the object *a*, is grasped at the very moment of its disappearance, when the object falls away in the logical moment of separation. This object, he says, supports the fact that through the signifier, sex and its significations are always capable of making death present. And like Spielrein, Lacan states that there is a distinction between the life drive and the death drive, which he also situates as two *aspects* of the drive, in so far as what emerges from all the sexual drives is ultimately death. Hence the destruction that is tied to the death drive, through the function of the object *a*, is precisely what raises the advent of the subject. And Lacan specifies this in the following way: "Through the function of the *objet a*, the subject separates himself off, ceases to be linked to the vacillation of being, in the sense that it forms the essence of alienation" (p. 258).

Spielrein refers both to philosophy and mythology to support her thesis. For instance, she cites Nietzsche when he writes in *Thus spake Zarathustra* that, "Man is something that must be overcome" (cited in Spielrein, 1912b, p. 176). That is, according to Spielrein, what we refer to as *man*—and here we can insert *child* in the place of *man*—serves as a bridge to the formation of Nietzsche's notion of the *Übermensch*. Spielrein's reading of the *Übermensch* in this context is a conception of the subject as the one that emerges from the act of destruction, or self-destruction—the destruction of the self, of the ego: "The procreative act per se leads to self-destruction" (p. 170).

But Nietzsche's *Übermensch* is not a superman, he is the one who allows himself, his *self*, to be overcome by the Dionysian song, that is, by jouissance. Again we find this in little Hans' experience of being subjected to sex, when he is overcome by what Lacan refers to as his turgescence, as well as some equivalent of orgasm. Such an experience of sex is, for Hans and for each and every subject, a source of distress and anguish as much as it is of enjoyment. Thus this coming into being is an experience of being subjected to sex, of jouissance, of a type of *coming*. This is also the subject's experience of the *en plus*, the surplus that cannot quite be grasped but must be harnessed in some way.

Spielrein also uses Wagner's versions of mythology to demonstrate this duality, citing both his *Siegfried* and *The Flying Dutchman*. Uncannily, Spielrein here cites the work of "Dr. Graf", in other words, Max Graf, little Hans' musicologist father, to support her reading of *Siegfried*. She concludes in the following manner: "For Wagner, death is often nothing other than the destroying components of the instinct of coming into being" (p. 178). Thus to create, for the subject to be created, requires that something—the *child*—be destroyed.

What is of most interest here is that this paper of Spielrein's was written at the very time of her endeavour to free herself from her analyst, Carl Jung, a relation, as is well known, that had become complicated by a love affair. Sabine Richebächer, in her biography of Spielrein, has the following to say: "'Destruction as the cause of coming into being' can be read like a balance-sheet, a retrospective and an attempt to comprehend and assimilate painful experiences" (2005, p. 172, translated for this edition).

It was through Spielrein's act of writing—of the "Destruction as the cause of coming into being" paper, her psychiatry thesis, as well as the writings in her personal diary and letters—that she was able to articulate and enact the end, the destruction, of her analysis, in order to accede to the position as analyst. It was by virtue of her writings, in particular that of her psychiatry thesis, that she was recognised as an analyst and accepted into the Vienna Psychoanalytic Society. Moreover, if terminating her analysis in this way allowed her to leave Jung, it also effected a separation from her own parents. Richebächer, for instance, writes the following regarding this moment:

> Sabina Spielrein decided in Zürich to remain in the enlightened and paternal Western world; she did not want to return to 'Mother Russia'. On the immigration form in Munich, like on the police records from Vienna, she filled in the category 'Religion' with 'no religion'. (p. 183)

We cannot concur with this simplistic division into the maternal homeland and the paternal West. Nonetheless, what we may take from this is the separation that Spielrein makes from her parents and from her childhood in Russia, as well as the separation from the Other of her parents' religion. They had originally sent her to Zürich when she was still a teenager for psychiatric treatment and potentially to study at university. After terminating her relationship—and hence effectively her analysis with Jung—Spielrein did not return to Russia as her parents wished. She took, on the contrary, the step of following another path, that of not returning to them, nor to her homeland, nor following their religion. The path that she chose was one that involved Vienna and Freud. Hence the question of the termination of the analysis is not just that of leaving the person of the analyst, but one in which there is a fall of the object, a conclusion that has effects on many levels.

Here we are approximating the moment of leaving behind the place as *child* and the correlative advent to the place of subject, to the end of an analysis through what Lacan designated as the *passe*. Robert Lévy similarly equates the analysis of the child's symptom to the *passe* in his work *L'Infantile en Psychanalyse*. What is interesting to consider here is that through her writing, not only does Spielrein effectively terminate her analysis with Jung, but she also grows up and leaves her parents, finishes her studies, and moves away from Zürich. Yves Lugrin has already suggested that Spielrein's writing was a new but makeshift procedure that contained a type of secret intuition regarding the *passe* that Lacan was to invent some fifty-five years later (2009). We would consider this to be a rather misplaced and anachronistic proposition that in fact distorts the originality of Spielrein's creative act. Moreover, to equate Spielrein's act to Lacan's *passe*, in its insistence on the modality of transmission through speech, overlooks the fundamental nature of writing in this conclusion of analysis, which is the essence of Spielrein's method of termination of her analysis.

Spielrein's method also evokes the importance of the scribblings and writings of children and adolescents. Through Sabina Spielrein's productions, we might give greater importance to the place of writing for each child and adolescent as an act by which he may be able to accede to the place of subject. We think of the diaries that children and adolescents often keep, diaries that are more or less private: sometimes, in a moment of crisis, they are left out for parents and others to see. Often adolescents write poems and songs—not to mention numerous unfinished stories and novels—in an effort to articulate sensations and thoughts that cannot quite be captured. And now the writings of adolescents have expanded exponentially with the advent of text messages, social-networking pages, and blogs on the internet. Such writings also include inscriptions on the body with tattoos, often undecipherable messages in foreign scripts. The writings that are private are thus also directed elsewhere—even if sometimes misdirected—to an Other, or to Others who might then intervene in relation to the subject. That is, the writings reveal a type of *ex-timacy* in the structure of the adolescent subject.

Spielrein states in her "Destruction" paper that "I have come to the conclusion that the chief characteristic of an individual is that he is 'dividual'" (1912b, p. 160). Thus in her writing, Spielrein also negates, or destroys, the common notion of the individual. She substitutes for this the notion of the "dividual", in other words, the subject as divided. To be a subject is to destroy the concept of the individual, which is an imaginary form of undivided being, the common idea derived from the philosophical tradition of a self-reflexive subject who is always identical to himself. The linguist Ferdinand de Saussure was also critical of this traditional notion of subject as ego, giving the following critique: "Is it not ridiculous and even intolerable to be constantly enclosed in one's particular ego [*moi*] and subjected to this very little me [*moi*]?" (cited in Rastier, 2006, translated for this edition). Thus to destroy the individual, and similarly to raze the *child*, is to emerge from the enclosure of this imaginary shell of the ego—with its correlative imaginary identifications with the parents and their ideals—into the place of the subject.

What we have described here as a *moment* of the advent of the subject is not to be reduced to any moment or period in the development of the child. Rather, such a moment is a logical moment which might occur at any time, and many times, throughout one's life. This needs to be asserted against any notion of a *process of separation*, but instead separation might be located in these very specific moments, such moments being *acts of separation*. This also puts an emphasis on the advent of the subject as an act, something active, rather than the passivity of a developmental phase which always refers back to the illusory individual as ego. Such acts of separation primarily occur through language, through acts of speech or writing. Such an act is, at the same time, an annihilation of the image in which the *child* is held. For a subject to emerge from the child, something must be broken or destroyed.

Such moments also occur in clinical practice through the speech of the child. When the child is presented for assessment or treatment in clinical practice, it is not the child presenting him- or herself for treatment. We refer back to Hermine Hug-Hellmuth's initial proposition that the child does not come of his own accord to the analyst, as the grown-up does, but owing to the wish of his parents. Rather, one or both parents present the child to the clinician as having a particular problem or symptom in reference to them. It is the adult, the mother or father, who requests the consultation. In such a presentation there is a child, but not yet a subject. Nonetheless, at some point the child has the possibility of articulating his or her own demand for treatment. For there to be analysis, the *child* must be overcome. It is in such a moment that lies the possibility of the advent of the subject and of the subject's assumption of the responsibility for his or her own suffering and its treatment.

The child and the others

We have cited Lévi-Strauss' famous formula that the prohibition of incest is the fundamental step because of which, by which, but above all in which, the transition from nature to culture is accomplished. Thus the first relation with the primordial Other is marked by a prohibition. For Lévi-Strauss the function of the prohibition of incest is to facilitate exchange and reciprocity, such that what is promoted by the prohibition of incest is the rule of exogamy. And exogamy is precisely what allows the child, ultimately, to move beyond the family, to move beyond the microcosm of society that is constituted by the family. That is, it is the prohibition of incest that promotes, for the subject, the place of the *Others* beyond the immediacy of the family.

In a recent paper, Isidoro Vegh defined the prohibition of incest as the limit of the subject with the first body of enjoyment, or jouissance (2013). For Vegh, however, exchange and exogamy, with their resultant greater social cohesion, are only the secondary social benefits of the prohibition of incest. The primary function pertains to the subject, the speaking being, who is described by Vegh as "the living being who comes to place of subject through language". His proposition is that this subject "requires the loss of the first object to allow the emergence of the indestructible desire to obtain it" (p. 5, translated for this edition). This "obtain it" clearly evokes Freud's notion that the object is not to be found, but refound. Here it is no longer a question of the renunciation of the object, but rather of the endeavour to retrieve it, which constitutes desire itself.

Vegh also refers us back to the often cited ending of Lacan's paper, "The Subversion of the Subject and the Dialectic of Desire in the Freudian Unconscious", regarding the question of castration, of which the prohibition of incest is the fundamental exemplar. Here I cite from the Sheridan translation which conveys the French original: "Castration means that *jouissance* must be refused, so that it can be reached on the inverted ladder [*l'échelle renversée*] of the Law of desire" (Lacan, 1966c, p. 324).

Lacan's notion here of the jouissance that is refused in order to be sought elsewhere, is an elaboration of Freud's concept of the lost object that is to be refound. With Lacan this ladder is the retrospective belief that there was once, outside memory, outside history, a jouissance obtained as a child or infant, or maybe as a foetus, *in mummy's tummy*. This jouissance is, in one sense, the imagined wishful union with the mother. The inverted ladder is the means of endeavouring to attain this jouissance, rather than renouncing the prohibited object. This *surplus*, the refused jouissance, continues to function in the structure of the subject in the attempt to reach it, in the endeavour to put it to use. This is also what we have elaborated here, through the title of Badinter's book, as the *en plus* or surplus that remains elusive but nonetheless must be harnessed by the subject to make his own.

The individual who remains in the place of the *child* is precisely one who has difficulty in inverting this ladder, in being able to refuse the jouissance that can lead on to desire and putting the surplus to work. This *child* occupies a perverse position in relation to the parents. Interestingly, Freud himself in his "Foreword" to August Aichhorn's *Wayward Youth*, places the *child* together with his perverse counterpart in the following way: "The child, even the wayward and delinquent child, should not be compared to the adult neurotic" (1925, p. vii). Freud tells us elsewhere that "[T]he child lives on almost unchanged in the sick patient as well as in the dreamer and the artist" (p. v). It is obvious here that Freud is not referring to "the child" as an age or a stage of development—since this *child* can just as easily be an adult—but rather as a particular psychic structure.

In his work, *La Perversion Ordinaire* (2007), Jean-Pierre Lebrun writes of the contemporary tendency for the child to remain in limbo—in other words to remain a *child* or minor—to which we referred at the end of the previous chapter. Lebrun theorises this difficulty as a failure of the function of Others (*Autrui*) for the child. Deleuze proposed that we need to attach the greatest attention to the conception of Others (*Autrui*) as structure: "... not at all a particular 'form' inside a perceptual field ... but rather a system which conditions the functioning of the entire perceptual field in general" (1969, p. 356). Without this structure of *Others*, the child remains in a perverse position in which, as Deleuze writes, "[H]e apprehends others sometimes as victims and sometimes as accomplices, but in neither case does he apprehend them as Others" (p. 358). We can articulate this as a logical position, one that Freud designates as polymorphous perversity, that the *child* necessarily occupies, and out of which he must come into being as a subject.

Freud goes on to tell us in his "Foreword" to *Wayward Youth* that the possibility of psychoanalysis with a child or young delinquent depends on quite definite conditions that he characterises as the analytic situation. Of particular interest here is the fact that Freud explains that the possibility of an analytic situation "requires the formation of certain psychic structures and a special attitude toward the analyst" (1925, p. vii). We can conclude that it is precisely the formation, or rather the *de-formation*, of the subject from the *child* that allows the possibility of the transference and thus of psychoanalysis itself. Here again we can draw together the question of the training or formation of the analyst with that of the child's advent to the place of subject. We are reminded of Lacan's words, "I never spoke of the analytic formation, I spoke of the formations of the unconscious" (1975, p. 191, translated for this edition). And in the analysis of a child, it is precisely through the particular moments of the emergence of the formations of the unconscious, or the *unbeknownst*, through *ablunders*—the slips of the tongue, dreams, bungled actions, and so on—that the subject may be structured.

The child and time

It is from the adult's retrospective and nostalgic viewpoint that it is possible to speak of the *child*. Such a viewpoint, like a developmental model, can target particular attributes and tasks to specific ages and stages. However the child is not a static entity, nor form. To be a child is never an endpoint, it is a transitory position that is always being left behind. The girl who is four years old, for instance, waits all year for the moment in which she turns five. But following her fifth birthday party she is already anticipating the next birthday when she will turn six: she will again turn into something different. Furthermore, the child is always anticipating what it will be like to be an adult, encapsulated in the formula *when I grow up*, or even, *when I am a grown-up*. That is, the subject in the child is he who is constantly anticipating no longer being one. If we can say that the adult lives in the nostalgia of *childhood*, or the nostalgia of what might have been, then the *child* is one who lives in anticipation of the future to come.

Such an anticipation is not self-evident, but, as we have seen, needs to be responded to by the parent, that is, by the Other. As we have noted, Bergès and Balbo refer to this as the function of symbolic anticipation. The demand of the child is present from the very beginning, in the cry. This cry becomes a call or appeal [*appel*] to the Other: "… only to the extent that it is answered, otherwise it returns to silence and henceforth no longer has any meaning. But if it is answered by a word, by a look, by a gesture, it henceforth becomes a demand" (1994b, p. 7).

The parents and educators must overcome their own ideals to allow this to occur, for there to be *paring* and *renting* of the place that the child occupies in each of their ideals. If not, the child risks being frozen in the fantasms of the mother and father, of assuming a static form for the parents. The anticipation, then, allows a place to remain open for the child to come into being, for the child to not remain in limbo.

Since the question of anticipation is also that of *time*, we need to examine this more closely. We have elaborated Freud's notion of the *infantile* as pertaining to a time outside history, a time, indeed, that carves out a hole in the history. In the history of psychoanalysis, this time of the *infantile* is postulated clinically as a past time, evoked by such phrases as *when I was a child, when I was a baby*, and *when I was in mummy's tummy*. From a theoretical perspective, Freud also evoked this time as a time past, through speaking of it as the prehistory, the archaic, the phylogenetic, or even in his archaeological approach to the theory and practice of psychoanalysis.

These notions of the *infantile* in Freud are precursors to Lacan's conceptualisation of a logical exception that is able to underpin the very notion of history itself, both the clinical history as well as the history of psychoanalysis. What we call the *prehistory* of psychoanalysis of the child forms a logical exception to the contemporary practice of psychoanalysis of the child. This logical exception occurred in the case of Little Hans, as well as the early practice of psychoanalysts analysing their own children. In the same way, in the case of each singular subject, the *prehistory* functions in order to ground the history. This is what we have elaborated as the *hole in history* which is the logical exception upon which the history itself is founded. The logical exception is *necessary* in order to approach the *impossible* profession of the analysis of the child. This impossible is an inherent part of discourse, as Lacan wrote of it in his four discourses. This *impossibility* is no longer that of a profession or task, but part of discourse. And what is referred to as the *child* is effectively a fact of discourse. For this reason it has been necessary to examine the prevailing discourses pertaining to the child in our itinerary.

If the time of the *infantile* always evokes something beyond the tangible, it does so in calling up an object that remains out of reach. But for the child as subject, this time does not need to remain a time past. This *time* is also evoked in the child's speech by such phrases as: *when I turn five, when I'm big, when I grow up,* and so on. These are the means by which the subject allows a space to remain open, and to be able to evoke this object as missing, or rather, as being out of reach. The object does not have to be located as a thing or a time to be refound: it is not just the object of a retrospective nostalgia. There does not need to be a search for a lost place, posited as having existed in the mists of time. Rather, there is an object that drives the child forwards. In this way the subject anticipates something to come, some prospective joys. The subject becomes animated by the inextinguishable desire to obtain the thing that cannot quite be grasped. The child as subject is driven forward in the endeavour to apprehend an object that lies ahead. The time of the singular subject that emerges from the *child* is a time of the future.

EPILOGUE

The idea for this book arose from the seminars that Tine Nørregaard and I have conducted together for a number of years now, convened under the title *Psychoanalysis and the Child*. It began from a question of what to do with the leftovers of our seminars, the notes we had made, and our ideas and ways of thinking about the child—ideas that we had generated through our work and talks together.

Like a love-affair, we began with an exchange of phone calls, messages, and conversations. Even before embarking on the seminar, we had already had many discussions regarding how we would conduct it, what we wished to work and present. These fertile discussions pertained to questions that posed difficulties for us, in our clinical work and theorisation, and the problems that we considered had beset the whole arena of clinical practice with children. The seminar, then, also began as a way of not refusing or foreclosing on these questions, but rather to utilise them as a motor to drive our questioning and elaboration. We then put our words into action as a type of pledge to our discussions and preparatory work together. But as with any love affair there was always the question of a pregnancy. Our work was already expectant with the persistent and guiding question that imposed itself despite ourselves: *what is a child?*

Our pledge involved the sharing of our conversations, which were now generating new conceptualisations, with others. Our conversations began to involve others, most particularly the participants of the seminar who have become a part of our ongoing conversation, and have thus made their own contributions to it and ultimately to this book. We may also hear in these *others*, the *others* evoked again by the title of Maud Mannoni's book *The Child, His "Illness", and the Others*, and also the Others or *autrui* in Tournier's novel *Friday* and Deleuze's working of it. These others are the people beyond ourselves with whom we endeavour to enter into discourse through the work I present here.

As well as the seminar, along the way we have also published papers that have sprung from our work. I have presented some of these as conference papers in Australia, Europe, and Latin America. Some of these papers, by necessity, are given reference here. Additionally, we have given talks here in Melbourne, as well as in Copenhagen, Denmark. Some of these talks have been in our workplaces or in the community to which our families belong. Others have been more formal presentations in the context of The Freudian School of Melbourne, and the psychoanalytic school Freuds Agorá in Copenhagen, as well as to the Dansk Selskab for Psykoanalytisk Psykoterapi med Børn og Unge or Danish Association of Psychoanalytic Psychotherapy with Children and Adolescents. So our conversation has spread to others outside the seminar, which we continue to convene. This book is a further endeavour to allow our ideas, and the thinking from our seminar, to involve yet others again.

This book results from a love affair. But if it was conceived of a love affair, it is an affair that Freud referred to as transference-love. It is then an affair of psychoanalysis. Our transference has been embodied in the conception of this book, which has been a copulative endeavour. It is transference in deed, transference in act, but a transference to work, as Lacan said, that has provided the impetus for this work. So it is not facile to say then that this book is also the product of a fertile meeting between a man and a woman. There is something of our own sexes that we bring to bear upon our collaboration. And it is important to insist on this point: the project of work for this book results from an encounter of a man and a woman, lovers of psychoanalysis, but not an imagined unity of *parents*.

Our work continues to be marked by our own histories and the enigmas that we find therein and by which we continue to be confronted.

Along the course of the production of the book each of us has lost a parent, which has underscored the place for each of us as *child* of our own mothers and fathers. And each of us also continues in our own lives to struggle with—and take joy in—educating and bringing up our own children, a profession that Freud designated as impossible. This is the basis of this work: the residues from our lives, the remainders of our own analyses, as well as the leftovers from the work that we have pursued, both together, and of course, alone.

There is a point at which one finds oneself alone, and perhaps it is only from this point that something is written. Tine Nørregaard echoed the words of Kant to me: *you can, since you must!* I took up this responsibility as it was I who found myself in a position to be able to respond to the theses that were generated by our encounter. Of course it is one thing to speak and to plan, it is another to write. And in the writing something more is produced, something that could not be foreseen in the speaking of it. This *child* was put to the test in the writing of it: one way of raising it is abandoned, and another attempted. My task was to endeavour to commit this *child* that had been conceived onto paper: to get it to survive infant mortality, in order to bring it to the point of civil registration and baptism. So inevitably this progeny is also marked, not just by its conception, but also by the tender care with which I nurtured it, as well as by my forcing it to take shape when it proved unruly.

Therefore what I have produced from this transference-love is a body of work that first a man and woman wrestled to produce, and which I then brought to fruition. To do so I have had to face the impossibility of raising a child, the failure of never being able to produce the work one imagines. I made do with what I had and raised this child from the surplus of my own clinical experience and theoretical work. Hence it is inevitable that the resulting infant is marked by my singular style. This book, then, has been a response to being left with a remainder, the *en plus* that is left over, that continues to be left over, from our seminars. To write I have had to find a way to overcome the resistance, including that of my own impotence, in the face of the struggle with this surplus, in order to make something of it, in order to make something more from it.

I put this body of work, this child conceived by two and tended by one, into the world so that it can make its way, which will not be easy. In order to find its own path, a child needs to no longer rely on those who generated him, to not have to defer to them. Grandfather Freud also told us that it is not the *attachment*, but rather the, "detachment from parental authority … that alone makes possible the opposition, which is so important for the progress of civilization, between the new generation and the old" (1905d, p. 227). The child, after all, is not owned by his parents, whether they are his guardians or carers. The mother and the father conceive of him or her with love and desire. But whoever can, must bring up the child as best he is able. And then the day arrives when this child must be allowed to go forth. The act of making, of engendering this child, whilst imbued with excitement and joy, has not also been without pain. The separation in the aloneness of writing, as well as in the releasing of the child and leaving it to go and encounter *others*, is also tinged with sadness and regret for any other possible child that might have been but was not.

The reader, through his or her own transference-love, might also encounter this book, not as an ideal or polished work, but rather as a work in progress with which he or she can also contribute and continue to work. From a lucky encounter, but after a difficult gestation and painful labour, a child now enters the world.

REFERENCES

Agamben, G. (1978a). Time and history: Critique of the instant and the continuum. In: Agamben, G. *Infancy and History: On the Destruction of Experience* (pp. 97–116). L. Heron (Trans.). London: Verso, 2007.

Agamben, G. (1978b). In Playland: Reflections on history and play. In: Agamben, G. *Infancy and History: On the Destruction of Experience* (pp. 73–96). L. Heron (Trans.). London: Verso, 2007.

Alexandre-Bidon, D., & Lett, D. (1997). *Les Enfants au Moyen Âge: V^e–XVe Siècle*. Paris: Hachette.

Allouch, J. (1995). *Érotique du Deuil au Temps de la Mort Sèche*. Paris: E.P.E.L.

Allouch, J. (1998). How Lacan invented the object (a). P. Anderson (Trans.). *Papers of the Freudian School of Melbourne, 19*: 47–70.

Allouch, J. (2007). *Lacan Love: Melbourne Seminars and Other Works*. M. -I. R. Zentner & O. Zentner (Eds.). Melbourne: Lituraterre.

Anzieu, D. (1959). *Freud's Self-Analysis*. P. Graham (Trans.). London: Hogarth & Institute of Psychoanalysis, 1986.

Ariès, P. (1960a). *Centuries of Childhood: A Social History of Family Life*. R. Baldick (Trans.). London: Jonathan Cape, 1962.

Ariès, P. (1960b). *L'Enfant et la Vie Familial sous L'Ancien Regime*. Paris: Seuil, 1973.

215

Australian Bureau of Statistics (2009). *Home and Away: The Living Arrangements of Young People*. www.abs.gov.au/AUSSTATS/abs@.nsf/Lookup/4102.0 Main+Features50June+2009 (last accessed 1 February 2014).

Badinter, É. (1980a). *Mother Love: Myth and Reality: Motherhood in Modern History*. Foreword by F. du Plessix Gray. New York: Macmillan, 1981.

Badinter, É. (1980b). *L'Amour en Plus: Histoire de l'Amour Maternel XVIIe-XXe Siècle*. Paris: Flammarion, 1981.

Barnes, J. (Ed.) (1984a). Aristotle's *Prior Analytics*. In: *The Complete Works of Aristotle: The Revised Oxford Translation* (*Volume One*) (pp. 39–113). Princeton, NJ: Princeton University Press.

Barnes, J. (Ed.) (1984b). Aristotle's *Metaphysics*. In: *The Complete Works of Aristotle: The Revised Oxford Translation* (*Volume Two*) (pp. 1552–1728). Princeton, NJ: Princeton University Press.

Bergès, J., & Balbo, G. (1994a). The treatment setting: Demand, transference and the contract with the parents and for their child. T. Nørregaard Arroyo & M. Plastow (Trans.). In: L. Clifton (Ed.), *Papers of the Freudian School of Melbourne* 2012, 24: 105–116.

Bergès, J., & Balbo, G. (1994b). *L'Enfant et la Psychanalyse: Nouvelles Perspectives* (*2nd edn*). Paris: Masson, 1996.

Bergès, J., & Balbo, G. (1998). What does transitivism consist of? *Écritique* 2011, *8*. www.fsom.org.au/ecritique2011%20 index.html (last accessed 5 March 2014).

Boukobza, C. (1993). Faut-il relire Anna Freud? In: *L'Enfant et la Psychanalyse* (pp. 41–64). Paris: Esquisses Psychanalytiques.

Burgelin, P. (1969). Émile ou de l'éducation. In: B. Gagnebin & M. Raymond (Eds.), *Jean-Jacques Rousseau: Œuvres Complètes* (*Vol. IV*). Paris: Gallimard, La Pléiade.

Carr, G. (1930). Translator's introduction. In: Condillac, É. B. (1754). *Condillac's Treatise on the Sensations* (pp. xix–xxvii). London: Favill.

Claparède, E. (1923). Preface. In: Piaget, J., *The Language and Thought of the Child* (pp. ix–xvii). M. Gabain (Trans.). London: Routledge & Kegan Paul, 1959.

Condillac, É. B. (1746). *An Essay on the Origin of Human Knowledge: Being a Supplement to Mr. Locke's Essay on the Human Understanding*. Mr. Nugent (Trans.). London: J. Nourse, 1761.

Condillac, É. B. (1754a). *Condillac's Treatise on the Sensations*. London: Favill, 1930.

Condillac, É. B. (1754b). Traité des sensations. In: *Œuvres Complètes de Condillac, Tome IV*. Paris: Dufart, 1803. (Reprinted as a facsimile edition by Elibron Classics, Chestnut Hill, MA, 2006.)

Cousins, M. (2011). *The Story of Film: An Odyssey* (*Episode 7*). Glasgow: Hopscotch Films.

Deleuze, G. (1969). Michel Tournier and the world without others. In: C. Boundas (Ed.), M. Lester (Trans.), *The Logic of Sense* (pp. 341–359). London: Bloomsbury, 2004.

Descartes, R. (1641). Meditations on first philosophy. (Reprinted in: E. Anscombe & P. T. Geach (Eds. & Trans.), *Descartes: Philosophical Writings* (pp. 5–151). Edinburgh: Nelson, 1954.)

Diderot, D. (1749). Letter on the blind for the use of those who see. In: *Early Philosophical Works*. Brooklyn, NY: AMS, 1973.

Dupont, G. (2013). Enfants maltraités: deux morts par jour. *Le Monde*, 15 June, p. 11. Available at: www.lemonde.fr.

Edwards, L. (2002). *How to Argue with an Economist* (*2nd edn*). Melbourne: Cambridge University Press, 2007.

Erikson, E. (1950). *Childhood and Society*. New York: W. W. Norton.

Falzeder, E. (Ed.) (2002). *The Complete Correspondence of Sigmund Freud and Karl Abraham 1907–1925*. C. Schwarzacher (Trans.). London: Karnac.

Fierens, C. (2002). *Lecture de L'Étourdit: Lacan 1972*. Paris: L'Harmattan.

Foucault, M. (1961). *Madness and Civilization: A History of Insanity in the Age of Reason*. London: Routledge, 1971.

Foucault, M. (1963). *The Birth of the Clinic: An Archeology of Medical Perception*. New York, Vintage, 1994.

Foucault, M. (1966). *The Order of Things: An Archeology of the Human Sciences*. New York: Pantheon, 1970.

Foucault, M. (1975). *Discipline and Punish: The Birth of the Prison*. New York: Vintage, 1977.

Foucault, M. (1976). *The Will to Knowledge: The History of Sexuality* (*Volume I*). London: Penguin. (First translation published under title *The History of Sexuality (Volume I), An Introduction*. New York: Random House. Reprinted under present title, Penguin, 1998.)

Freud, A. (1927a). Introduction to the technique of the analysis of children. In: Freud, A. *The Psycho-Analytical Treatment of Children* (pp. 1–52). London: Imago, 1946.

Freud, A. (1927b). *Einführung in die Technik der Kinderanalyse*. Leipzig, Wien, Zürich: Internationaler Psychoanalytischer Verlag.

Freud, A. (1965). *Normality and Pathology in Childhood: Assessments of Development*. New York: International Universities Press.

Freud, S. (1895). *Gesammelte Werke: Texte aus den Jahren 1885 bis 1938*. Frankfurt, Germany: S. Fischer Verlag.

Freud, S. (1896c). The aetiology of hysteria. *S. E., 3*. London: Hogarth.

Freud, S. (1899a). Screen memories. *S. E., 3*. London: Hogarth.

Freud, S. (1900a). *The Interpretation of Dreams. S. E., 4–5*. London: Hogarth.

Freud, S. (1901b). *The Psychopathology of Everyday Life. S. E., 6*. London: Hogarth.

Freud, S. (1905c). *Jokes and Their Relation to the Unconscious. S. E., 8.* London: Hogarth.

Freud, S. (1905d). *Three Essays on the Theory of Sexuality. S. E., 7.* London: Hogarth.

Freud, S. (1908e). Creative writers and day-dreaming. *S. E., 9.* London: Hogarth.

Freud, S. (1909b). Analysis of a phobia in a five-year-old boy. *S. E., 10.* London: Hogarth.

Freud, S. (1909c). Family romances. *S. E., 9.* London: Hogarth.

Freud, S. (1912–13). *Totem and Taboo. S. E., 13.* London: Hogarth.

Freud, S. (1914b). The Moses of Michelangelo. *S. E., 13.* London: Hogarth.

Freud, S. (1914c). On narcissism: An introduction. *S. E., 14.* London: Hogarth.

Freud, S. (1914d). On the history of the psycho-analytic movement. *S. E., 14.* London: Hogarth.

Freud, S. (1915c). Instincts and their vicissitudes. *S. E., 14.* London: Hogarth.

Freud, S. (1915e). The unconscious. *S. E., 14.* London: Hogarth.

Freud, S. (1918b). From the history of an infantile neurosis. *S. E., 17.* London: Hogarth.

Freud, S. (1919). *A Young Girl's Diary.* Fairfield, IA: 1st World Library, 2004.

Freud, S. (1925). Foreword. In: Aichhorn, A. *Wayward Youth.* Foreword by Sigmund Freud. New York: Viking, 1935. (First published in German with title *Verwahrloste Jugend*, Vienna: Internationaler Psychoanalytischer Verlag, 1925. Revised and adapted from the second German edition in 1935. Issued as Compass Books edition in 1965.)

Freud, S. (1925e). The resistances to psycho-analysis. *S. E., 19.* London: Hogarth.

Freud, S. (1925h). Negation. *S. E., 19.* London: Hogarth.

Freud, S. (1926d). *Inhibitions, Symptoms and Anxiety. S. E., 20.* London: Hogarth.

Freud, S. (1926e). *The Question of Lay Analysis. S. E., 20.* London: Hogarth.

Freud, S. (1927c). *The Future of an Illusion. S. E., 21.* London: Hogarth.

Freud, S. (1933a). *New Introductory Lectures on Psycho-Analysis. S. E., 22.* London: Hogarth.

Freud, S. (1937c). Analysis terminable and interminable. *S. E., 23.* London: Hogarth.

Freud, S. (1937c). Die endliche und die unendliche Analyse. *Gesammelte Werke*: XVI: 59–99.

Freud, S. (1950a). A project for a scientific psychology. *S. E., 1.* London: Hogarth.

Freud, S. (1950a [1892–1899]). Extracts from the Fliess papers. *S. E., 1.* London: Hogarth.

Freud, S. (2002). *Notre Cœur Tend Vers le Sud: Correspondance de Voyage, 1895–1923.* Paris: Fayard, 2005.

Freud, S., & Breuer, J. (1895d). *Studies on Hysteria. S. E., 2.* London: Hogarth.

Gagnebin, B., Raymond, M., & Osmont, R. (1959). Notes et variantes. In: B. Gagnebin, M. Raymond & R. Osmont (Eds.), *Jean-Jacques Rousseau: Œuvres Complètes (Vol. I).* Paris: Gallimard, La Pléiade.

Hamad, N. (2007). Schooling: Between knowledge and truth. N. Chavannes & F. Muller Robbie (Trans.). *Écritique* 2011, *8.* www.fsom. org.au/ecritique2011%20 index.html (last accessed 5 March 2014).

Harris, W. T. (1892). Editor's Preface. In: Rousseau, J. - J. (1762a). W. T. Harris (Ed.), W. H. Payne (Trans.), *Émile or Treatise on Education* (pp. vii–xvi). New York: D. Appleton, 1896. (Reprinted New York: Prometheus, 2003.)

Hegel, G. W. F. (1820). *Philosophy of Right.* S. W. Dyde (Trans.). Amherst, NY: Prometheus, 1996.

Heraclitus (1987). *Fragments: A Text and Translation with a Commentary by T. M. Robinson.* Toronto: University of Toronto.

Hölderlin, F. (2008). Rousseau. In: M. Chernov & P. Hoover (Trans.), *Five Hölderlin Translations. Revue Interval(le)es* 4/5. www.cipa.ulg.ac.be/ intervalles4/20_chernoff.pdf (last accessed 21 January 2014). Also published in: Hölderlin, F. (2008), *Selected Poems of Friedrich Hölderlin.* M. Chernov & P. Hoover (Trans.). Richmond, CA: Omnidawn.

Houllebecq, M. (2001). *Platform.* F. Wynne (Trans.). London: Vintage, 2003.

Hug-Hellmuth, H. (1912). The analysis of a dream of a 5½-year-old boy. In: G. MacLean & U. Rappen, *Hermine Hug-Hellmuth: Her Life and Work* (pp. 51–57). New York: Routledge, 1991.

Hug-Hellmuth, H. (1921). On the technique of child-analysis. *International Journal of Psychoanalysis, 2:* 287–305.

Hug-Hellmuth, H. (1924). The libidinal structure of family life. In: G. MacLean & U. Rappen, *Hermine Hug-Hellmuth: Her Life and Work* (pp. 267–274). New York: Routledge, 1991.

Hughes, A. (1992). Letters from Sigmund Freud to Joan Riviere (1921–1939). *International Review of Psycho-Analysis, 19:* 265–284.

Hyppolite, J. (1966). Appendix I: A spoken commentary on Freud's "Verneinung" by Jean Hyppolite. In: Lacan, J., *Écrits* (pp. 880–754). B. Fink (Trans.). New York: W. W. Norton, 2006.

Jaspers, K. (1913). *General Psychopathology.* J. Hoenig & M. W. Hamilton (Trans.). Chicago: University of Chicago Press, 1968. (Reprinted as

General Psychopathology (*Volume I & II*) with foreword by P. R. McHugh. Baltimore, MD: John Hopkins University, 1997.)

Jones, E. (1955). *The Life and Work of Sigmund Freud (Vol. II): 1901–1919: Years of Maturity*. New York: Basic Books.

Kahn, F., & Robert, F. (2006). Avant-propos à l'édition française. In: *Sigmund Freud: Lettres à Wilhelm Fließ 1887–1904* (pp. 7–12). Paris: Presses Universitaires de France.

Kant, I. (1784). An answer to the question: What is enlightenment? In: M. J. Gregor (Trans. & Ed.), *The Cambridge Edition of the Works of Immanuel Kant: Practical Philosophy* (pp. 11–22). Cambridge: Cambridge University Press, 1996.

Kaplan, H. I., & Saddock, B. J. (1981). *Modern Synopsis of Comprehensive Textbook of Psychiatry* (*3rd edn*). Baltimore, MA: Williams & Wilkins.

Klein, M. (1932). *The Psycho-Analysis of Children*. London: Hogarth. (Reprinted London: Vintage, 1997.)

Lacan, J. (1953–1954). *The Seminar of Jacques Lacan. Book I: Freud's Papers on Technique 1953–1954*. New York: W. W. Norton, 1991.

Lacan, J. (1956–1957). *Le Séminaire Livre IV: La Relation d'Objet. 1956–1957*. Paris: Seuil, 1994.

Lacan, J. (1957–1958). *Séminaire 1957–1958: Les Formations de l'Inconscient*. Paris: Seuil, 1998.

Lacan, J. (1962–1963a). *The Seminar of Jacques Lacan: Anxiety. 1962–1963. Book X*. C. Gallagher (Trans.). (Translated from unedited French manuscripts.) (Non-commercial edition.)

Lacan, J. (1962–1963b). *Séminaire 1962–1963: L'Angoisse*. Paris: Éditions de l'Association Freudienne Internationale, 2000. (Non-commercial edition.)

Lacan, J. (1964). *The Four Fundamental Concepts of Psychoanalysis: Seminar 1964*. A. Sheridan (Trans.). New York: W. W. Norton, 1981.

Lacan, J. (1966a). The function and field of speech and language in psychoanalysis. In: Lacan, J., *Écrits*. B. Fink (Trans.), (pp. 237–268). New York: W. W. Norton, 2002.

Lacan, J. (1966b). The instance of the letter in the unconscious, or reason since Freud. In: Lacan, J., *Écrits* (pp. 412–441). B. Fink (Trans.). New York: W. W. Norton, 2002.

Lacan, J. (1966c). The subversion of the subject and the dialectic of desire in the Freudian unconscious. In: Lacan, J., *Écrits: A Selection*. A. Sheridan (Trans.), (pp. 292–325). New York: W. W. Norton, 1977.

Lacan, J. (1970). Radiophonie. In: Lacan, J., *Autres Écrits* (pp. 403–447). Paris: Seuil, 2001.

Lacan, J. (1971–1972). *Le Savoir du Psychanalyste/The Knowledge of the Psychoanalyst: Séminaire 1971–1972* (*bilingual edition*). M. Plastow (Trans.).

Paris: L'Association Lacanienne Internationale, 2013. (Non-commercial edition.)

Lacan, J. (1974). Television. *October* 1987, 40: 6–50.

Lacan, J. (1975). Intervention dans la séance de travail "Sur la passe" du samedi 3 novembre. In: *Les Lettres de l'École Freudienne, 15*: 185–193. Accessible at: http://aejcpp.free.fr/lacan/1973–11–03b.htm (last accessed 2 March 2014).

Lacan, J. (1978a). The neurotic's individual myth. *Psychoanalytic Quarterly* 1979, *48*: 405–425.

Lacan J. (1978b). Le mythe individuel du névrosé ou poésie et vérité dans la névrose. (Transcribed by J. -A. Miller). *Ornicar?* 17–18: 290–307. Paris: Seuil.

Lacan, J. (1985). Geneva lecture on the symptom. R. Grigg (Trans.). *Analysis* 1989, 1: 7–26.

Lacan, J. (1986a). Deux notes sur l'enfant. *Ornicar?* 37: 13–14.

Lacan, J. (1986b). Note on the child. R. Grigg (Trans.). *Analysis* 1990, 2: 7–8.

de Lajonquière, L. (2013). *Figures de l'Infantile: La Psychanalyse dans la Vie Quotidienne Auprès des Enfants*. Paris: L'Harmattan.

Laplanche, J., & Pontalis, J. -B. (1967). *The Language of Psycho-Analysis*. London: Hogarth, 1985.

Lebrun, J. -P. (2007). *La Perversion Ordinaire: Vivre Ensemble Sans Autrui*. Paris: Denoël.

Lévi-Strauss, C. (1947a). *The Elementary Structures of Kinship*. J. H. Bell & J. R. von Sturmer (Trans.), R. Needham (Ed.). Boston: Beacon, 1969.

Lévi-Strauss, C. (1947b). *Les Structures Élémentaires de la Parenté*. Paris: Mouton, 1967.

Lévi-Strauss, C. (1949). The effectiveness of symbols. In: *Structural Anthropology* (pp. 186–205). C. Jacobson & B. Grundfest Schoepf (Trans.). New York: Basic Books, 1963.

Lévi-Strauss, C. (1955a). The structural study of myth. *Journal of American Folklore, 68*: 428–444.

Lévi-Strauss, C. (1955b). *Tristes Tropiques*. London: Penguin, 1976.

Lévy, R. (2008). *L'Infantile en Psychanalyse: La Construction du Symptôme chez L'Enfant*. Ramonville Saint-Agne, France: Érès.

Lugrin, Y. (2009). Sabina Spielrein et la transmission de la psychanalyse. *Le Coq-Héron, 197*: 93–104.

MacLean, G. (1986). A brief story about Dr. Hermine Hug-Hellmuth. *Canadian Journal of Psychiatry, 31*: 586–589.

MacLean, G., & Rappen, U. (1991). *Hermine Hug-Hellmuth: Her Life and Work*. New York: Routledge.

Malle, L. (1971). *Le Souffle au Cœur*. Paris: Nouvelles Éditions du Film.

Mannoni, M. (1964). *L'Enfant Arriéré et sa Mère*. Paris: Seuil.

Mannoni, M. (1967a). *The Child, His "Illness", and the Others*. London: Karnac, 1987.

Mannoni, M. (1967b). *L'enfant, sa "maladie" et les autres*. Paris: Seuil.

Mannoni, O. (1969). L'analyse originelle. In: *Clefs pour L'Imaginaire ou L'Autre Scène*. Paris: Seuil.

Masson, J. M. (1984). *The Assault on Truth: Freud's Suppression of the Seduction Theory*. New York: Farrah, Straus & Giroux.

Masson, J. M. (Ed. & Trans.) (1985). *The Complete Letters of Sigmund Freud to Wilhelm Fliess: 1887–1904*. Cambridge, MA: Belknap.

Morford, M., & Lenardon, R. (2007). *Classical Mythology (8th edn)*. New York: Oxford University Press.

Nørregaard Arroyo, T. (2012). Father can't you see that I am burning?: Interventions in the real of the parental couple. In: L. Clifton (Ed.), *Papers of the Freudian School of Melbourne, 24*: 125–134.

Nørregaard Arroyo, T., & Plastow, M. (2012). Psychoanalysis and the child. In: L. Clifton (Ed.), *Papers of the Freudian School of Melbourne, 24*: 99–104.

Nunberg, H., & Federn, E. (Eds.) (1967). *Minutes of the Vienna Psychoanalytic Society (Volume II): 1908–1910*. New York: International Universities Press.

Nunberg, H., & Federn, E. (Eds.) (1974). *Minutes of the Vienna Psychoanalytic Society (Volume III): 1910–1911*. New York: International Universities Press.

Pereira, D. (1999). The *infans* and the (k)not of history. *Papers of the Freudian School of Melbourne, 20*: 59–71.

Périn, J. (1995). Suis-je le propriétaire ou l'usufruitier de mon corps? *Journal Français de Psychiatrie, 2*: 7–8.

Pessoa, F. (n. d.). Là-bas, je ne sais où … In: *Obra Poética e em Prosa, (Vol. I): Poesia*, pp. 1040–1041. Porto: Lello & Irmão, 1986.

Pessoa, F. (1934). Untitled. In: *Obra Poética e em Prosa, (Vol. I): Poesia*, p. 411. Porto: Lello & Irmão, 1986.

Piaget, J. (1923). *The Language and Thought of the Child (3rd edn)*. M. Gabain (Trans.). London: Routledge & Kegan Paul, 1959.

Plastow, M. (2000a). Book review: Psychoanalytic psychotherapy of the severely disturbed adolescent by D. Anastasopoulos, E. Laylou-Lignos, M. Waddell (Eds.). *Australian Journal of Psychotherapy, 19*: 76–90.

Plastow, M. (2000b). From family myth to individual fantasm. *Papers of the Freudian School of Melbourne, 21*: 21–39.

Plastow, M. (2005). The rules of the game. *Écritique, 5*. www.fsom.org.au/ecritique0405.htm (last accessed 5 March 2014).

Plastow, M. (2005–2006). The era of lite. *Écritique, 6*. www.fsom.org.au/ecritique0506.htm (last accessed 6 March 2014).

Plastow, M. (2011a). Mother nature. *Écritique, 8.* www.fsom.org.au/ecritique2011%20 index.html (last accessed 5 March 2014).

Plastow, M. (2011b). Hermine Hug-Hellmuth, the first child psychoanalyst: Legacy and dilemmas. *Australasian Psychiatry, 19*: 206–210.

Plastow, M. (2012a). Once upon a time. In: L. Clifton (Ed.), *Papers of the Freudian School of Melbourne, 24*: 11–20.

Plastow, M. (2012b). The child and seduction. In: L. Clifton (Ed.), *Papers of the Freudian School of Melbourne, 24*: 71–78.

Plastow, M. (2012c). Freud and Faust. In: L. Clifton (Ed.), *Papers of the Freudian School of Melbourne, 24*: 185–193.

Plastow, M., & Nørregaard Arroyo, T. (2011). Book review: *L'Infantile en Psychanalyse* by Robert Lévy. *Écritique, 8.* www.fsom.org.au/ecritique2011%20 index.html (last accessed 5 March 2014).

Porge, E. (1996a). *Freud Fließ: Mythe et Chimère de L'Auto-Analyse.* Paris: Anthropos.

Porge, E. (1996b). Some cases of "Name of the father subject supposed of knowledge". M. Plastow (Trans.). In: L. Clifton (Ed.), *Intervention in the Real: Papers of the Freudian School of Melbourne, 24*: 117–123.

Porge, E. (2005). *Transmettre la Clinique Psychanalytique: Freud, Lacan, Aujourd'hui.* Ramonville Saint-Agne, France: Érès.

Pujó, M. (1996). Adolescence and discourse. M. Plastow (Trans.), *Papers of the Freudian School of Melbourne 1997, 18*: 55–68.

Quarfood, C. (1997). *Condillac, la Statue et L'Enfant: Philosophie et Pédagogie au Siècle des Lumières.* Y. Johansson (Trans.). Paris: L'Harmattan, 2002.

Rastier, F. (2006). Saussure, la pensée indienne et la critique de l'ontologie. *Texto!, XI*(1). www.revue-texto.net/Saussure/Sur_Saussure/Rastier_Inde.html (last accessed 3 March 2014).

Rastier, F. (2007). Le langage a-t-il une origine? *Texto!, XII*(3) (July). www.revue-texto.net/Dialogues/Dial_index.html (last accessed 5 March 2014). Also published in: *La Revue Française de Psychanalyse, 71*: 1481–1496 (2007).

Riché, P., & Alexandre-Bidon, D. (1994). *L'Enfance au Moyen Âge.* Paris: Seuil/Bibliothèque Nationale de France.

Richebächer, S. (2005). *Sabina Spielrein: De Jung a Freud.* D. Martineschen (Trans.). Rio de Janeiro: Civilização Brasileira, 2012. (Original title *Sabina Spielrein: Eine Fast Grausame Liebe zur Wissenschaft.* Zurich: Dorlemann Verlag.)

Robinson, T. M. (1987). *Heraclitus: Fragments. A Text and Translation with a Commentary by T. M. Robinson.* Toronto: University of Toronto Press.

Roudinesco, É. (2007). *Our Dark Side: A History of Perversion.* D. Macey (Trans.). Cambridge: Polity, 2009.

Roudinesco, É., & Plon, M. (1997). *Dictionnaire de la Psychanalyse*. Paris: Fayard.

Rousseau, J. -J. (1735). Fiction ou morceau allégorique sur la révélation. In: B. Gagnebin & M. Raymond (Eds.), *Jean-Jacques Rousseau: Œuvres Complètes (Vol. IV)*. Paris: Gallimard, La Pléiade, 1969.

Rousseau, J. -J. (1762a). *Émile or Treatise on Education*. W. T. Harris (Ed.), W. H. Payne (Trans.). New York: D. Appleton, 1896. (Reprinted Amherst, NY: Prometheus, 2003.)

Rousseau, J. -J. (1762b). *Émile or On Education*. A. Bloom (Ed. & Trans.). New York: Basic Books, 1979. (Reprinted London: Penguin, 1991.)

Rousseau, J. -J. (1762c). *Émile ou de l'education*. In: B. Gagnebin & M. Raymond (Eds.), *Jean-Jacques Rousseau: Œuvres Complètes (Vol. IV)*. Paris: Gallimard, La Pléiade, 1969.

Rousseau, J. -J. (1762d). *The Social Contract*. M. Cranston (Trans.). London: Penguin, 2004.

Rousseau, J. -J. (1771). *Pygmalion, Scéne Lyrique*. In: B. Gagnebin & M. Raymond (Eds.), *Jean-Jacques Rousseau: Œuvres Complètes (Vol. II)* (pp. 1224–1231). Paris: Gallimard, La Pléiade, 1964.

Rousseau, J. -J. (1780). Rousseau, Juge de Jean Jacques: Dialogues. In: B. Gagnebin, M. Raymond, & R. Osmont (Eds.), *Jean-Jacques Rousseau: Œuvres Complètes (Vol. I)* (pp. 657–989). Paris: Gallimard, La Pléiade, 1959.

Rousseau, J. -J. (1782a). *The Confessions*. J. M. Cohen (Trans.). London: Penguin, 1953.

Rousseau, J. -J. (1782b). Les confessions. In: B. Gagnebin, M. Raymond, & R. Osmont (Eds.), *Jean-Jacques Rousseau: Œuvres Complètes (Vol. I)*. Paris: Gallimard, La Pléiade, 1959.

Saramago, J. (1984). *The Year of the Death of Ricardo Reis*. G. Pontiero (Trans.). Orlando, FL: Harcourt Brace, 1991.

de Saussure, F. (2002). *Writings in General Linguistics*. C. Sanders & M. Pires (Trans.). Oxford: Oxford University Press, 2006.

Schröter, M. (Ed.) (1986). *Sigmund Freud. Briefe an Wilhelm Fließ, 1887–1904. Ungekürzte Ausgabe*. G. Fichtner (Trans.). Frankfurt, Germany: S. Fischer Verlag.

Shakespeare, W. (1598). *The Merchant of Venice*. In: S. Wells & G. Taylor (Gen. Eds.), S. Wells, G. Taylor, J. Jowlett, & W. Montgomery (Eds.), *William Shakespeare: The Complete Works (Compact Edition)* (pp. 425–451). New York: Oxford University Press, 1988.

Shakespeare, W. (1600). *As You Like It*. In: S. Wells & G. Taylor (Gen. Eds.), S. Wells, G. Taylor, J. Jowlett, & W. Montgomery (Eds.), *William Shakespeare: The Complete Works (Compact Edition)* (pp. 627–652). New York: Oxford University Press, 1988.

Smith, A. (1776). *An Inquiry into the Nature and Causes of the Wealth of Nations.* Oxford, Clarendon Press, 1976.

Spielrein, S. (1912a). Die Destruktion als Ursache des Werdens. *Jahrbuch für psychoanalytische und psychopathologische Forschungen, IV*: 465–503.

Spielrein, S. (1912b). Destruction as the cause of coming into being. *Journal of Analytical Psychology, 39*: 155–186.

Starobinski, J. (1957). *Jean-Jacques Rousseau: Transparency and Obstruction.* A. Goldhammer (Trans.). Chicago, IL: University of Chicago Press, 1988.

Tournier, M. (1967a). *Friday.* N. Denny (Trans.). Baltimore, MD: Johns Hopkins University Press.

Tournier, M. (1967b). *Vendredi ou les Limbes du Pacifique.* Paris: Gallimard, 1972.

Tumarkin, M. (2009). Mining the mother lode. *The Age, A2*, 18 April: 20–21. Available at: www.theage.com.au.

Vegh, I. (2013). Prohibición del incesto: Variables e invariante. http://lacano2013.org/docs/Vegh%20Isidoro%20Espa%f1ol.pdf (last accessed 11 March 2014).

Verhaeghe, P. (1998). *Love in a Time of Loneliness: Three Essays on Drive and Desire.* London: Karnac, 2011.

Weiss, E. (1970). *Sigmund Freud as a Consultant: Recollections of a Pioneer in Psychoanalysis.* New York: Intercontinental Medical Book.

Wilcken, P. (2010). *Claude Lévi-Strauss: The Poet in the Laboratory.* New York: Penguin.

Winnicott, D. W. (1977). *The Piggle: An Account of the Psychoanalytic Treatment of a Little Girl.* London: Penguin, 1980.

INDEX

For Product Safety Concerns and Information please contact our EU
representative GPSR@taylorandfrancis.com
Taylor & Francis Verlag GmbH, Kaufingerstraße 24, 80331 München, Germany

www.ingramcontent.com/pod-product-compliance
Lightning Source LLC
Chambersburg PA
CBHW070401270326
41926CB00014B/2652

*9 7 8 1 7 8 0 4 9 0 5 5 7 *